PITTSBURGH THEOLOGICAL MONOGRAPHS

New Series

Dikran Y. Hadidian

General Editor

D1738010

14

CONTEMPORARY POLITICAL ORDERS AND CHRIST

Karl Barth's Christology and Political Praxis

contemporary political orders and christ

KARL BARTH'S CHRISTOLOGY AND POLITICAL PRAXIS

BY ROBERT E. HOOD

Foreward by
John Macquarrie

PICKWICK PUBLICATIONS
Allison Park, Pennsylvania
1985

Copyright© 1984 by **Pickwick Publications**
4137 Timberlane Drive, Allison Park, PA 15101

Library of Congress Cataloging in Publication Data

Hood, Robert E. (Robert Earl), 1936–
    Contemporary political orders and Christ.

    (Pittsburgh theological monographs; new ser. 14)
    Bibliography: p.
    Includes index.
    1. Christianity and politics—History—20th century.
2. Jesus Christ—History of doctrines—20th century.
3. Barth, Karl, 1886–1968. I. Title. II. Series.
BR115.P7H585   1985   261.7'092'4   84-26525
ISBN 0-915138-56-5

Printed and Bound by Publishers Choice Book Mfg. Co.
Mars, Pennsylvania 16046

In **THANKSGIVING**

for my father (deceased) and my mother
who nourished me with all that they had
that I might begin this journey

CONTENTS

Chapter Four - cont'd

FOREWORD

It is a great privilege to commend this important book by Dr. Robert Hood. It occupied him for several years, some of them spent in the calm reflective atmosphere of Oxford, others amid the social and political tensions of Berlin. The result is a work which is both scholarly and closely related to the practical problems of our contemporary society.

Few people would deny that Karl Barth stands as the greatest Protestant theologian of modern times. From the very beginning, his theology was tied to the situations of everyday life. Ethics, in his view, is a branch of dogmatic theology, and it has often been said--and I think, rightly--that this was what enabled him to stand up to the ideology of the Nazis. Their regime of deceit, violence, aggression and repression was founded on the false dogma of the inherent superiority of the Nordic race and its right to world-domination. Barth opposed to that the central Christian dogma of the incarnation--that the nature of God and so of ultimate reality is to be learned from Jesus Christ.

Barth's position, of course, is a controversial one. In his lifetime he was severely criticized by Reinhold Niebuhr, Paul Tillich and many others. However, a theologian has got to take the risk of being wrong about some things. Nothing brings theology into disrepute more than the blandness of those who try to please everyone and give offense to none.

The more a theologian particularizes and devotes himself to concrete issues of moral and social concern, the more he exposes himself to the possibility of error, and the more controversial he becomes. Barth certainly did not shrink from such matters.

Today, I think we are coming to a new appreciation of Barth's greatness. This will not mean that we shall come to accept all his positions--far from it. But we are more and more seeing his theological work as a vast quarry of Christian wisdom, from which we can get guidance for our problems.

But the very vastness of the quarry is a discouragement to those who might feel themselves attracted to it. Barth's **Church Dogmatics** alone is said to contain six million words. To read it intelligently is a most demanding task, calling for constant efforts of judgment and also of memory as one tries to hold each new pronouncement in relation to those already made. Furthermore, the **Church Dogmatics** is only part of the incredible output of this incredible theologian.

Dr. Hood has performed a Herculean labor in working through Barth's essential teaching (his Christology) and in showing the political theology that emerges from it.

It is sometimes said that American theology has not yet come to terms with Barth. Certainly there is a great deal still to be explored, sifted, criticized and appropriated from the work of this theological giant. Dr. Hood has made a very significant contribution to this continuing task, and in so doing has also made his own outstanding contribution to political theology.

John Macquarrie
Lady Margaret Professor of Divinity
University of Oxford, England

PREFACE

This book examines the development of Karl Barth's political theology as it emerges from his christology. As early as 1911, in a speech to the Arbeiterverein in Safenwil, Switzerland, entitled, "Jesus Christ and the Movement for Social Justice," Barth insisted that all theological reflection about the significance of Christ has to include an ethical dimension. This dimension should lead to political concern and active involvement by Christians and the Christian community in the political order:

> Jesus **is** the movement for social justice and the movement for social justice **is** Jesus in the present. . .The essential content of the person of Jesus can actually be summarized by the words: "movement for social justice." [1]

Throughout his career Barth continued to insist on establishing ethical issues in human society which grew out of his understanding of the person and work of Christ. Jesus Christ became crucial in shaping the character and direction of Christian political and social praxis, particularly as that praxis led to a partiality on behalf of the poor and downtrodden in society. That is, there are political and ethical dimensions connected with any hermeneutical appraisal of the New Testament. In 1946, Barth pointed this out in an article:

> The Church is witness of the fact that the Son of Man came to seek and to save the lost. And this implies that casting all false impartiality aside--the Church must concentrate first on the lower and lowest levels of human society. The poor, the socially and economically weak and threatened, will always be the object of its primary and particular concern, and it will always insist on the State's special responsibility for these weaker members of society. [2]

This thesis will seek to demonstrate the contents of the dynamic or link existing in Barth between Jesus Christ as servant, lord, and witness, His work in justification, sanctification, and vocation, and the political directions and goals emerging from the ethical dimensions of such a dynamic or link. Hence one may speak of political implications, since Barth consistently ties theological reflection and the consequences of that reflection to consideration of and action about the social, economic, and political structures, institutions, and ideologies shaping and influencing the concrete situation of humankind. As Barth himself noted when he joined the Social Democratic Party in Switzerland whilst still a pastor in Safenwil:

> I have now become a member of the Social Democratic Party. Just because I set such emphasis Sunday by Sunday upon the last things, it was no longer possible for me personally to remain suspended in the clouds above the present evil world, but rather it had to be demonstrated here and now that faith in the Greatest does not exclude, but rather includes within it, work and suffering in the realm of the imperfect. [3]

The event which links God and man as His chosen partner is Jesus Christ. This leads Barth to insist that theological anthropology must be founded on christology, which he also connects with the kingdom of God already present in man's world. Because the kingdom is already at work through Jesus Christ in our world, God does bring about change and transformation in our society.

Such an anthropology has two consequences for Barth. First, it means that the Christian and the Christian community have to take note that God in His graciousness and His righteousness as witnessed in scripture stands preeminently at the side of the low and the lowly, the poor and the disinherited, i.e., to the left. Secondly, the man of faith has a particular political responsibility in light of his knowledge of the right revealed by a righteous God. The man of faith cannot evade the issues of justice and human rights, for to do so is to reject the divine justifications in Jesus Christ.

But the political implications of such an anthropology also point to particular goals, directions, structures, and institutions in society which allow Barth to speak of a dialectic between two kinds of societies found within the one society. They might be called the "redeemed" and the "unredeemed" societies. Those goals and directions of the first more often than not resemble some form of social democracy or socialized democracy. Those goals and directions of the "unredeemed" society more often than not are characterized by the injustices and ethics of exploitation, selfishness, and class divisions associated with capitalistic societies and private enterprise.

Yet Barth is careful not to confuse the Christian faith or Christian political dogmatics with any specific political party or position. Just as Barth warned in his **Epistle to the Romans** that the revolution of God must not be confused with revolutions taking place in our world, even though such revolutions may reveal some of the truths of God's revelation, so he is quite deliberate about not identifying his political theology with Social or Christian Democratic politics. Barth does not accept the classic Marxist definition of socialism nor can his position be described as that of Marxist socialist as Prof. Frederick Marquardt in his important but controversial book on Karl Barth is wont to do. Instead a wider definition of socialism or social democracy as provided by C. Wright Mills might be more appropriate for understanding Barth's political dogmatics:

> Socialism [is] the demand for a planned, economic order, producing for use rather than profit, and subject to central administration and budgetary accounting. This involves a fusion of economic and political orders by the extension of democratic practices to the economic order, which, in turn, makes for the elimination of property and income class privileges in favor of economic equality. [4]

The danger of this kind of theological analysis is that more deliberate political theologians relying on pragmatism or, like Reinhold Niebuhr, on "Christian realism" will dismiss it as irrelevant. As Niebuhr noted in his harsh criticism of Barth's political position before he later changed his mind:

> [Barth] is certainly neither a 'Primitive anti-communist' nor a 'secret pro-communist.' He is merely a very eminent theologian, trying desparately to be impartial in his judgments. The price of this desperation is of course moral irrelevance. [5]

But as Dr. Joseph Bettis points out, such a critique says more about Niebuhr's problem than Barth's. It is because the beginnings, options, and methodology employed by Barth do not conform to the liberal and pragmatic categories of Niebuhr that Barth's arguments are not dealt with. Rather only a model founded on modern political liberalism and pragmatic "Christian realism" is held up as a filter through which to hear and interpret Barth. [6]

Bettis notes rather acutely that what Barth really does in linking political responsibility with theological reflection is to relocate the whole ethical question. That is, instead of pursuing the traditional line of moral theologians in trying to discover the right or developing casuistry based on the choice between what is right and what is wrong or trying to conceptualize Christian ethics in such a way as to avoid the dogmatism and authoritarianism of previous moral theologians and ethicists, which the liberal theologians of this century such as Niebuhr rightly understood as demonic, Barth relocates the ethical question by insisting that all human existence and actions fall under the command of God. This command is founded on the grace of God and is intrinsic in all human existence and action. This command is the basis of creation and therefore, for Barth, it is not comparable to the Enlightenment or liberal choice of deciding to obey or disobey it. Obedience to the command of God means to do authentic ethical action. Disobedience is death and inauthenticity. The command of God is the heteronomous law essential in the very fabric of man's existence and society. [7]

In II/2, Barth gives the criteria for what he would consider authentic ethical action under the command of God, pointing out that ethical reflection itself is an ethical act. Ethical reflection carries with it an awareness of its consequences which accompany it at all times.

First, ethical action means that we confess an ignorance of being able to apprehend or decide about God's command without the aid of God's grace. It means accepting the possibility of being mistaken, reversed, renewed, and enlightened, which can happen over and over again as the concrete situation demands it. (II/2, 645-649)

Secondly, ethical action means that man's obedience is to a command which transcends his actions. The command is alien to man, outside himself, whose truth is not subject to the conditioning of man. It establishes its own validity. But unlike the Kantian imperative it is not only the highest duty to obey it, rather it _is_ the highest good. (II/2, 649-653)

Thirdly, ethical action means that it is communal, not individualistic. There is an intrinsic solidarity between fellowmen. This communality has two consequences: first, there is always a personal involvement, thereby excluding the possibility of the questioner being a spectator. Secondly, the individual, as important as he is, stands under the divine command together with his fellow-man as a joint-covenant partner elected by God in Jesus Christ. Without this communality, the questioner in asking the question of what ought he to do, can become detached, irresponsible, and uncaring. (II/2, 653-657)

Fourthly, ethical action means that it is concrete, not abstract. It has a relationship to past decisions which shapes future ones. Reflection is not the goal of ethical action; concrete living and acting are the goals. That is, theory and practice are one in concrete situations. (II/2, 657-661)

The component which links God in Jesus Christ and man, man's redeemed society and his unredeemed society, the ethically responsible Christian engaged in political praxis to the non-Christian in the world with socio-economic structures and complexes is Barth's concept of solidarity. All his doctrines about the consequences of the work of Jesus Christ have the component of co-humanity, or what may be called solidarity. This concept is all the more important for the Christian as well as the Christian community engaged in seeking to realize the directions and goals in the redeemed, and therefore, the obedient society.

NOTES

1. "Jesus Christus und die soziale Bewegung," Vortrag gehalten im Arbeiterverein Safenwil am 17. Dezember 1911, Der Freie Aargauer, 6. Jg. 23rd December 1911, 1. English translation in **Karl Barth and Radical Politics.** George Hunsinger, editor and translator. (Philadelphia: Westminster Press, 1976), 19.

2. "The Christian Community and the Civil Community," **Community, State and Church.** With an Introduction by Will Herberg. Ronald Gregor Smith, trans. (Gloucester, Mass.: Peter Smith, 1968), 173.

3. **Revolutionary Theology in the Making: Barth-Thurneysen Correspondence, 1914-1925.** James D. Smart, trans. (Richmond, Virginia: John Knox Press, 1964), 28.

4. Hans Gerth and C. Wright Mills, **Character and Social Structure: The Psychology of Social Institutions** (New York: Harcourt, Brace & World, Inc., 1953, 1964), 452. Cited in **Karl Barth and Radical Politics,** 185.

5. "Barth's East German Letter," The Christian Century 76 (February 11, 1959), 147-148. Cited in Joseph Bettis, The Scottish Journal of Theology 27 (1974), 300.

6. Ibid., 301-304.

7. Ibid., 296.

ACKNOWLEDGEMENTS

This work was begun several years ago as a venture in faith and scholarship at Christ Church, University of Oxford. After a number of interruptions, including a teaching career in West Berlin, Germany, and my current teaching post at a theological seminary, research on the work was resumed and completed finally in 1981.

An enormous amount of gratitude and appreciation is extended to Professor Dr. Helmut Gollwitzer, now retired Professor of Evangelical Theology at the Free University, West Berlin, Germany, who encouraged me to resume research. He patiently assisted me in revising the topic and directed me most conscientiously to resources and other doctoral students interested in Karl Barth at the Free University. Both his seminars and the collegiality which he extended to all his doctoral students allowed for a kind of counsel and dialogue which has proven to be most valuable in testing ideas, hearing and exploring new perspectives, and sharing a common enthusiasm for one of the most significant theologians of the twentieth century, Karl Barth. Professor Gollwitzer's extensive knowledge of Karl Barth and his own example of being an engaged, politically involved theologian gave me both an impetus and a model by which I understood better the dynamics and importance of the interplay between theological knowledge and political praxis. Professor Gollwitzer's mentor, of course, was Karl Barth, with whom he had studied during Barth's teaching days in Bonn. I would hope that I have captured part of the key to Professor Gollwitzer's living example of theology and praxis by examining Karl Barth's testimony to Jesus Christ being the key.

Without the deliberate and persistent encouragement by the Reverend Professor John Macquarrie, Lady Margaret Professor of Divinity and Canon of Christ Church at Oxford, the final completion of this work may have been delayed even more. His willingness to read critically each of the chapters and his wise counsel fulfilled in every sense the German understanding of a Doktorvater. Also his suggestions about new sources and important critical ideas which enabled me to examine Barth's thought from different theological perspectives were always forthcoming. Most of all, his ability to work with me on the basis of our being colleagues rather than he being the schoolmaster and I the pupil provided envigorating discussion all the times we met. For his wise counsel and theological nourishment I am indeed most grateful and indebted.

Much thanks is extended to Mrs. Lee Hennessy, who typed the final copy of this work, and to her husband, the Reverend John Hennessy, who very conscientiously proof-read the text and made very helpful suggestions about style. Likewise, great appreciation is expressed for the devoted proof-reading and corrections of Mr. David Aherne, whose thoroughness in linguistic matters was very important for the final submission of the work, as well as that of the Reverend David Green, a valued colleague at the General Theological Seminary in New York.

Finally, gratitude is due the Episcopal Church Foundation in New York City which granted me the fellowship in order to begin this study at Oxford as a post-graduate.

Robert E. Hood
New York, New York

July, 1983

Chapter One

BEGINNINGS AND BOUNDARIES OF BARTH'S CAREER

When Karl Barth made his first journey to America in 1962, he wished more than anything that when Americans actually saw him in the flesh--the feared giant of the supposed "negative" dialectical theology of the twenties which was still the prevailing American opinion and appraisal of him--they would begin to discuss his theological writings not as a bit of undigestible theological pons asinorum but as ideas from a "normal human being." As Barth noted in his recollections about America, he considered himself to be like anyone else,

> considerably involved in all sorts of human affairs and distinguished from all other men only by the simple fact that he chiefly has devoted his days to a special emphasis on the question of the proper theology and that he would be happy if others would also devote themselves in all seriousness to this question again and again. [1]

A rehearsal and repetition of Karl Barth's already well-known biographical data and pilgrimage may be necessary only to establish the seriousness with which Barth himself obeyed this charge. A number of books have already been produced devoted to Barth's early life before he left Germany in 1935 as well as to the early influences and developments in his thinking. [2]

Born in the latter part of the nineteenth century (10th May, 1886) in Basle, where he also died in 1968 (9th December), Karl Barth was surrounded by and schooled on the liberalism of Friedrich Daniel Ernst Schleiermacher (1768-1834), Isaac August Dorner (1809-1884), Albrecht Daniel Ritschl (1822-1889), Wilhelm Herrmann (1846-1922), Adolph von Harnack (1851-1930), Ernst Troeltsch (1865-1923), and the Religionsgeschichte school in biblical studies. This was a time which Barth later characterized as "open doors" - a desire to listen to and to understand the various new emphases and disciplines which were coming to light in the sciences, philosophy, and history. [3] He described it as a time when theologians felt apologetic about the seemingly unrelatedness of the Christian faith to the other disciplines in the rapidly developing cultural areas.

> The interest of these theologians focused on the believing man in his past and in his present, in his confrontation and association with Jesus Christ. Theological discussion with the contemporary world centred around the existence of the believing man, and in philosophy of religion particularly around the possibility of this existence. [4]

In 1904, young Barth went to the University of Bern and later to Germany, where he attended universities in Berlin, Tübingen, and Marburg. The most prominent scholars during his university career were Harnack, Gunkel, and Troeltsch at Berlin, Herrmann and Adolf Jülicher (1857-1938) at Marburg where Barth along with another student named Rudolf Bultmann later assisted Martin Rade (1857-1940) in editing Die christliche Welt in 1908. There he also became acquainted with Eduard Thurneysen, his life-long friend. [5]

Barth was enthusiastic about going up to Marburg, which he described as "my Zion". [6] The real joy was the opportunity to study under Herrmann, whom Barth in a letter described as **the** theologian during his time at the university, and under whom Barth heard Dogmatics I (Prolegomena to the Concept "Religion"), his Ethics as well as his Dogmatics II. [7] In a momentary burst of youthful enthusiasm, Barth acclaimed: "I took Herrmann into my very pores": [8]

> (His theology) was to be differentiated from old Liberalism as well as from all "Orthodoxies" and all "positivistic" theology; we despised both. To the left and to the right we felt free and thoughtful, in order to continue on the thin edge. [9]

Barth was ordained to the ministry of the Reformed Church in Bern in 1908 after returning to Switzerland to sit for his theological examinations. He went on to Geneva in 1909 as Hilfsprediger at the German-speaking congregation. It was during this time that he wrote an article about his own uncertainties regarding the content and method of theological training of clergy under liberal professors. Entitled "Modern Theology and Work for the Kingdom of God," [10] Barth observed that his colleagues who had been trained under liberal theological faculties experienced more difficulties in beginning their ministry in the parish than those trained under more conservative and orthodox faculties. The first reason for this difficulty Barth found in the individualism engendered by the liberal theological insistence that one should think for himself, "calling true only what he himself sees to be true, proving all things, finding his salvation on his own." [11]

> It is not obedience to laws which come to man from without, but it is meditation and concentration upon a truth which reveals itself within him. [12]

This very personal and self-determining faith made it problematic for such clergy to subscribe to any tradition.

Secondly, the historical approach common to liberal theological faculties made all of theology and dogmatics appear as relative, meaning that the very foundations of the Christian faith were seldom embraced for their uniqueness; Jesus Christ was simply the "founder" of another religion.

> Whosoever keeps himself to "modern" theology must know that the question is: to be or not to be. For science deprives him of that entire historical outfit of ideas and concepts which were the "motive and quietive" of the religion of the past; he is vigorously compelled to come to a decision about them, i.e., to ask himself whether they are expressive also of his belief. [13]

Consequently the liberally trained were more insecure and experiencing constant bewilderment about the firm and absolute truths of the Christian faith which their more orthodox colleagues were able to affirm.

These early strains came even more to the surface after Barth became the pastor in Safenwil, Switzerland, an industrial and agricultural area in the canton of Aargau, in 1911. The main employer in the town was a member of Barth's congregation, the Hüssy family, who owned the textile factories and weaving industry. [14] Barth held talks at the Arbeiterverein in Safenwil, which was an educational organization established in various localities for the purpose of discussing topics and ideas held to be important for the worker by the Social Democratic Party in Switzerland. [15] In the local newspaper, the Freier Aargauer, a speech of the young pastor was published in which he said:

> The correct Socialism is the correct Christianity in our time; of course the correct Socialism is not that which the Socialists now do, rather what Jesus does--and what the Socialists want to do. [16]

The factory owner in the congregation, Walter Hüssy, attacked Barth as an uninformed idealist, to whom Barth immediately replied. Eventually a cousin of Hüssy who was also President of the Safenwiler Kirchenpflege protested officially about Barth's speech and conduct. [17]

Barth also renewed his acquaintance with a former friend at Marburg, Eduard Thurneysen, who had become pastor of a neighboring church in Leutwil. During the same period he began laying the foundations for his future theological ethics. [18] Barth described this friendship, which was sustained by a correspondence of some 1000 letters:

> Indeed we wandered incessantly back and forth in order to meet one another, but that did not suffice. We had that pressing need as very brothers to exchange ideas about everything which, as we said at that time, happened in the Church, the world, and the Kingdom of God. And because there was no telephone connexion between our houses . . . , there resulted a lively letter correspondence which was carried on almost week by week. [19]

Thurneysen was also apparently the person who brought Barth in contact with the Religious Socialists. [20]

During the early part of his ministry at Safenwil, Barth began to single out some ideas about the absolute character of God, ideas which would later be given substance in his **Römerbrief**. In an article in 1914 called "Der Glaube an den persönlichen Gott", ("Belief in a Personal God,") Barth, after criticizing 19th century theology, remarked:

> We must speak of God as free from finitude and condition, as these states are necessarily connected with space and time. The polemic of A. Ritschl against the use of the term absolute in theology is justified only in so far as it opposes the one-sided emphasis upon the negativism of God made by mysticism. But it is entirely contrary to the facts when Ritschl asserts, that the absolute is not a product of religious reflection, but a metaphysical concept that is foreign to the Christian. For there is hardly a religious reflection which could really do without the negation of God's limitedness. Of course, when one takes the absolute in its liberal meaning, as being dissolved from given reality, one is guilty of mythologoumenon . . . . Pure abstractness becomes pure origin. It is the . . . truth and validity of the apriori which has proved itself the positive component of the God-idea. [21]

There is a Feuerbachian tone in this article which criticizes and is impatient with all abstract notions separating God and man as participants in the same history, although he does not agree with Feuerbach's idea that God is in fact an abstract projection of man himself:

> The God-idea of religion cannot be something that we have projected from ourselves, but only the reflection

of a fact which has been created by us. This fact is
the life which is given us by God and mediated to us
through history. Our being conditioned by history is our
religious experience. [22]

There are in fact a number of themes in this essay: Liberalism,
Feuerbachianism, Herrmannism, Kantianism. Nonetheless, the
strong emphasis of the Christian living and working within this
history and this world both for the good and for the bad was
to be pronounced some seven years in the **Römerbrief** thusly:

What is true of the generality of man is true also of
the men of God. As men they do not differ from other
men. There is no fragment or epoch of history which
can be pronounced divine. . . . There are no saints in
the midst of a company of sinners, for where men have
claimed to be saints, they are thereby marked as not
saints. [23]

Curiously enough Barth came full circle when in an essay
on Feuerbach in 1926, some four years after the **Römerbrief** and
some twelve years after this article, he supported Feuerbach
in his criticism of the liberal theologians, which he accused of
laying the groundwork for "speaking of God simply by speaking
of man in a loud voice." [24] Barth also attacked the notion of
an abstract God removed from man's history and time, lauding
Feuerbach's insights:

He is concerned with the whole reality of heart and
stomach of man. It is only when one is thus concerned
that one can in truth speak of God. [25]

In 1915 Barth joined the Social Democratic Party of
Switzerland in his area, a move which he claimed was directly
related to his pastoral work in Safenwil. This party, which was
organized in 1880 as one of the first workers' institutions aimed
at furthering the political and economic interests of the working
classes along with the Allgemeine Schweizerische Gewerkschaftsbund
(SGB), did not succeed nationally. In 1888 the Social Democratic
Party of Switzerland (SPS) was established as a people's party
(Volkspartei) intended to further the political goals of the workers.
[26]

In the programme of 1904 the SPS insisted on the classic
socialistic aim of removing the means of production from private
ownership and placing them under community control as well
as emancipating the working classes from the "oppression" and
"exploitation" of the capitalists, but all of this through democratic
means as maintained by the hitherto western industrial democracies.

[27] Barth justified his membership in the SPS as the consequent step resulting from his pastoral work in his parish:

> Because I try very hard Sunday after Sunday to talk about the last things, I am no longer permitted to sweep merely' in the clouds above the wicked world of today; rather it must be shown that belief in God does not exclude labour and suffering in this imperfect (world), but includes them. [28]

Immediately Barth as Social Democrat got involved in a working class event because shortly thereafter some 55 female workers at the yarn machine factory were threatened with dismissal because they had formed a trade union. Barth went to the villa of the owner and talked with him as Moses with Pharoah, to ask him to let the people go into the desert." [29] Barth had little success, as the meeting broke up apparently in a shouting match, [30] but a few weeks later the "red pastor", [31] as he was afterwards called, could report:

> The membership has more than doubled. The owner defends himself mightily, soon by means of individual firings, soon by means of individual wage rises. On Saturday another assembly was held at which I also spoke. This evening it continues. It is a time in which some stand the test and some do not. [32]

This new phase in the cure of souls led to Barth's renewed interest and acquaintance with the Religious Socialists, particularly Hermann Kutter (1863-1931), Leonhard Ragaz (1842-1919), whom he had first met during his student days at Tübingen (December, 1907) and again in Bad Boll, Germany (April, 1915) as he and Thurneysen were returning from the wedding of his older brother, Peter, who had married the daughter of Barth's former professor and editor of Die christliche Welt, Martin Rade. [33] This whole period appears to have had a telling effect on Barth's thinking about the relation of social problems and eschatology. In a letter to Thurneysen in 1915, Barth wrote that he saw the connection between religious socialism and community problems to lie in the fact that whilst the religious socialist worked for the realization of the Kingdom of God, he also had to be concerned for our time, the relation of that time to God's time, and the practical application of such a concern. [34] This theme of the eternality of God which also includes our existence, history and institutions even with their transitory and non-permanent nature, is mentioned again in an address in 1919 which startled and aroused the Religious Socialists in Germany, who were encountering the young Swiss pastor for the first time, entitled "Der Christ in der Gesellschaft" ("The Christian in Society"). [35] But Thurneysen said that initially the two of them became members of the SPS because they saw in the movement the possibility of making the Kingdom of God a reality in a tattered, insecure world during the unsettledness throughout all of Europe at that time. They understood the increasingly dark events to be a judgment on a culturally oriented bourgeois Christianity which simply had become an "ism" amongst other "isms". The shaking of the foundations of religious socialism occurred at the time of the war, and as their festering disillusionment with religious socialism increased, these two young pastors began to read the Bible anew:

> We did not seek in it our bourgeois or socialistic, cultural or conservative opinions. We read it with the eyes of the shipwrecked people whose everything had gone overboard. [36]

But prior to this, both Barth and Thurneysen joined the Religious Socialists Conference, possibly more for theological reasons due to Ragaz's influence than for practical reasons; in fact in 1916 Barth was elected President of the Conference. [37]

The year 1916 was also the year in which Barth began working on his commentary on **Romans,** which was eventually published in 1919. [38] Barth's feeling of discomfort with his theological teachers and with Kulturprotestantismus was made all the more acute with the outbreak of World War I. In August, 1914, 93 German intellectuals published a petition supporting the war policies of Kaiser Wilhelm II and his Government, amongst whom were all of Barth's former professors whom he had admired and sought to imitate in some cases:

> I experienced a Götterdämmerung as I studied how Harnack, Herrmann, Rade, Eucken, etc., positioned themselves with regard to the new situation. [39]

> In despair over what this indicated about the signs of the times, I suddenly realized that I could not any longer follow either their ethics and dogmatics or their understanding of the Bible and of history. [40]

The second source of discomfort was the incongruity between his theological principles and the hearing of scripture, especially as he tried to exegete texts for his Sunday sermons. Kulturprotestantismus appeared to come undone for the young Barth, as he pointed out many years later:

> For twelve years I was a minister, as all of you are. I had my theology. It was not really mine, to be sure, but that of my unforgotten teacher, Wilhelm Herrmann, grafted upon the principles which I had learned with less consciousness than unconsciously in my native home--

the principles of the Reformed Churches. . . . Once in
the ministry, I found myself growing away from those
theological habits of thought and being forced back at
every point more and more upon the specific minister's
problem, the sermon. . . . It simply came about that
the familiar situation of the minister on Saturday at
his desk and on Sunday in his pulpit crystallized in my
case into a marginal note to all theology, which finally
assumed the voluminous form of a complete commentary
on the Epistle to the Romans. . . . Naturally and evidently
there are many subjects mentioned in the book--New
Testament theology, dogmatics, ethics and philosophy--but
you will best understand it when you hear through it
all the ministers' question: what is preaching?--not,
how dare one do it? but how can one do it? [41]

Professor Smart comments that the **Romans** of 1919 moved
against the stream of New Testament exegesis which trimmed
Paul of his contemporary features in order to fit the liberal mind
of the new day. [42] But it was also a note of jubilation, joy,
and resurrection for Barth. [43] Some forty years later Barth
noted that the one thing which spurred him on toward producing
the **Romans** was his observation that God, who had freely given
Himself to man and had freely given man a history and a hope,
was being reduced to a "pious notion, a mystical expression and
symbol of a current alternating between a man and his own heights
or depths." [44]

During this period of working on **Romans**, Barth began
to be more critical of the Religious Socialists as well as liberal
theology, although he continued to be active in the SPS; indeed
he was an official delegate to the party's conference in Bern
in 1919. [45] He had already been quarreling with Ragaz over
the need to dissolve the Religious Socialist Conference for a while
in order to rethink the role and task of the group. [46] As Barth
wrote in his first edition of **Romans**:

It was always complete without God. God was to be
always good enough for the carrying through and crowning
of all that which man had begun by himself. The fear
of God did not stand at the beginning of our wisdom,
rather His consent was sought always only when passing
by. [47]

In August, 1919, Friedrich Naumann and Christoph Blumhardt died, and Barth wrote for the two of them a common obituary
with the title, "The Past and the Future" (Vergangenheit und Zukunft) in which he suggested that they themselves had abandoned
"Christian social" principles for "national social" principles. [48]

Barth was beginning to concretize his departure from and unhappiness with Christian Religious Socialism, an unhappiness which came to a head at the Tambach Conference of the Religious Socialists in September (22nd-25th) in Germany. [49] Ragaz and Kutter had originally been invited, but they were unable to appear, so that Alfred de Quervain (1895-1968) suggested Barth as a substitute. [50] Insisting that Jesus Christ is the raison d'être for all theological thinking and ethical actions, Barth at Tambach criticized the "Bindestrich-Christentum". [51] The philosopher, Hans Phillip Ehrenberg (1883-1958) from Heidelberg, who, in converting from Judaism to Christianity, became interested in theology as well, was present at the conference and was so impressed with the talk that he obtained the rights to print it as the first publication of his "Patmos-Kreis". [52]

This talk was all the more remarkable when one recalls that just prior to this Tambach conference, the main employer in Safenwil, the Hüssy family, who were active members of the congregation, along with others left the congregation because of disagreement with Barth's role in the general strike in 1918. Amongst other things Barth was accused of glorifying the strike as well as Bolshevism and Spartacism, to which he replied. [53] This was used by some of his opponents to deny him an entitled rise in salary, a struggle which he later won. [54]

The second edition of the **Romans** was written after Barth had left the congregation at Safenwil and taken up the new chair in Reformed Theology at the University of Göttingen, which had been recently endowed by American Presbyterians [55] through the good offices of a Dr. James Good, Philadelphia. Professor August Lang at Halle, whom Barth at the time did not know, but was later to meet in 1923 at an assembly of Reformed theologians, a meeting characterized by Barth as a meeting of "very traditional German Reformed theologians", [56] had visited the United States twice and had persuaded the Board of Foreign Missions of the Presbyterian Church to endow the chair. [57] Barth took up his appointment in February, 1921.

Barth was both apprehensive and uncertain about his entrance into German academic theology. In a letter to Thurneysen at the time of the appointment, Barth wrote that the current orthodox thrust of liberal theology at the universities was embarrassing to him in light of the practical needs and problems of the time, particularly as demonstrated by the Socialists and the Humanists. Later in 1925, he reflected on the academic theological profession as a possible drive into the "tunnel of dogmatics" which could well signify the end of his summons as a Christian minister. [58] He was most apprehensive about his own scholarly talents, [59] remarking once in a letter to his friend Thurneysen that, whilst on the one hand, he was fearful that he might end up a "grotesque failure", on the other hand, he could not return to the parish situation.

> For after one has chewed wearily for twelve years on the half of the sour theological apple in the pastoral office, (and) now all at once to have the other, the academic half, presented to him,

this can be overwhelming. [60] In 1922 the second edition of **Romans** was published, the same year in which Barth was named doctor of theology by the Evangelical Theological Faculty at the University of Münster, an honor about which Barth some years later mused as "academic legitimation". [61] In honor of the news, which, according to Barth, was granted for his "important fundamental contributions to the deepening of the formulation of religious and theological questions," he wished only a good cup of coffee. [62]

Professor Smart claims that the second edition of **Romans** was so radically different from the first edition because Barth had been impressed with Franz Overbeck (1837-1905), a New Testament scholar and church historian at Basle from 1870-1897. [63] Barth was acquainted with him and his wife. Indeed, after a particularly disagreeable encounter with his former teacher Harnack, Barth went to Frau Overbeck, "who sketched a picture of her husband, which corresponded to our conception." [64] Barth saw in Overbeck's sharp negative criticism of the historical critical direction in biblical studies exactly the opposite positive point from which theology should be re-examined anew. [65] Barth had received a publication of Overbeck's fragments in 1919, entitled "Christianity and Culture," which he reviewed for a pamphlet in 1920. [66] He saw in primitive Christianity the claim for the radical antithesis between man's world and God's Kingdom as revealed in Jesus Christ. The Church abandoned this radical eschatological faith with the advent of apologetics and entered a time of a "postapostolic degeneration". [67] Overbeck had a notion of what he called the Urgeschichte, which both precedes and participates in man's history, even with that history's entanglement with sin. This means a break with man's history, a vast difference between God's eternity and man's time. The Urgeschichte is the telos toward which all of history is moving; yet, it is not an abstraction from history. Rather, by its participating in history, it calls the very existence of man into question and offers the possibility of a new existence. [68]

> Barth warned his readers that Overbeck's book was dangerous for them. It would shake them out of their false religions and theological securities and set them in motion, leaving them nowhere to rest ever in history. . . . . The

understanding reader hears himself called away from all the fleshpots of Egypt to venture forth into the wilderness. To become a Christian theologian, is not to find or to construct a theology in which the mind and spirit can come to rest, but, rather to recognize all such human bases of security as idolatry and to be perpetually launching out into an unknown future. [69]

He enlarged upon this radical difference between God's world and man's along with Kierkegaardian ideas about the "qualitative difference" between the two worlds, although as Smart rightly points out, Kierkegaard's influence disappeared from Barth's writings almost as quickly as it appeared. [70] Barth himself pointed out in his Dankrede for the Sonning Prize at the University of Copenhagen in 1963, that although he first purchased a book of Kierkegaard's in 1909 (The Instant), it made very little impression on him. It was between the writing of the two Romans that Kierkegaard took on an importance because, as Barth said:

What attracted us particularly to him, what we rejoiced in, and what we learned, was the criticism, so unrelenting in its incisiveness, with which he attacked so much: all the speculation which blurred the infinite qualitative difference between God and man, all the aesthetic forgetfulness of the absolute claims of the Gospel and the necessity to do it justice by personal decision . . . he became and was for us one of the cocks whose crowing seemed to proclaim from near and far the dawn of a really new day. [71]

But Kierkegaard was soon abandoned because Barth recognized what seemed to be more and more of a 19th century figure reflecting on 19th century Pietism to which Barth himself was utterly opposed. [72]

His teaching is, as he himself once said, "a pinch of salt" for the food, not the food itself, which it is the task of right theology to offer to the church and thus to me. The Gospel is firstly the glad news of God's Yes to man. It is secondly, the news which the congregation must pass on to the whole world. It is thirdly the news from on high. These are three aspects, in relation to which I had to do further study, after my meeting Kierkegaard, in the school of other teachers. [73]

Thurneysen credits part of the reason for the radical change in the second Romans to Christoph Blumhardt, [74] particularly his emphasis on God being an active power in our earthly and therefore daily life; to understand our existence, therefore, we must first understand the ways of God. This meant a reversing of the direction from our subjective religious experience to the ways of God. [75]

As an active power in the here and now, God's Kingdom also interrupts our life and situation in spite of our resistance.

> The present situation had constantly to be seen as an era between the victory of Christ in his cross and resurrec-tion and the coming victory when his sovereignty over the world would be complete. In this time between the times we are in the midst of a life-and-death struggle between God and the forces of evil. [76]

As such, the Christian cannot be utopian because he knows that the present is not the fullness of time; he cannot, at the same time, despair because he knows that the final victory must belong to Jesus Christ. "Warten und eilen was the watchword of Blum-hardt." [77] "The Blumhardts," wrote Barth later in the **Church Dogmatics**, "gave a central position to the prayer: 'Thy kingdom come' and 'Even so, come, Lord Jesus,' and therefore to post-temporal eternity." [78]

Another aspect of Blumhardt's faith was his political activism: a Social Democrat in the Württemberg Landestag, who insisted that the evil was social as well as individual. [79] Thus inspired to move against the stream once again, particularly in seeking to avert dangers Barth saw in his first edition of the **Romans,** he noted unmistakingly in his second edition:

> There is no human righteousness by which man can escape the wrath of God. There is no arrangement of affairs or department of behaviour, no disposition of mind or depth of feeling, no institution or understanding which is by its own virtue, pleasing to God. Men are men and they belong to the world of men: that which is flesh is flesh. The kingdom of men is without exception, never the kingdom of God. [80]

Our hope for gaining some direction toward the good and the right can come only through and by means of the grace of God granted by God Himself: "God Himself propounds the problem of God and answers it." [81] The polemical style and attack on the prevailing theology of the day by this young, thirty-six-year old don was not only his emancipation from the cultural Christianity, but also was to stereotype him for a long time in the non-German religious world as the negative dialectical theolo-gian, a characterization which, as noted, did not go unheeded by Barth when he visited America some forty years later. Yet, as Barth himself suggested, he was trying to overcome the "stone wall" of theology, seeking to assert the absolute independent, free, and uniquely different character of God and His structuring of the relationship between Himself and us and between us and the world, not that ordered and initiated by us. [82]

The second edition of **Romans** was reviewed by the rising young New Testament scholar, Rudolf Bultmann, whom Barth had come to know at Marburg when they assisted Martin Rade with the editing of Die christliche Welt. Bultmann liked the book, although he disagreed with Barth's stress on the distance between God and man and his method of exegesis. [83] When Barth was told of Bultmann using his commentary as the basis for some of his own university lectures, writing to Thurneysen, Barth said: "So there is still all manner of old leaven to be swept out, even in Marburg." [84] In fact, in an article published in 1924, entitled "The liberal theology and the most recent theological movement," Bultmann appeared to be in basic agreement with Barth. [85]

Barth began to receive invitations to discuss his theology throughout Germany and Switzerland, more often than not at Pastor's Conferences. At one of the conferences in October, 1922, the term "dialectical theology" found its way into the theological landscape identifying Barth and others. [86]

> We should as theologians speak about God. We are, how-
> ever, men and as such cannot speak about God. We should
> know both our should-ness and our not-being-able-ness
> and thus give the honour to God. [87]

Barth claimed that the actual name was attributed to him by a spectator. [88]

From 1925 to 1930, Barth taught at the University of Münster, although he apparently was still uncertain whether the academic life was to be his final calling. [89] These were formative, somewhat painful, as well as fruitful years for Barth. Included in these years was the well known "false start", namely, the **Christian Dogmatics,** the beginning of a change in his theological method signaled in his lectures about Anselm's **Cur deus homo?,** the beginning of the long friendship with Fraülein Charlotte von Kirschbaum. They were also the years in which Barth first ventured outside Germany and Switzerland. [90] It was an important break with the familiar Germany and German-speaking Switzerland, for it meant that Barth broke out of his insularity. Looking back on this period some years later, Barth commented,

> I sat at the same desk in a small house of my own in
> Münster in Westphalia--a Prussian in Germany, nearly
> on the point of becoming something like a "good German".
> [91]

In 1923, Thurneysen suggested to Barth that he consider giving a series of lectures on his own dogmatics based on reformed theology. Barth himself had hinted in a letter shortly before this that reformed theology always had to be re-examined from time to time in order to be able to speak to the cultural existence at particular moments in history: "a trumpet blast which needs to be blown in our sick time." [93] He also began to have second thoughts about the lecture system being adequate for dealing thoroughly with theological ideas. [94] Already at Göttingen he had held "open evenings" during which he discussed 19th century theology with the students, particularly Schleiermacher. [95] Yet, in reply to Thurneysen's suggestion about a reformed dogmatics, Barth realized that sectarian dogmatics would always prove unsatisfactory, and as such would restrict the Christian faith's ability to speak to the whole of man's situation in the world. [96] In 1924, he had prepared lectures on a Prolegomena to Christian dogmatics. [97] During the summer holidays of 1927, he finished the first stage of his projected dogmatics, which was entitled **Christliche Dogmatik im Entwurf (Band I: Prolegomena zur christlichen Dogmatik: Die Lehre vom Worte Gottes)**. The title was intended to express his apprehensiveness about a beginner being presumptuous enough to publish a dogmatics so early in his career. [98]

The rebellion against the burden of Herrmann and Schleiermacher came fully to the front. Barth modestly described this first effort as only an examination of what God had made available to the Church in scripture and of the ways in which the Church responds to that content in her theology. He sought to understand the standard for judging both the content of theology and the faithfulness of theology to that content. [99] Thus, with the question of where one can know God's Word, what form does the Word take, what evidence is there that the Word has in fact been revealed to us, and how is humankind to respond to the Word, Barth undertook to demonstrate that theology was, first of all, human language about a subject which has been revealed to us. This provided it with an objective character not dependent on our self-understanding or some similar subjective norm as was often the case with the 19th century liberal and pietistic theologians. Secondly, theology was formed by and assumed its methodology according to a logic inherent in the subject itself, i.e. the Word of God. The Word of God cannot, therefore, be dependent on the language or the structure of a particular theology, but rather the subject matter controls both the approach and the shape of the final utterance; indeed the Word of God is not founded on the Christian faith, but rather the Christian faith is founded and sustained by the Word of God. [100] This insistence on the objective character of the Word of God is a decided rupture with the hitherto liberal approach to Christian theology:

> [Dogmatics] is concerned with the situation set up between
> the speaking God and the hearing man in which man
> is both questioned before God and is given the answer
> to that questioning and therefore it is concerned to trace
> out the way of the knowledge of God actual in that
> situation which it finds to be the way, not of man's
> cognition so much as recognition of God, not of knowledge
> so much as of acknowledgement of God, in making Himself
> known. [101]

Barth is thus anxious to refute Feuerbach's methodology and anthropology, as well as to rescue Christian theology from what he called the "sting of Feuerbach's question." [102]

A second major stress of the **Christian Dogmatics** was the expected obedience of theology to the Word heard in the Church where the concrete, actual person is found. This does not mean that we can use our experience to speak of knowing God, for God still remains hidden from our knowledge. But the hearing of that Word means that our whole existence is shaken by God's judgment upon it, which is proclaimed in His Word. And in hearing God's No to our existence, we can either reject that Word or respond to it in faith, which in turn reveals God's Yes to our existence. "Not Christian faith, but the hidden Word of God to which faith responds is the object of theology." [103] This hidden Word is particularly revealed in Jesus Christ through whom the Urgeschichte of God invades man's history and overcomes the contingent, ambiguous nature of existence. [104]

A third emphasis was God's intervention being witnessed in Jesus Christ. Yet even in Jesus Christ God's Word has a hiddenness about it, especially whenever we, who still remain sinners in spite of faith, try to claim that we "know" God:

> The human word is never in itself God's Word. It becomes
> God's Word only when God himself speaks in it. [105]

To claim more than this means that one actually only worships a historical figure with certain cultural attributes whilst never knowing Him to be both God and man. Barth stressed that this movement of revelation from God to man as seen in the Trinity, where God as subject reveals Himself, is the revelation, and also provides the means for responding to that revelation. As such God establishes His freely independent lordship over us and our world. Here one notices the beginning of Barth's insistence that the knowledge of God and of the Godhead is revealed primarily in christology.

Still a fourth characteristic of the **Christian Dogmatics** was the objective character of scripture. The truth of scripture depends neither on the language of the writers nor on the interpretation of the exegete, but rather is itself the criterion which tests the faithfulness of the Church's theological language to the revelation.

> It is because we cannot speak of a direct identity of the Scripture as such with Revelation, although we cannot separate the Scripture from that Revelation, that our knowledge of the Bible as the Word of God is itself an event, an ever-new breaking-through to the Revelation of faith and obedience. [106]

One must indeed learn about and witness to this revelation in scripture as it is proclaimed in the Church. But that proclamation also has to test its truthfulness against the truth in scripture and its obedience to that truth.

Finally, Barth included what came to be called an "existentialist" methodology in the **Dogmatics.** In trying to guard against the hearer of scripture only understanding the Word of God as some abstract principle, Barth insisted that the Word does become a "happening" in our life through the freedom of the individual to respond to the Word, depending on the peculiar circumstances and situation of the person. This is not an individually determined response on the model of Kierkegaardian subjectivity; rather it is a response heard in the fellowship of the Church and re-examined from time to time within that community. One's freedom to respond is bound by the freedom of others in the community which is under the authority of the Word. [107]

The **Christian Dogmatics** was a systematic attempt to think through the implications of Paul's theology in **Romans,** as well as the issues included in the Fathers, the Reformation, and liberalism. Barth later abandoned this method in order to start fresh on a completely new Prolegomena to the re-named **Church Dogmatics.** Commenting some five years later on the motivating force compelling him to change course, he noted:

> I could and wanted to say the same thing as before, but now I could no longer say it in the way in which I had said it before. What else was left me except to begin at the beginning and here, to say the same thing over again, but the same thing over again in a different way. [108]

Still sensitive to this change-over in 1951, he described the first **Dogmatics** as "my well-known false start". [109]

Between the two **Dogmatics,** several events occurred which were to play important roles in Barth's theological career.

First, he took on Fräulein Charlotte von Kirschbaum (1899-1975) as an assistant and began a life-long friendship which was not without its problems with respect to his relationship with his family and especially his wife. [110] He had met Fräulein von Kirschbaum earlier in Germany and had indeed come to know her better in 1925 when they were in the same area on holiday. [111] She came from Munich, where she was a nurse and also a daughter of a Bavarian general who had fallen during the First World War. She attended a secretarial school in Munich and used this talent to assist Barth with some of his university administrative work one summer at Göttingen, after which she accompanied him to Münster. Barth's dependence on her was explained by himself some years later:

> [She] provided not only the liveliest participation in this area (of theology and the Church), but also a noticeable understanding and intelligence and an untiring work capacity each day, without whose assistance, which she especially provided for the orderliness and execution of my correspondence, I would have been able to do only a small particle of the work. [112]

Secondly, Barth acquired German citizenship, a decision which was to bring him into conflict with German laws for civil servants under the fascists later. [113] Thirdly, he was called at the age of forty-four in 1930 to the professorship of systematic theology at the University of Bonn, a particularly pleasant appointment, since Barth felt that he could work well with the evangelical theologians there. [114] His first lecture was packed with over 160 students and his informal open evenings, which he continued at Bonn, were almost getting out of hand because of the numbers. Eventually, he had to institute admission tests for his seminars. [115]

In June, 1930, he received his second honorary doctorate in theology from Glasgow University. [116] The British custom of granting hoods with degrees so fascinated him that when he returned to Bonn, he wore it to various faculty functions:

> Wenn schon, denn schon, dachte ich und erklärte hier den staunenden Medizinern etc.: ich sei nämlich der päpstliche Legat. [117] (If I am going to do it, I thought, I may as well do it up right. So I declared to the astonished medical professors and others: I am the papal legate.)

In 1930, he began a series of lectures which were to have a telling effect on his own theological method and which he eventually published, Anselm's **Cur Deus Homo?**. [118] Barth described these lectures as the turning point in his increasing unhappiness with the prevailing philosophical and naturalistic approach and orientation to theology and dogmatics. [119] These were "a vital key, if not the key" to a reversal in his own theological thinking. [120]

Several emphases are to be noticed in this little book. First, God's revelation is given by God Himself and faith in that revelation is also given by God. The existence of faith takes on a rational character (in the sense of _ratio_) as a reality independent of human responses seeking to know God. One begins with faith and moves to an understanding of that faith rather than first having an understanding of human nature and then moving to faith. "Credo ut intelligam means it is my faith itself that summons me to knowledge." [121] Faith therefore is a gift provided by God, which, once heard in the Church and in scripture, is to be understood and grasped in one's daily existence before God and in the company of others. [122]

Secondly, theology is not only a human response to the Word heard in the Church, it is also an obedient servant of the Church. Theology is to be an explication of the Credo of the Church.

> Intelligere will not go beyond the limit of the inner neces-
> sity of the articles of the Credo, beyond the limit of
> faith's essential nature which corresponds to these articles.
> [123]

Theology, therefore, cannot, indeed, must not rely on other disci-plines outside the spoken and revealed Word for verification either of its language or of the nature of the faith which is its content. Theology's beginning and boundary is the Word, which, whilst not limited by language, uses language and conceptualization to make explicit the fact of the revelation of that Word to us and the implications of that revelation in our faith and ethics.

Thirdly, as the Word is the source of and the boundary or limit for theology, then theology qua theology has an historical relativity inherent in its very structure and function. Theological statements cannot be absolutized, but must be re-viewed and re-examined from time to time in different historical circumstances:

> Any statement that is really theological, that is to say,
> not covered by biblical authority, is bound by this rule;
> such a statement is not final; fundamentally it is an
> interim statement, the best that knowledge and conscience
> can for the present construe; it awaits better instruction
> from God or man. [124]

Fourthly, Barth sees the need for clarifying the relationship between the givenness of revelation, the language describing that revelation, and the possibility of that language bearing "truth" about the nature of that revelation. This relationship is found in Anselm's idea of "correspondence" or analogia fidei. The Word as truth "conveys" upon human language the possibility of a semblance to its truth and allows for this possibility through the structures and conceptions of language. There is a peculiar rationality in the nature of the Word itself which becomes the criterion for the accuracy and faithfulness of theological statements. This rationality, which is understood to be the comprehension of existence as it conforms to a particular "law", is a part of faith itself and becomes the means by which our existence and that of our world is understood and questioned. The possibility of theological language bearing truth about God and about His relationship to us is given freely by God Himself:

> One form of the revelation is obviously also the occurrence of intelligere, of the vera ratione quaerere veram ratio-nem . . . to which even the inner text discloses itself, inasmuch as the conformity of ratio (meaning the particular character of something which makes it intelligible to another and also the capacity of one to grasp the existence before him, according to Barth's interpretation of Anselm's model) [125] to truth depends neither upon the object nor the subject, but on that same revealing power of God which illumines faith and which faith encounters as authority. The antithesis between auctoritas (origin of truth, i.e., God) and ratio does not coincide with the antithesis between God and man, but represents the distinc-tion between two stages of the one divine road along which man first attains faith and on the basis of that faith attains knowledge. [126]

Consequently, when Anselm speaks of the name of God as something beyond which nothing greater can be conceived, Barth understands this to mean that Anselm is speaking from within the situation of a believer before his creator. To try and conceive something greater than one's creator would be absurd.

> It concerns the choice of the concrete limit which, so far as this question is concerned, appears to make knowledge possible. [127]

Finally, Barth sees in Anselm's method a rejection of apologetics as a possibility for Christian dogmatics. Anselm does not accept the idea that within the Church the voice of the Church and other voices have equal rights. [128] Dogmatics is to speak from within the Church about the truth given by God to the Church about the relationship between Him and us:

> Perhaps, desiring to prove, (Anselm) did not really remain standing on this side of the gulf between the believer

and non-believer but crossed it, though on this occasion not in search of a truce as has been said of him and has often happened, but as a conqueror whose weapon was the fact that he met the unbelievers as one of them and accepted them as his equal. [129]

Prof. Smart suggests that with the study of Anselm, Barth saw the crucial issue between the liberalism of his earlier days and his newly developing approach to theology via christology to center on whether theology was to be primarily concerned with the Word of God (which in turn shapes the faith given to man, but is neither limited by nor given credence by man's response to that faith) or whether theology was to be concerned with the faith-response by man to that Word. [130] Barth's idea of the objectivity of God's Word, now supported by the theological method learnt from Anselm, certainly had an effect on his epistomology because the place of Jesus Christ in man's knowledge of God is looked at afresh, the first clue being provided in the **Church Dogmatics** published in 1932.

Barth was to justify this redirection several years later as a compulsion which grew as the result of the work on Anselm. Between the two **Dogmatics**

I had to learn that Christian doctrine, if it is to merit its name and if it is to build up the Christian church in the world as she must needs be built up, has to be exclusively and conclusively the doctrine of Jesus Christ-- of Jesus Christ as the living Word of God spoken to us men. If I look back from this point on my earlier studies, I may well ask myself how it ever came about that I did not learn this much sooner and accordingly speak out. How slow is man, above all when the most important things are at stake. [131]

In the first part of the first volume of the **Church Dogmatics**, Barth suggests that he felt it necessary to begin anew for several reasons:

First, he wished to make certain that scripture was understood to be the controlling written authority for dogmatics and exegesis in their entirety, i.e., for understanding not only the text, but also the situation in which the text was written.

Secondly, he thought it necessary to affirm that dogmatics was the servant of the Church, rather than an apologetics of some kind.

Thirdly, he desired to refute any criticism of his first **Dogmatics** as being scholastic because of the emphasis on the Trinity and epistomology.

Fourthly, he wished to provide the Evangelical Church with a new foundation for its theological ethics as the Body of Christ in its cultural and political surroundings. [132]

Barth insisted that the "dogma" of the Church was the "stuff" of dogmatics, that is, the testing of the Church's past and contemporary teachings and the truth or lack of truth therein. Dogmatics is a necessary control within the Church in service to the Church. [133]

Just the year before the publication of **Church Dogmatics**, Barth had said in an address entitled, "The Dilemma of the Evangelical Church," that the Church may have to part ways from its cultural situation at times, for should the Church persist in seeing its message and that of the world as identical, eventually the two would become one and the Church would be betraying the Gospel for the aims of the state. [134] For this remark, Barth was publicly rebuked by church officials, [135] but he retorted later in the first part of the **Dogmatics** that the Evangelical Church in Germany ought to reconsider its own theological ethics and the basis for that ethics in order to be able to play a role in the affairs of state with an evangelical identity. [136]

This disagreement about the basis of theological action in the state between Barth and the Evangelical Church officials was only the beginning of what Barth came to see as the inevitable conflict between the ideological claims of the state and the theological claims of the Church. In order to further a kind of warning system about this conflict, he and Thurneysen established a journal, Theologische Existenz heute. In an article published in 1933, Barth stressed the centrality of the Word as the absolute beginning of the Church's life and work in the world. The Church cannot seek God nor understand its task in any age from any source other than the Word and cannot know that Word other than in Jesus Christ, who cannot be known other than in scripture. [137]

In December, 1930, Günther Dehn, a pastor in Berlin-Moabit, a working class district, and a former religious socialist--indeed he was at the Tambach conference at which Barth was first introduced to Germany--was invited to be Professor of Practical Theology at the University in Heidelberg. Dehn had become well-known because of a lecture he had given in November, 1928, called "The Church and the Reconciliation of the Nations," in which he sought to explain the theological reasons for a Christian's opposition to war. Germany was still very much insecure nationally and embarrassed over the loss of face suffered as the defeated country of World War I. The excessive demands for war reparations by the victorious allies only exacerbated matters. Dehn suggested in that lecture that soldiers trained by the state to kill others, even though they were killed in combat, could not expect honors and recognition by the religious community because such training violated Christian teachings. In the heated atmosphere of Germany at the time, this 1928 speech not only was disapproved by the higher church officials in the dominant Prussian Church in Berlin, but also was remembered by the church officials when he was called to the professorship. [138] The theological faculty at the university eventually rescinded the call under pressure, but Barth along with Martin Dibelius, Otto Piper, Karl Schmidt, and a few others, publicly defended Dehn and his right to preach freely and unhindered when he felt he was being loyal to the Word. In a newspaper article entitled, "Why Does One Not Conduct the Struggle Straight Across The Line," (Frankfurter Zeitung, 15th February, 1932), Barth, in his first public political article, claimed that two things were at stake in the Dehn case: First, the opponents of dialectical theology were only using Dehn to get at the advocates of that theological position and at the opponents of the tendency to identify the goals and interests of the state and church as one and the same. Second, the attack on Dehn was only a foretaste of the increasing conflict between church and state in Germany. [139] It was also in 1932 that Barth joined the Social Democratic Party in Germany (SPD).

In June, 1932, the Glaubensbewegung deutscher Christen was emerging. This movement called for a "new order" in the Evangelical Church, summoning all evangelical Christians of German stock to renew the German spirit of Luther, to stand against Marxism and socialism, to support the anti-miscegenation laws and pure racial laws of the state, and to move against pacifism and internationalism. [140]

Also, in 1932 a two-volumed work entitled, **Die Kirche und das Dritte Reich: Fragen und Forderungen deutscher Theologen,** appeared. This book sought to create a dialogue between the Evangelical Church and the state and amongst its contributors were Emil Fuchs, Otto Piper, Martin Rade, and Paul Tillich. The official comment from the Reich's Office of Church Affairs in dismissing the book was that it was an "accumulation of ignorance, superficiality, presumption and malicious enmity to the German Freedom Movement." [141]

Events began to move quickly after Hitler became Chancellor in January, 1933. This sharpened Barth's resistance to the fascist direction in Germany all the more. [142] The office of Reichsbischof was established, largely with the support of the Lutherans and "German Christians", since the Reformed wing of the Evangelical Church opposed such an establishment. On 27th May, 1933, Friedrich von Bedelschwingh, a Lutheran pastor and director of the Bethel Institute, was elected as the first Reichsbischof. On the day he took office Barth and several Reformed theologians issued the "Düsseldorf Theses". [143] Opening with the question, "What is the Evangelical Church?" this group defined the Church as a community born of the Word of God whose only voice is that of the Word of God as evidenced in the Old and New Testaments and as revealed in Jesus Christ. The Church's sole authority is Jesus Christ and the existence of an episcopal office with authority over all the congregations does not correspond to the biblical idea of God's Lordship alone. The Theses apparently aroused latent sympathies and support amongst a number of Evangelical Christians in Germany, for they were later included in the Confession of the German Reformed Churches' Alliance in 1938 (Die Bekenntnisschriften und Kirchenordnungen der nach Gottes Wort reformierten Kirchen).

On 24th June, 1933, a State Commissar for supervision of the Evangelical Church was appointed, an appointment which also was to have influence on the other Landeskirchen in Germany. The Commissar immediately dismissed the properly elected church officials and put "German Christians" in their offices along with the issuance of a notice that efforts to frustrate the state's authority in Church affairs would be viewed as treason. [144] Just prior to these events, in March after the fascist government had passed a new law re-ordering the rights of civil servants (Beamten) in Germany and political parties, the Social Democratic Party (SPD), which Barth had joined in 1932, released its civil servant members from having to declare loyalty to that party since such a declaration could endanger their status as civil servants. Barth, as a civil servant, corresponded with Paul Tillich and insisted on maintaining openly his party membership: "Wer mich nicht so haben will, der kann mich überhaupt nicht haben." ("Anyone who does not want to have me like this cannot have me at all.") [145] He also wrote to the Prussian Minister of Culture, asking whether his party membership would be a hindrance to his continuing his teaching duties in the summer of 1933. The minister, who was acquainted with Barth through his Romans agreed that he could do so only if he would not build up any cells of support at the university. [146] In June the SPD was dissolved and forbidden by the fascists. When asked by the rector of the university whether such would affect his status, Barth replied:

> Ich habe die Sache mit dem Herrn Minister in Ordnung
> gebracht. Und so bin ich vielleicht faktisch der letzte
> SPD-Mann im Dritten Reich gewesen. [147] ("I have
> arranged things with the Minister himself. So perhaps
> I was the last man in the SPD in the Third Reich in
> point of fact.")

Near the end of June SA troops occupied the buildings of the Federation of the Evangelical Churches in Berlin and the government issued a "Decree for the Removal of the Critical State in Church and Nation," saying that the state was taking over the administration of the Federation "for the sake of the Church and its Gospel" and was intent on being obedient to the "pure Gospel of Jesus Christ." [148] Just prior to this action, Barth and Thurneysen had published the first issue of their pamphlet Theologische Existenz heute (25th June, 1933). Describing his intentions about the publication of this magazine-pamphlet many years later, Barth said:

> I still had nothing essentially new to say. At that time I said rather just what I had always tried to say, namely, that beside God we can have no other gods, that the Holy Spirit of the Scriptures is enough to guide the Church in all truth, and that the grace of Jesus Christ is all-sufficient for the forgiveness of our sins and the ordering of our lives. But now, suddenly, I had to say the same thing in a situation where it could no longer have the slightest vestige of an academic theory. Without my wanting it, or doing anything to facilitate it, this had of necessity to take on the character of a summons, a challenge, a battle cry, a confession. [149]

The two of them also attacked both the office of Reichsbischof as the controlling force in Evangelical Christian life and the continuing divisions between the Lutheran and Reformed wings of the Evangelical Church. The crucial issue, as Barth and Thurneysen saw it, was not the political pressures being applied to the administration and program of the churches; rather the vital issue was the freedom of the churches to preach the Word of God and to conduct their own theology in obedience to the revealed Word in scripture. [150] On 1st July, Barth sent a copy of the pamphlet to Hitler himself, which meanwhile was being published in increasing numbers until it was finally confiscated on 28th July, 1934. [151] Hermann Albert Hesse (1877-1957), the Reformed representative on the Collegium of Three, which, along with the representatives from the Lutheran and United Churches, had rewritten the new constitution for the Evangelical Church Federation, [152] said after reading Barth's article:

> As I read, the scales fell from my eyes. Here lay my mistake since my early days under Schlatter. Besides Holy Scripture, another side of revelation had been authoritative for me, namely, nature. . . . I could only give the professor [Barth] my hand and say, "You are right." [153]

On 11th July, 1933, the new Constitution was accepted by the representatives of the various Landeskirchen in Berlin, and on 14th July, the government ratified the Constitution as law and published it. The "German Christians" began to campaign for a "new Church of Christ in the new state of Adolph Hitler,"

[154] and on 23rd July, in elections held throughout the churches, the "German Christians" won most of the offices. Barth, along with Karl Ludwig Schmidt, Ernst Wolf, Hans Weber, Gustav Hölscher, and Otto Bleibtreu had drawn up another list of candidates to oppose both the "German Christians" and a sympathizing group called "Evangelium und Kirche". The list won some ten percent of the votes, and one of the successful candidates in Bonn was Barth. [155] On 27th September, 1933, Ludwig Müller was elected President of the Prussian Federated Church with the title of bishop, which occurred only some three weeks after the Prussian synod decided that non-Aryans and Germans married to non-Aryans could no longer be employed in church positions. [156] With this development, Barth declined an earlier offer from the government to be a member of a newly organized theological commission in the Prussian Church and resigned his position on the examination commission in the Rhineland church's Consistorium. [157]

The immediate reaction to this legislation and direction amongst some German Evangelical pastors was the organizing of the Pfarrernotbund in Berlin under Pastor Martin Niemöller in Berlin-Dahlem. This group was immediately joined and supported by some 1300 clergy, all of whom subscribed to a four point pledge:

1) to be a minister of the Word solely bound to Holy Scripture and to the Reformation Confessions as true expositions of Scripture,

2) to protest regardless of the cost any violation of this Source of authority,

3) to assist the victims who have been or are being persecuted by the state because of their support for this pledge, and

4) to oppose the Aryan legislation. [158]

In Berlin in November, 1933, the consequences of the alliance between church and state became clearer with the famous address of Reinhold Krause in the Berlin Sportpalast at a "German Christian" rally. Krause, a district superintendent in the Berlin-Brandenburg Landeskirche, said on that occasion that the Third Reich would complete the reformation of the Church begun by Martin Luther and would bring to an end all the internal quarreling and divisions within the Evangelical Church. A "people's Church" would be established which would be a non-confessional German national church not bound to restrictive confessions, but to the German people. The movement toward such a church meant that the immoral "Jewish" Old Testament had to be abandoned and the New Testament had to be expurgated of "all perverted and superstitious passages," including those of the Jew Paul. [159] The rally approved propositions calling for the removal of all non-Aryan

Christians from the Evangelical Church, the abolition of all non-Germanic elements from the worship and confessions, especially where they referred to the Old Testament, the redefinition of the image of Jesus as a hero who was conscious of the divine within Himself, thereby arousing consciousness within His followers, and support for the fascist state. [160] Barth sought again to warn the Evangelical Christians of the signs of the times:

> They (the government) could do it (make concessions to the church leaders who had asked for condemnation of Krause's speech) because the substance of the "German Christian" faith is not affected one bit. For this reason, it is senseless to conclude from the concessions made that a serious change has taken place in the nature, attitude, and character of the "German Christians" or of the "German Christian" government. . . . The resistance has to go farther and be directed against the ecclesiastical-theological system of modern Protestantism which in no way is embodied in the "German Christians" alone if everything is not to have been in vain. [161]

Barth saw a continuation of a theological tendency he had attacked just some six days previously (6th November) at a Pastor's Conference when the "Rengsdorf Theses" of the newly founded Evangelical bishopric of Cologne-Aachen dominated by "German Christians" were discussed. Barth had attacked the notion of the state and the Church making up two divine orders within God's creation to which loyalty was to be given by the Christian as an expectation from God. He also attacked in that speech, the claim of the Nazis that Christian discipline included a "healthy family life," loyalty to the state and obedience to God: [162]

> For obedience toward God, Jesus Christ alone has given his life as a substitution for the disobedience of us all. Discipleship of Jesus Christ can indeed mean that we give our life for the blessings we have received from God, but it can also mean that we surrender them.
>
> Whoever today uncritically mentions in the same breath the giving of one's life in obedience to God and for the good things of the German people denies the fact of sin, reconciliation through Christ, and the freedom of the divine commandment, and places himself outside the Evangelical Church. . . . [163]
>
> Conclusion: the "theology" of the Rengsdorf Theses is clearly not a theology, but a specimen of a gnosis that operates with Christian concepts but which neither understands nor deals with the first, second, or third articles (of the Creed) as a Confession of God's Word, but treats all three as explications of human reason (with the current

> emphasis upon the national factor). In addition, it has
> put itself in possession of outward Church authority by
> an act of usurpation. For both reasons it is not a philosophy
> to be discussed, but to be entirely rejected and opposed
> just for the sake of Christian love. [164]

Finally, in late 1933, Barth in a "Memorandum" to the Pfarrernotbund called the principles of the "German Christians" a heresy. [165]

On 4th January, 1934, the Reichsbischof decreed that clergy were not to speak of church controversies in their sermons, but were to preach only "the pure Gospel". He also insisted that the sorting out of Aryans and non-Aryans in the Church was to be brought forward. Pastor Niemöller (1892-1984) led the Pfarrernotbund in protesting this new action from his pulpit, saying:

> When we oppose his decree, we do so in agreement
> with the Augsburg Confession, which in the article concern-
> ing the power of bishops declares the following: "When
> bishops teach or ordain anything contrary to the gospel,
> we have God's command not to obey them in such a
> case. Even properly elected bishops are not to be followed
> when they err." We too must act in relation to the Reichs-
> bischof according to the text: "We must obey God rather
> than man." [166]

After this, Hitler personally summoned Niemöller and some other church leaders, and reminded them that the care and guidance of the state was exclusively within his realm. [167] On 26th-27th January, the Lutheran bishops said in a declaration that they were "unconditionally loyal" to the Third Reich and to Hitler and that they condemned all criticism of the state as a danger to the German nationhood. [168] On 27th January, Pastor Niemöller was removed from his parish in Berlin-Dahlem by the Reichsbishof and on 10th February he was stricken from the list of active clergy.

The year 1934 also saw the coming together of mostly Reformed churchmen at Barmen-Gemarke in the Rhineland for the first Free Reformed Synod, where a major declaration written by Barth was adopted as the "Declaration Concerning the Right Understanding of the Reformation Confessions of Faith in the German Evangelical Church of the Present (Gegenwart) by the Reformed Synod in Barmen-Gemarke." [169] This was a fore-beacon to the later All-Churches Barmen Synod of the Confessing Church. The Declaration insisted on the absolute independence of God's revelation from all human sources and reminded the people that the Church as the Body of Christ had to be concerned not only with the spiritual welfare of her members, but also with the historical situation in which they were expected to witness to and serve the Word of God. The Church "serves men and people, state and culture, when it is concerned about being obedient to the Word of God prescribed for it." [170] This service is a command from God revealed in Jesus Christ, the only Lord and Ruler of the Church. As Jesus Christ is the same for all peoples and races, so His Church must be the same inclusive community for all peoples and races. The state is not an order, but has been given an assignment by God as a human institution to assist in fashioning man's temporal existence; yet Jesus Christ is also Lord over the state as He is also over the Church. [171]

On 29th-31st May, 1934, the first Confessional Synod of the German Evangelical Church met in Barmen and Barth along with seven others made up the Theological Commission, which wrote the now famous "Theological Declaration Concerning the Present Situation of the German Evangelical Church," in short the "Barmen Declaration". Although the synod met in a reformed church, it included all parties and churches amongst its 138 delegates gathered "with a common word to utter," namely, that "the unity of the Evangelical Churches in Germany comes only from the Word of God in faith through the Holy Spirit." [172]

In his usual incisive way, Barth understood this action to have deeper significant implications. He saw it as the first important attack on natural theology:

> The Confessional Church was, so to speak, only the witness of a situation in which simultaneously there took place a remarkable revelation, as there had not been for a long time, of the beast out of the abyss, and a fresh confirmation of the only old revelation of God in Jesus Christ. It was only a witness to this event. . . . What it noticed on this occasion was the fact of the unique validity of Jesus Christ as the Word of God spoken to us for life and death. The repudiation of natural theology was only the self-evident reverse side of this notice. [173]

Yet the implicit connection between dogmatics and ethics in concrete situations was revealed to Barth in a most poignant way: the requirement by the government that all lectures at the university were to begin with an "Heil Hitler". [174] Unable to do this, Barth conplained both to the rector and the Minister of Culture. This matter became even more troublesome when, on 7th November, 1934, Barth as a civil servant of the state was asked to swear loyalty to the Führer (Treueid). Barth declined and was suspended from teaching on 26th November, whereby a "German Christian" professor, Schmidt-Japing, was presented as Barth's successor. As he was formally introduced to the students at Barth's seminar on 7th December, some of his students read a petition signed by some 200 of them refusing to accept a successor to Barth. On 20th December, Barth was dismissed from his position by the Dienststrafkammer in Cologne. [175] Together with his assistant, Helmut Gollwitzer, but also including Ernst Wolf, Günther Dehn, Dietrich Bonhoeffer, and Karl Schmidt at other places, Barth's and their careers in German universities were effectively at an end. Bultmann had asked Barth to reconsider his refusal to pledge loyalty to Hitler. [176] Barth appealed the ruling and asked the Berlin church for support, which declined to do so.

On 1st March, 1935, Barth was forbidden to speak or preach in public. [177] The University of Utrecht, however, invited him to lecture there on weekends on the subject, "Central Problems of Dogmatics", which formed the basis of his book, **Credo**. [178] Barth wanted to continue to teach in Germany, although there were offers to teach in Switzerland. On 14th June, 1935, Barth's appeal against the Cologne judgment was granted, but Barth was fined because of his refusal to make the Hitler salute and some remarks he had made at the house of Gerhard Jacobi in October, 1933. Barth was appointed Professor of Systematic Theology at the University of Basle, so he left Germany, since the Minister of Culture had effectively retired him. Remarked Barth sardonically on the transition from Bonn to Basle:

> Es war . . . so, dass ich an einem Samstag in Deutschland abgesetzt wurde, und schon am Montag hat mich der Regierungsrat von Basel zum ordentlichen Professor ernannt, so dass ich also nur über den Sonntag arbeitslos war. . . . "Dei providentia et hominum confusione Helvetia regitur". . . [179] (It happened . . . that I was dismissed on a Saturday in Germany and already on Monday the Regierungsrat in Basle had appointed me a professor ordinarius, so that I was only unemployed over Sunday. . . Dei providentia et hominum confusione Helvetia regitur. . . .)

Barth's chair was done away with and the funds transferred to the Technical College in Berlin (Technische Hochschule). Together with Barth and his family went also Fräulein Kirschbaum to Basle, never again to return to Germany until after the end of World War II, with one exception: the acceptance of an invitation to come to Barmen in 1935, to deliver the lecture himself. It was read, however, by a Pastor Immer with the police in the over-crowded church observing because the German officials forbade Barth to read it himself. [180]

In 1938, Barth published the second part of the first volume of the **Church Dogmatics**. Germany was moving toward war and Barth saw fit to remind his readers of the relativity of all human structures, including that of the Church as most people knew it. It is not man who sustained creation or the Church, but Jesus Christ. [181] Barth's mother also died in 1938 after being unwell for a long time. [182] Oxford made him an honorary doctor in that year as well, and in March, he gave the second part of his Gifford Lectures in Aberdeen.

Barth remained in Switzerland for most of the war years, except for an occasional journey to other countries. He maintained regular contacts with the Confessing Church in Germany and also assisted in relocating Jewish refugees in Switzerland. In 1940, at the age of fifty-four, Barth volunteered for the Swiss national army and did sentry duty as well as preaching amongst his fellow soldiers. He was also a member of a secret organization devoted to the defence of Switzerland should the Germans invade. [183] He also managed to write the first part of the second volume of the **Church Dogmatics,** entitled **Doctrine of God,** in March, 1942.

Barth returned to Germany for the first time after the war in 1945 for a conference on the reorganization of the post-war Evangelical Church. He was rather disappointed with what he saw of the theological and ecclesiastical interests and tendencies in the Church, for the Church appeared to have learned little from the events of the past ten years.

> I realized more clearly than before that men--Christian
> men also, and especially Christian men--are by nature
> tough and cannot easily be brought to repentance. [184]

In 1946, he returned to Bonn as a guest lecturer in dogmatics, and Emil Brunner (!) was his substitute in Basle. Because of Bonn, Barth declined to be the Rector of the university for that year. [185] In 1947, he met up with one of his chief American critics, Reinhold Niebuhr, an encounter to which Barth looked with some anxiety and wonderment. [186]

Barth went to Hungary in 1948 to lecture as well as raise questions about the allegiance expected of Christians by the rising socialist countries in eastern Europe. He felt that the historical conditions of the churches were different from those of Nazi Germany and that the communists did not make the theological claims of the fascists. He detected an openness about the churches in eastern Europe facing a new post-war situation which he failed to notice in post-war Germany amongst the Evangelical Christians. [187] It is now well known that Barth was heavily criticized in other western countries for not standing against communism with the same fervor displayed in his resistance to the fascists, but Barth warned his critics against embracing western democracy as a kind of kingdom of God come to earth.

> Were we so unsure of the goodness of the Western cause
> . . . that we could bring ourselves to admit only senselessly

unequal alternatives--freedom and the dignity of man
as against mutual atomic annihilation--then venture to
pass off this latter alternative as a work of true Christian
love. [188]

The Barthian caution about embracing any single system still lingered. He also journeyed to the First Assembly of the newly organized World Council of Churches in Amsterdam, although he initially was suspicious of the whole ecumenical movement. [189] Amongst others he met there were Michael Ramsey of England "über die Beziehung zwischen diesem Mann und mir fiel von dritter Seite das Wort: wenn es so weit sei, dann müsse das Millennium 'around the corner' sein", ("A third party described the relationship between this man and me with these words: If things are this far, then the millennium must be 'around the corner'.") [190] Nygren, Florovsky, and John Foster Dulles, "sein Blick war dabei kalt und abweisend und er gefiel mir auch sonst nicht", ("his look was cold and absent and I did not like him at all"). [191]

Barth continued to write his **Church Dogmatics** until the last part of the fourth volume, entitled **Doctrine of Reconciliation,** was published in 1959. In 1953 he wrote his now famous letter to a pastor in the German Democratic Republic. His **Dogmatics** was translated into English under the editorship of G. W. Bromiley and T. F. Torrance and published in Scotland. In 1962, Barth, now 76 years old, made his first trip to North America for some lectures, having just retired from his professorship at Basle (1st March). [192] Just prior to this journey there had been a controversy about his successor. The theological faculty had selected his former assistant at Bonn and friend, Helmut Gollwitzer of the Free University of Berlin; but the choice was vetoed by the Minister of Education in the canton because of Gollwitzer's political background and embrace of socialism and peace movements. Heinrich Ott was appointed instead. The Junge Kirche observed in an editorial:

The so-called "free West" has shown that even in the
appointment of a chair of theology it is not the relevant
qualifications that are decisive, but political criteria derived
from the cold war. [193]

In 1963, the Sorbonne, which has no theological faculty, honored Barth with a doctorate from the Faculty of Letters and Humanities, describing him as "a creator of comprehensive scientific work" in the Laudatio written by the philosopher, Prof. Paul Ricoeur. [194] Just prior to this he had also received the Sonning Prize in Copenhagen for his advancement of Kierkegaard. [195]

Barth suffered a heart attack in December, 1964, from which he recovered. Four years later on 9th December, Karl Barth died in his sleep, to be discovered by his wife as she went into his room to put on a record of his favorite composer, Mozart, to awaken him. [**196**] On 13th December, Barth was buried in the Hörnli cemetery in Basle and on the 14th December, at the Münster in Basle a memorial service was held which was broadcast on the radio. The service was attended by such persons as Max Geiger, Dean of the theological faculty, Lukas Burckhardt, the President of the local government, Helmut Gollwitzer, representative of the German churches and universities, Joseph Hromadka from the eastern European churches, Hans Küng, representing the Roman Catholic Church, Eberhard Jüngel, representing the younger academic generation, and Willem A. Visser't Hooft from the World Council of Churches were present. Between each talk was played Mozart's Concerto for Flute in G Major. [**197**]

Chapter Two

THE EMERGING MODEL FOR POLITICAL DOGMATICS

That young Karl Barth very early on in his career understood the Christian faith implicitly and explicitly to include a
social ethic has been documented in several sources. [1] As pointed
out previously, Barth not only was an active lecturer in the Continuing Education program of the Safenwil Arbeiterverein, [2] but
also joined the local branch of the Social Democratic Party in
Switzerland, as well as preached on many political subjects. Such
actions were unusual at the time for an Evangelical pastor. Barth
was struggling to understand the political responsibility of a Christian in society. He was also searching for guidelines to establish
and measure the relationship between responsible political action
and Christian theology. As his life-long friend, Eduard Thurneysen,
observed:

> Already at that time in Safenwil alongside with the great
> interest in the Bible, the newspaper was read and the
> Bible was related to current events. All of this was under-
> stood as a sign and witness of the fact that God in
> Christ not only wants to save souls in a world which
> remains sinful, but also that God loved this sinful world
> and that this sinfulness was placed under judgment (richten)
> in the cross and resurrection of His Son; His overcoming,
> however, is as we like to say with a quote from (Chris-
> toph) Blumhardt, an overcoming in the proper direction
> (ein Zurechtrichten). . . . At that time in Safenwil princi-
> palities, dominions, and powers which "appeared to be
> endured" (schautragen) by Christ, were very much talked
> about. . . . Of course, the victory has been revealed
> only to the believer, it is thus veiled from our eyes.
> But the day will come in which the time of the veiling
> will be at an end, in which the victory of the kingdom
> will be clearly visible. So even then Karl Barth understood
> the coming again. [3]

This eschatological connection between the Christian faith in our world and society persisted in young Barth and, indeed, linked not only theology and politics, but also provided a frame of reference for what would now be called a "political theology." Barth first acknowledged political interests and political activism because of pastoral problems confronting him as vicar in the small industrial town of Safenwil. In a speech to the Safenwil Arbeiter-verein in 1911, he pointed out that in light of the injustices being carried out by the local factory owners, one of the most prominent of whom was a member of his congregation, Jesus Himself was more socialistic than the Socialists because of His comments on the ease with which a camel could go through the eye of a needle compared with the possibility of a rich man coming into heaven:

> Jesus taboos the conception of private property; about
> this I have no possible doubt. He taboos the basic principle
> (of capitalism): "What is mine is mine." [4]

Yet this was also the beginning of Barth's efforts at co-ordinating his politics with Christian theology, that is, finding an authentic theologically grounded social ethic. This is the clue to his seemingly contradictory directions in the two editions of **Romans.** It is also the clue to his claim some 21 years afterwards that "ethics belongs not only to dogmatics, but to the doctrine of God." [5]

> Ethics so-called I regard as the doctrine of God's command
> and do not consider it right to treat it otherwise than
> as an integral part of dogmatics. [6]

Thus, it is significant that in each of his major dogmatic divisions there is a section on ethics: in the prolegomena under the theology of the Word of God is the ethical section of this doctrine called "The Life of the Children of God"; [7] under the heading "Doctrine of God" is the ethical part called "The Command of God"; [8] under the "Doctrine of Creation" is "The Command of God the Creator"; [9] under the "Doctrine of Reconciliation" is the section "Ethics as the task of the doctrine of reconciliation." [10] Why this connection?

Barth, after an examination of the traditional method which usually separates theological issues from dogmatics--a separation based on the presupposition that goodness is a "natural" norm apart from Christ as the revelation of true goodness and therefore discernible by all--decided that the consequence of such a separation had been that theological ethics became the norm for controlling and interpreting biblical exegesis. This was ironic, because biblical exegesis was intended itself to provide the norm for determining the good:

> Its standard ceases to be the Word of God. It is the
> idea of the good which controls its investigation of the
> goodness of the Christian character. The Word of God
> is retained only in so far as it can be made intelligible
> as the historical medium and vehicle of this idea. The
> Church which sanctions this theology has subjected itself
> to an utterly alien authority. [11]

But there is also a methodological error in such a separation, and here one notices Barth's continued denial of the claims of Kulturprotestantismus. The logical consequence of such a methodology was the practical action taken by so many of his former liberal professors who so disappointed young Barth when they signed a petition supporting the militaristic policies of Kaiser Wilhelm and the German state during the First World War. [12] Barth felt that such actions were inevitable because through such a separation humankind became the constitutive principle instead of God or His Word: "the book of the holy man which is the sequel to that of the holy God." [13]

> In his book (Bible) the holy man has no independent
> existence. Therefore, he never becomes an independent
> object of thought. He exists only in the course of the
> existence of the holy God and of the study of His speech
> and action. [14]

The coordination of dogmatics and ethics means that there can be no reversal of the grace/redemption relationship between God and us: God turns toward us initially and only through His grace are we as sinners set free, redeemed, and made capable of turning toward God. However, such is not to assume that both are on an equal plane. Dogmatics, and therefore the study of the revelation of God, takes precedence:

> Included in the reality of the Word of God, (theology)
> obviously has to present the reality of man to whom
> the Word is turned and who is redeemed by it. What
> is theologically impossible is a study of these two realities
> (ethics and dogmatics) as though they are on the same
> plane, as though there can be between them coordination,
> continuity or interchange, or, as though, in the last resort
> they are somehow identical. . . . We cannot coordinate
> in this way God's Word on the one side and the man
> who hears God's Word on the other. . . . It is not true
> that believing man must work for the coming of God's
> kingdom. It is not true that he is related to the Word
> of God as the subject to the object. All these are ideas
> which are possible only on the basis of the view which
> ruined the Catholic Church, that there is coordination,
> continuity, interchange and finally identity between nature

> and supernature. It may all be very true with regard to "nature" and "supernature". But theology is concerned, not with the encounter between nature and supernature, but with the encounter between nature and grace, or concretely, with the encounter between man and the Word of God. The reality of the man addressed by the Word of God cannot be related to the reality of the latter as a subject to an object, but only as a predicate to a subject. [15]

As such, the positive aspect of this connection is that the Word of God has always to do with human existence and therefore with ethics, which is the question of right and proper conduct. The theme of dogmatics is the revelation of the Word of God and the relationship of that revelation to God's concern and care for us, i.e., for our existence. It is about the relationship between the Creator and His creature, the Holy One and the sinner, the Commander and the commanded. Thus, only for analytical purposes there may be a technical or systematic separation, but there cannot be an actual separation of the two in fact. [16]

> Therefore, the theme of dogmatics is always the Word of God and nothing else. But the theme of the Word is human existence, human life and volition and action. This is challenged by the Word of God, questioned as to its rightness, and brought into the right way. It is for this reason and in this sense, not in virtue of its own previous competence, but by the Word of God, that human existence acquires theological relevance. . . . A reality which is conceived and presented in such a way that it does not effect or claim men . . . , i.e., a theoretical reality, cannot possibly be the reality of the Word of God. . . . Dogmatics has no option: it has to be ethics as well. . . . [17]

In order to understand the development of this component of Barth's methodology, one has to begin with his early years and move to the period when he began his academic career as a university professor at Göttingen. The entrance into the academic theological world was the start of a new theological direction in his life. The period included Barth's emerging understanding of political theology and political action as they relate to society and the state. This is an important factor to recount when noticing the difference between the two editions of **Romans.** This difference has particularly irritated several critics of Barth, such as Niebuhr and Brunner.

Several questions must be raised in this connection when tracing this development. First, how does Barth understand society/ state or the world? Secondly, how does he understand the action of the creature in the society/state? Thirdly, what, if any, are the political implications and consequences of this action?

Barth and Blumhardt

In 1919, in an essay commemorating Friedrich Naumann and Christoph Blumhardt, both of whom had died in August of that year, Barth complained that the Religious Socialist Naumann had awakened the social consciousness of many through his understanding of the coming of the new age by God and God's concern with the political problems of particular social situations.

> It was a beautiful, hopeful springtime for many serious Christians far beyond Germany's borders as Naumann at that time began, together with his friends and with that equally enlightened preacher to the Imperial Court, Stöcker, to ask these questions. . . . One felt something: here is a coming strong, great new something. [18]

But, lamented Barth, this anticipated "new great thing" never arrived. A secularization of the evangelical social intentions occurred which made little distinction between a "Christian-social" goal and a "national-social" goal. [19] Barth felt that Naumann and the other Religious Socialists had betrayed the New Testament by lacking such a distinction, because a "new Trinity" was instituted: democracy, industry, and world power as the worthy goals for socially-active Christians:

> Either that is God whom the New Testament identifies. That means, however, not only the conversion of some things, rather of all things, the renewal of the whole world, a permanent change (Veränderung) of this life. . . . Then the Social Democrats are right and not the social reformers, indeed the most radical Social Democrats are not radical enough; indeed the confession of social democracy is only a small, to be sure, very insufficient poorly prepared partial payment of that to which a Christian today is indebted to his faith. Or Naumann must have said to himself: "God is that who binds man to His own nature and to the general laws of nature, which hurls him into the struggle of existence. . . . There is nothing new under the sun." "Socialism, indeed the more radical it is, touches a fatal recognition of reality: social reform with the careful consideration of capitalism, democratization, with deep respect for the Kaiser and the military, the unfolding of the personality . . . is the highest and last thing to expect, to demand, to achieve." Naumann has decided for that "or". [20]

The consequence of this secularization of Christian social principles--a trait which Barth felt to be characteristic, or at least tendentious, of most German religious socialists--was the logical willingness to support the German State and Kaiser in their war policy of 1914:

> (Naumanns) Gestalt ist die Verkörperung der tragischen Grösse, Schuld und Beschämung nicht nur seines Volkes, sondern unserer ganzen Zeit. ([Naumann's] figure is the embodiment of the tragic greatness, guilt, and shame, not only of his people, but of our entire age.) [21]

Barth lauded Blumhardt, however, for Blumhardt understood not only the victory of God in Jesus Christ in all spheres of human and social endeavor ("Jesus ist der Siegeschild!--nicht bloss der Seilenfreund oder Moralprediger, sondern der Verkündiger und Träger der göttlichen Macht auf der Erde." - "Jesus the victorious hero!", not merely the friend of souls or the preacher of morality, but the herald and bearer of divine might on earth.), [22] but also that all social institutions stand under the biblical judgment of God and therefore are not to be infused with any kind of quasi-divine or godly character. [23] In contrast to Naumann, young Blumhardt did not secularize the universalism of the New Testament, that is, the seeing of the divine or the Christ in social institutions as a possibility; social democracy was not "christianized" as Naumann was prone to do with Religious Socialism:

> Blumhardt's secret was his ever true movement between hurrying and waiting, between the new attack in the middle of abundance (Fülle) and the astounding inner listening of that which wants to become by means of strength from on high. He had a high living relationship to his period, which was founded in God. No world war and no revolution could penalize him as a liar. [24]

In other words, Barth was impressed with Blumhardt's sense of the eschatological, for it provided Barth with an emerging and distance from, but also an intense concern for, social institutions and structures. This distance is evidenced in his eventual break with the Religious Socialists--a break first displayed by his notorious speech in Germany at a Religious Socialist conference on "The Christian in Society". This speech not only brought the hitherto unknown Swiss pastor to the attention of the German theological circles, [25] but it also permitted him to introduce the eschatological note into his understanding of ethics--a connection which was to be explored further in his first edition of **Romans.** The eschatological theme was not new; Barth's early sermons often centered around this theme. But the attempt to relate the eschatological character of Christian dogmatics to an ethical realization of that character in society was a new departure.

Tambach: Barth's First Theological Rebellion

At Tambach, Barth sought to clarify and define three issues: 1) the nature and content of the summons to be a Christian in society, 2) the nature of the society/state/world in which the Christian has to act and exist, and 3) the basis for political action by the Christian. The Christian in society means, first of all, Christ in society--Christ in us and therefore acting through us as in the Pauline text. This is not an idea of exclusiveness for a few chosen, but conveys a universal inclusiveness which is almost ontologically true for all people:

> The congregation of Christ is a house, which is open on all sides; for Christ is always for the others, for the ones outside, the ones who are dead. Christ is in us, over us, behind us, this side of us--a consciousness of the purpose of life, a reminder of the origin of man, a return to the Lord of the world, a critical No and a creative Yes to all the areas of our consciousness, a turning from the old to the new aeon. Its mark and fulfillment (is) the cross. [26]

But this inclusiveness does not mean a "Christian" certification of all human actions and institutions in the state/society, a secularization of Christ, or what Barth called hyphenated (Bindestrich) Christianity:

> All combinations like "Christian-social", "evangelical-social", "religious-social", are conveniently handy, but it is especially important to ask the question, whether the hyphens which we use with reasonable boldness are not dangerous short cuts. The paradox that God's service (Gottesdienst) is or must become service to mankind (Menschendienst) is very ingenuous, but whether our hasty service to mankind becomes through such an enlightenment service to God, even when it occurs in the name of purest love, such is another book. The evangelical reminder is very true that the seed is the word and the world the field, but what is the word and who from us possesses it? . . . The divine is something total, something closed, something in the nature of the new, the different over against the world. It cannot be glued on and conformed to something. It cannot be separated or divided up because it is something more than religion. . . . It is all or it is nothing. [27]

The word "God" includes both humankind and its existence in this world and society. Barth agreed with Blumhardt; to believe in God, is also to believe in mankind: to believe in humankind leads to believing in the real renewal of our world. [28] But there is no reversed identification, that is, from us to God. Nor is there any reversed identification of our world being in fact synonymous with God's world:

> "God"--He stands always near that which moves us: exalted, solemn, but always incomprehensible, discomforting, almost threatening. [29]

Society has its own "logos", its own center which may rule the life of its members, even though such a rule is relativized under the judgment of God's rule. This is what the medieval Church failed to realize as it tried to "clericalize" society. [30] This is seen in the self-sufficient culture which human society devises, as well as in the laws and economic ordering of the internal life of that society. [31]

> Already there are (similar) signs amongst protestants: let us build a new church with democratic allurements and a socialistic direction. Let us build parish houses, begin youth programs and sponsor discussion evenings and musical devotional programs. Let us climb down from the high throne of the theologians and put the laymen in the pulpit. Let us with new enthusiasm go the old way which began with the pietism of the Inner Mission and which will with deadly certainty end with the liberalism of Naumann. . . . The society will be deceived about God's help when we want to start over again learning to wait on God instead of hurrying with the building of our little churches (Kirchen und Kirchlein). [32]

Yet both human achievements and human society have a relativity about them because of what Barth calls the movement--the movement of the knowledge of God as revealed in the resurrection of Jesus Christ. [33]

This "movement" is grounded in what Barth calls the Ursprung, the source or Quelle. This Ursprung is the key to transforming our perception of God in God's divine history with us (Gottesgeschichte). This Gottesgeschichte invades and intervenes in human history and its world so that all efforts to make human institutions like the divine, that is eternal and on-going, or what Barth identifies as secularization, can be only a myth for Christians:

> Because the soul recalls its origin in God, it recalls also the origin of society. Because it remembers, it finds the sense of life in a wide area. . . . This awakening of the soul is the movement in which we are standing, the movement of the divine history or divine knowledge, the movement of life throughout life. . . . [34]

Yet Christians must be and act in such a society. What is the basis for their affirming their being and acting in such a society? When one recalls the negativism toward participation in the state expressed in **Romans,** which was just completed before he wrote the speech for Tambach, then this is a recurring and necessary question, particularly when dealing with some of the early criticisms of Barth's alleged anarchism or political inactivism. Also a systematic description of the basis for Christian action and being from this speech is not an altogether simple task.

First, the Christian in society must recognize the impermanence of society under the power and judgment of the Ursprung. The Christian cannot bring a solution; that only God can bring and the Christian can transmit the message of hoping and waiting on God. [35] Our time and our society must be seen in light of the Movement (Bewegung) which goes through and penetrates all human movements. This is the Movement of the knowledge of God revealed in the resurrection of Jesus Christ. [36] One can only point to the Ursprung, since it is not in our power to control it or to direct it:

> Christ is the necessary newness from above, the way, the truth and the life of God amongst mankind, the son of man in whom mankind is conscious of its direct link with God. But maintain distance. No very fine psychic objectification (Dinglichkeit) of the form of this consciousness must replace or hide the true transcendence of this content. The step from Jahweh-experience to Baal-experience is very short. [37]

Secondly, this breaking of the divine into the human brings discomfort, disquiet, critique into life and this becomes the frame of reference with which the Christian views his society and its institutions, whether it be the culture, the economy, or the art, or even the banal presuppositions of society like drinking and eating. The Christian cannot be indifferent to even the minimum laws of society.

> ... the soul is conscious of its origin in God, that is, however a lost and again to be won origin of all things, relations, orders (Ordnungen) and forms in God. For in that the soul remembers once again its origin in God, it also knows the source (Ursprung) of society. In that it comes to know and understand itself, it finds the purpose of life in its widest areas. . . . This awakening of the soul is the movement in .which we are standing, the movement of the divine history or the recognition of the divine, the movement of life within life. In that we are touched (begriffen) by this awakening, we can no more neglect to throw aside all legalities of this life

> or to test them for their connection with that which
> alone can be legal or valid (gültig). [38]

When seized by this fact, the Christian has to assume a critical position in society, for God's coming into his world brings judgment and disquiet. This is positive action by God which evokes negation in his world. [39]

> We are moved by God. We acknowledge God. God's history takes place in us and on our person. And thus it is the light of triumph in which our hope and need is steeped. Over against our need, hope is the decisive, prevalent moment. No more indifference about divine and worldly interests, tendencies and powers. God drives the wedge in order to exalt the world. (Gott setzt den Hebel an, um die Welt zu heben). . . . God's history is a priori victorious history. [40]

This is the sign under which the Christian stands and which accompanies him in his societal life and action:

> The last word is called the Kingdom of God, creation, redemption, completion of the world through God and in God. [41]

Thirdly, whilst an affirmation of God's judgment and critique of society can and often must take the form of protest by the Christian, which may in fact be an integral part of the movement toward the kingdom of God and a necessary attack on the existing society and its institutions, nonetheless God's kingdom stands beyond protests and movements growing out of protests:

> It is a revolution which is beyond all revolutions, as it is beyond all existing things. . . . In that we find ourselves in God, we find ourselves also with the task of affirming Him in the world as it is and not in a false transcendent world. Only out of this affirmation can the real, radical denial (of the world) take place, which is apparently intended with our protest movements. [42]

> God could not save the world, if he were not its Creator. Only because it is his property can it become his property. Real eschatology moves backward as well as forwards. Jesus Christ yesterday, not just today. [43]

But Barth cautions about identifying societal protests with God's intentions, even when they bear apparent truths about the nature of the existing society. The eschatological character of God's judgment upon man's world includes a far more serious negation than an affirmation:

> We are standing deeper in the No than in the Yes, deeper in the critique and protest than in the naivete, deeper in the yearning after the future than in a participation in the present. We cannot honour the Creator of the original world (ursprüngliche Welt) than to shout for the Redeemer of the present world. . . . Our Yes with regard to life carries within it the divine No. . . . Real recognition of life is hostile to all abstractions. It can say Yes, but only in order that out of that Yes it can say louder and more urgently No. . . . [44]

Professor Marquardt maintains that Barth was using a methodology which was the beginning stage of a developing revelation-oriented approach. [45] This had already been hinted at in **Romans**(1) and was further developed in **Romans**(2). In **Romans**(1) the "revolution of God" was mirrored in the proletarian revolution as the "wholly Other" standing over against the existing capitalistic relationships, that is, a more politicized approach. In Tambach, Barth appears to be reflecting upon a more theological approach based on God's revelation, particularly in Jesus Christ, the vehicle in which humankind becomes aware of its direct relation with God. [46]

If this is so, then the emphasis on the resurrection of Jesus Christ as the motor of the Movement makes sense, particularly when one recalls that throughout his years as pastor Barth sought to fill the void which had been created by his abandonment of liberal theological axioms for exegesis and social acting and being. The Hegelian scheme of the dialectic is begun and resolved in God and not in an abstract idea of the Spirit or the Absolute. [47]

> In the power of the resurrection naivete and critique have possibilities, their warranty, and their necessity. The resurrection of Jesus Christ from the dead is the world-wide moving power which also moves us because it is the appearance of a totaliter aliter--more we cannot say--of a bodily existence or corporality (Leiblichkeit) in our life. [48]

Because of this, the Christian has both the strength and the power to bear the social and political problems and dilemmas of his society, yet not only to bear them, but also to break through them. [49] The society stands under the theological standpoint of spes futurae vitae, which has practical consequences for the Christian and for the theologian, since the resurrection has to do with renewing society as well as revealing God's No and Yes to that society and to us in that society. [50] The Christian's

Yes and No to society and particular problems means that he will avoid abstractions and will be forced to deal with the Feuerbachian "real" man, for the regnum gloriae will redeem and renew our world/society. Knowledge of the regnum gloriae provides the Christian with a perspective and a distance as well as an involvement, both of which allow him to avoid the absolutism of the Right and the Left and to be able to say Yes as well as No to the society. [51]

Ragaz, at the time, criticized this form of the dialectic as "doppelseitig", complaining that Barth's understanding of the dialectic could imperil the Religious Socialist movement. [52] Adolph von Harnack, who was also present in Aarau at the Student Conference in 1920 where Barth continued his theological explorations in the direction already displayed in the **Romans**(1) and at Tambach in a speech entitled, "Biblical Questions, Insights and Viewpoints", [53] was shaken and deeply disturbed by the tone of this theology. In some recollections of her father's reaction to young Barth, which was also characteristic of much of the German theological world's reaction to him, his daughter wrote:

> There was not a sentence, not a thought which he could go along with. He recognized the deep earnestness with which Barth spoke, but he shuddered at this theology. [54]

Harnack, in a letter to Eberhard Vischer in Basle, described Barth as a meteor which had exploded and whose religion was irrelevant to the daily life. [55]

Carl Mennicke, editor of an influential Religious Socialist journal, responded to Barth's Tambach speech with a rather polemical critique published in 1920. He complained that Barth appeared unaware of modern problems and difficulties which he sought to dismiss or relativize by insisting on God's revelation in Jesus Christ. [56] He described Barth's view of revelation as "out of date": "a knowledge of God is only possible through the participation in this revelation (in man's time)," [57] and added that his view was so abstract as to remove God from the whole living process and to make him totally removed from man, often tending toward paradoxical thinking. [58]

Marquardt suggests that in early Barth, the resurrection is given both a theological and a political function, for in the resurrection the new world addressed in the New Testament is founded and established by and through Jesus Christ: [59]

> Der einzelne, aus dem die Auferstehung den "ersten Be-
> wegten" macht, kommt überhaupt nur als "Subjekt der
> Gesellschaft" in Frage. Unter ihrem Zustand und Druck
> "leidet" er: in bezug auf sie kommt er aber durch die

> Auferstehung auch zum "Handeln" und zur "Erkenntnis"
> (Man bemerkte diese Reihenfolge: gesellschaftliche Erkennt-
> nis folgt dem gesellschaftlichen Handeln) und erfüllt leidend,
> handelnd, erkennend seine Gesellschaftlichkeit wie seine
> Subjektivität in der Neuprädikation, die die Auferstehung
> als Vergebung der Sünden, Befreiung von der alten Welt,
> an ihm vollzieht--"das ist Ostern". [60] (The individual
> who by the resurrection is made the "first moved" [ersten
> Bewegten] comes only into question as a "subject of
> society." He suffers under its conditions and pressures;
> but also it is with respect to society that the individual
> is brought by the resurrection to action and "knowledge,"
> [One should notice this sequence: societal knowledge
> follows societal action] fulfilling in suffering, action,
> and knowledge his social role as well as his personal
> identity in the new predication which the resurrection
> as forgiveness of sins and liberation from the old world
> accomplishes in him--"That is Easter."

Because Barth wished to demonstrate how the resurrection was the mediating power between the divine and the secular realities, he was able to identify secular "reality" with man's historical achievements, thus moving toward a kind of theological Marxism. [61] It is the infamous totaliter aliter which mediates both God's reality and the secular reality and which, according to Marquardt, was originally the new world of God that would overturn the existing bourgeois society:

> Totaliter aliter ist ursprünglich im Denken Barths die
> neue Gesellschaft im Widerspruch gegen die stürzende,
> und das Ursprüngliche in diesem Widerspruch ist "Gott",
> wie Barth ihn damals versteht. [62] (Totaliter aliter
> in Barth's thinking is originally the new society which
> stands in contradiction to the collapsing society. The
> first point of origin in this contradiction is 'God,' as Barth
> understood him at the time.)

Renate Breipohl, perhaps rightly, points out that the question about the purpose of society in early Barth can be answered only in looking to Christ and not to history, for Christ ensures the eternal connection between the divine and the human and thus is a guarantee for the purposefulness of human history and society. [63]

The First Volcanoes of Romans

Although chronologically the first edition of **Romans** was written before Barth wrote his Tambach address, this edition will be examined after the Tambach speech in order to show systematically the connection, as well as the contrast with the second edition of **Romans,** published in 1922. The first edition of **Romans** emphasized the eschatological and krisis (judgment) nature of God's Word over against human society, as is usually known. This book, whose manuscript Barth finished on 16th August, 1918, according to his diary [**64**] and which was declined by three Swiss publishers, [**65**] initially was first printed in December, 1918, but only later released in 1919 by the Bern publisher, G. A. Böschlen. [**66**] One thousand copies were printed; but after only 300 copies were sold, the sales decreased. Georg Merz (1892-1959), a pastor in Bavaria and an acquaintance of Albert Lempp (1884-1943), owner of the Christian Kaiser Verlag in Munich persuaded Lempp to buy up the rest of the unsold first edition in Switzerland and to sell them eventually in Germany. This was carried through. Lempp then urged Barth to write a second edition, which eventually was published in 1922. [**67**]

Although the important part of **Romans**(1) regarding our acting and being in society is his exegesis of Rom. 13, early on in the book Barth mentions a point which was also noticed in the Tambach address--the Ursprung as the source of the totaliter aliter:

> Our thought of God is the living arm of God under which nature, history, mankind, we ourselves (we ourselves as possessors of the "fruits of the spirit" Rom. 8:23) are placed. The Ursprung, which was always claimed, known, yearned for, and under pain sought after, opened its mouth again. The divine word, "it shall be" is again fulfilled. Thus nothing new, rather the old; nothing special, rather the usual; nothing historical, rather the precondition of all history. That which was hidden in the not-understood appearances of nature is now however revealed, so that it is known in the eyes and ears of men as in the beginning and thus in the world, whose head and centre is man. Hence not just the old familiar, but the new, not the universal, but the special, not just a precondition, but history itself: the opening of a new aeon, the beginning of a new world in which God once again has power. This power of God stands behind us. This is our evangelium that we announce. [**68**]

This coming of God into our world ushers in the new, and thus divine history precedes, envelopes, and succeeds human history, which continues to persist under God's wrath. Yet clothed in that wrath is His love for the creature, even if humankind continues to reject that love. Standing under God's wrath, the relations within society are characterized by the "wantonness" and injustice (Frevelhaftigkeit) of humankind. This wantonness is characterized by our yearning to be divine and our injustice evoked through our making ourselves the center of history and of our world--"ein prometheisches Ansichreissen": [69]

> This is the resistance of man under which his whole world suffers: he always seeks God and always finds false gods (Abgötter), he always means to serve God and always serves himself. [70]

Thus the relationship between God and us and between God and our world/society is a negative one, since our world/society stands under Krisis, which is manifested in God's wrath. Barth says the judgment under which we constantly stand is the result of our exhibited disobedience before the Fall. [71] And all subsequent social problems, such as hunger, war, pestilence, have their origins in our fall from grace and our resistance to that grace:

> So der jetzige Staat, wie er an der Stelle des ursprüng-lichen und im Christus zu erneuernden Gottestaates getreten ist. Sein Name heisst "Gewalt", denn ausgesprochen und anerkannt ist seine reine Macht und Zwangscharakter im Gegensatz zu der Gerechtigkeit und Freiheit des Gotte-staates. [72] (So the present state, as it has taken the place of the original civitas dei is to be renewed in Christ. Its basic character is expressed and recognized to be that of power and coercion in contrast to the righteousness and freedom of the civitas dei.)

This is also the character of our institutions and politics, which Barth characterizes as the "devilish art of the majority (Major-isierung)", whether they be those of Gustav Adolph or Napoleon or Cromwell or Friedrich the Great or Bebel: "Es ist ein garstig Lied, pfui, ein politisch Lied. . . . Es lohnt sich, nicht zu unter-scheiden." [73] (It is a repulsive song, for shame, a political song. . . . It makes no difference if one makes distinctions.)

For this reason, wrote Barth, Paul reminds the Christians that they should have nothing to do with supporting the existing structures in the state, since his state and home is in heaven. The present state/society must be replaced:

> The power of the unjust (is) to be dissolved through the power of the just. You have moral obligations with regard to the present state, but from a positive appraisal. [74] The Christian's real Vaterland is in God. The state is out of order for the believers in its fundamental func-tions. [75]

Yet Romans 13 reminds the Christian that everyone is subject to the governing powers. This means that through his

48

freedom in God, the Christian cannot identify any nation or party of the existing structures with absolute truth for the state. Rather the Christian must concentrate on what Barth calls "the absolute revolution of God", [76] which means essentially bringing down the present state/society:

> Es konkurriert nicht mit dem Staat, es negiert ihn. . . . Es ist mehr als Leninismus. Es handelt sich für das Christentum in der Tat um das Programm. . . . Alles oder nichts. . . . [77] (It does not compete with the state. It denies it. . . . It is more than Leninism. It is concerned with the problem of Christianity. . . . All or nothing. . . .)

Barth disallows for an evolutionary process to take place which would move the state toward goals and ends that could be affirmed and supported by the Christian:

> This program cannot become a part of an "Ethic". The body of Christ must grow under its own power. The "Sons of God" must mature in accordance with the revelation of their being. [78]

Thus the Christian may act in the affairs of state in expectation of the revolutionary dissolution of the present state by the revolution of God:

> Können and müssen sie sich persönlich "unterziehen" (nicht aus Achtung, sondern aus radikaler Verachtung des Bestehenden, nicht aus Opportunismus, sondern um der Sache Gottes willen, "um des Gewissens willen," 13:4!). [79] (They themselves can and must personally go underground [not out of respect for the existing order, but rather out of radical contempt, not because of opportunism, but rather for the sake of God's interests, for the sake of conscience. 13:4!)

The revolution will come according to God's own plan, but Christians can prepare the way by acting in solidarity amongst themselves over against the existing society and its institutions. The evil on which the state/society is structured can easily overcome the single person trying to revolutionize or reform the state simply because he stands alone. [80] Such a demonic force can be defeated only through the good which is in Christ alone and as perpetuated by Christians acting in solidarity. Barth recoiled from individual action since this would lead to anarchy, which in turn would simply allow the structural evil of the existing state/society to continue to reign in other forms. [81] It is the Christians acting in solidarity who can prepare for a new society which will be ordered and structured according to the plan and order of God. [82] "We can only do good with God and make preparations for the final dissolution of evil into a new world--or become traitors to God." [83] Making preparations as such, the Christians must always stand to the left in political and social matters, but at the same time not totally losing themselves in any ideology:

> Dass ihr als Christen mit Monarchie, Kapitalismus, Militaris-
> mus, Patriotismus und Freisinn nichts zu tun habt, ist
> so selfstverständlich, dass ich gar nicht zu sagen brauche,
> "Die wir der Sünde gestorben sind, wie sollten wir in
> ihr weiterleben können? . . . Die Sache der göttlichen
> Erneuerung darf nicht vermengt werden mit der Sache
> des menschlichen Fortschritts. Das Göttliche darf nicht
> politisiert und das Menschliche nicht theologisiert werden,
> auch nicht zugunsten der Demokratie und Sozialdemokratie.
> [84] (That you as Christians are to have nothing to
> do with monarchism, capitalism, militarism, patriotism,
> and liberalism is so obvious that I need not say anything.
> "The sin to which we are dead, how can we still live
> in it?" (6.2) . . . The cause of divine renewal is not
> to be mixed up with the cause of human progress. The
> divine is not to be politicized and the human is not to
> be theologized, not even for the sake of bourgeois de-
> mocracy and social democracy.)

Yet Barth does not appear to encourage Christian support for an active political overthrow of the existing state in this first edition of **Romans,** although he does insist that the revolution of God will replace the existing state. There is an ambivalence here which is comparable to the race between the tortoise and the hare: at one point the Christian is expected to maintain a slow pace awaiting the coming revolution of God; at another point the Christian is urged to hurry toward preparing for the Kingdom.

> Whether you want to protect or overthrow the bourgeois
> society's gaps, you are moving in any case in that danger-
> ous area of the ordering of God, strengthen that which
> will make use of the authoritative force. . . . You ought
> not to expect that God's protection and victory power
> accompany you in such self-chosen and final steps. You
> ought not to wonder when the evil overcomes you in
> spite of all personal pureness. [85]

He warns against "Christian" politics or a "Christian democratic" party, reminding his readers that God's revolution is not to be bound to a political theology. [86] God cannot be controlled by human societal aims and intentions since a real "Christian" politics points beyond this present society to a new aeon. [87] One cannot mix the politics of the state which is founded on an evil with the absolute eternal claims of God's Kingdom: [88]

> The Kingdom of God must go its own way: also with
> the ascetic turning away from the state there would
> not be much accomplished as indeed (would be the similar
> case) with a premature Civitas dei experiment. [89]

Thus, neither a revolutionary secularization of the divine intentions nor a clericalization of human structures and aims can be identified as "Christian".

What is to be the Christian's position and work in the state? What does the Christian understand by the institution "the state"? Barth insists then that the state is a necessary order, as maintained in Romans 13, for issuing and executing laws--a needed institution as long as the "old man" lives. This does not mean that the Christian as a "new man" can disregard the laws. The continued existence of the "old man" and evil means that Christians show their cognizance of this by observing these laws of the state/society:

> As long as you remain obligated to God "the love one
> another", which is the positive being of the coming new
> world (Rom. 13:8a), you must not neglect the obligatory
> attention to the law of God and His "office-holders"
> (Rom. 13:6), whether he is the animal from the abyss.
> So long as the Kingdom of God also through your indebted-
> ness cannot come nearer, you must, with part of your
> being . . . pay tribute to the ethic. [90]

Thus, to withdraw from the political affairs of state or remain indifferent to them will not hurry up the revolution and Kingdom of God, nor will the new aeon come any sooner. Only God alone can and will bring in this aeon. [91] Within its own arena and its own time, the state has the right to insist upon respect for and obedience to its order and laws from Christians as well as from non-Christians. But when that time or era is at an end, so is the respect for such order and laws also at an end:

> Give to them everything which because of the basis
> of the general situation between God and the world
> can be now demanded of us: Taxes to whom taxes
> are due, customs to whom customs are due, respect
> to whom respect is due, honour to whom honour is due,
> but not a step further! . . . Civil initiative and civil
> obedience, but no combination of throne and altar, no
> Christian patriotism, no democratic crusade frame of
> mind. Strike and general strike and street fights when
> it must be, but no religious justification and glorification
> thereunto! Military service as a soldier or officer when
> it must be, but under no circumstances as chaplain! Social
> democratic, but not religious social! The betrayal of the
> evangelium does not belong to political duties. [92]

Now having warned the Christian about embracing a
societal ethic that gives total support to the existence of the
state/society, which is structured on disobedience of and resistance
to God's Word, Barth sees society as standing under the constant
judgment of God's wrath. At the same time having reminded the
Christian about his dialectical position of having to affirm and
to continue the existence of the state by virtue of conforming
to certain political duties expected of all citizens, such as taxes,
miltary service, adherence to the laws, etc., Barth suggests that
there is indeed an ethic which ought to guide the Christian even
in this dialectical dilemma. This is what he calls "the positive
principle" of love:

> All opposition and all negation over against the ruling
> forces is ambiguous . . . love is that unambiguous word
> which will be understood by mankind. [93]

Love is the driving force for both the creation and the resurrection
and has political consequences in society for overcoming the evil
within our society/state. This is the particular task of Christians
as the body of Christ, the "germ cell of the coming world," "the
new world community in Christ." [94]

Marquardt maintains that this exegesis of **Romans** not
only parallels Lenin's conception of the state, [95] but notes
that significantly it also appeared at the same time as Lenin's
"State and Revolution". This leads him to infer that Lenin's writings
may have had a limited influence on Barth as well as provided
him with a political form of revolution to which he reacted. Just
as Lenin, writing during the time of the Bolshevik revolution,
fought against the reconstruction of the bourgeois state according
to Marx's definition and opposition to the state and insisted on
the dictatorship of the proletariat as the revolutionary transition
force between capitalism and socialism causing the eventual withering away of the state, so Barth negated and declassified the state
as "Gewaltstaat", (a state rooted in violence), thereby dismissing
it as unworthy of preserving. Barth describes its politics and structures as "die teufliche Kunst der Majorisierung," i.e., the oppression
of the underprivileged, [96] by a powerful bourgeois minority
acting as the majority. (Likewise Barth's criticism of taxes and
duty collections as examples of exploitation of the ruled by the
rulers, is parallel to what Lenin was also writing at the time. [97])
But this can be no more than an inference by Marquardt. Nowhere
does Barth give evidence that Lenin influenced his thought, although
he does pay great respect to Marx as will be demonstrated later.

He further suggests that there is a noticeable ideological
parallel between Lenin and Barth, namely, the resistance to a
deification of the state. Engels and eventually Lenin refuted the
Hegelian thesis that the state is a realization (Verwirklichung)

of the Idea. Instead, they maintained that it was the product
and structure of historical class economic needs and conflicts
which were held under control by the ruling classes in various
epochs as a means of imposing interests and power on the powerless
so as to protect and maintain their own status and authority.
Barth warns also against such a deification of the state, indeed
insisting that Christians should starve out (aushungern lassen)
the state. [98]

Yet, according to Marquardt, Barth cannot be fully identified with Lenin since he failed to advocate dissolving the state
in order to repress the bourgeois. Barth insists on dissolving the
state because its very roots are evil and its structures built on
the power of evil (böse Gewalt) and replacing it with the Gottestaat
or the "Gewalt der Gerechtigkeit". Barth understands that the
problem of evil in society is not solved through a revolution by
humankind, but through a total revolution pointing toward ending
the very structure of the state whether bourgeoise or proletariat.
[99]

Thus there are hints of anarchistic tendencies in Barth
similar to those in Lenin and Engels. [100] Marquardt claims
that such parallel a subversive tactic advocated by Lenin, which
was to participate in the affairs of the bourgeois state for the
sake of moving toward Lenin's particular ideological or theological
goal. [101] And it is within this context that Barth understands
the role of the "Revolution Gottes":

> Die "im Christus" kommende Revolution ist eigene Barthsche
> Ausdrucks und Vorstellungsweise, die auf einen Zusammen-
> hang von Christologie und Revolution hinweist. Das Stich-
> wort "Welt-revolution" soll den Bolschewismus assoziieren. . .
> Bei Barth erhalten die im Sprach--und Vorstellungsgebrauch
> wirksamen Motiven begriffliche Schärfe eben durch den
> leninistischen Rahmen, genauer: durch die genau zu
> bestimmende Funktion, in der von der "Revolution Gottes"
> innerhalb einer leninistischen Grundvorstellung gesprochen
> wird. [102] (The coming revolution "under Christ" is
> a peculiar Barthian manner of expression and thinking
> which links christology and revolution. The catchword
> "world revolution" is associated with Bolshevism. . . . For
> Barth the motifs at work in the realm of language and
> thought are given conceptual sharpness precisely by their
> Leninistic frame of reference or, more exactly, by the
> precisely defined function in which the revolution of
> God is talked about from a basically Leninistic frame
> work.)

Therefore Barth understands the revolution of God to have the
function similar to that of the revolutionary dictatorship of the

proletariat in that it makes possible the removal of the unjust and the victory of the good over the evil, thereby revolutionizing not only the institutions within the state/society, but also all social relationships as well. [103] But it is not restricted to this model:

> The "revolution of God" functions as an ethical criterion, which breaks through the absolutism that the Leninistic dictatorship of the proletariat establishes. The "revolution of God" is not the negation, rather it is the necessary ethical, consciously established concretisation, that is, a relativising of the dictatorship of the proletariat. [104]

The Dutch Roman Catholic van Dijk maintains that there is a certain ambivalence in Barth because of the unbridgeable difficulties in writing a theological ethic based on the "great qualitative difference" between God in heaven and man on earth. [105] An ethic needs a positive norm and, as Barth in **Romans**(1) understands God to be the Krisis standing over against all human undertakings, it is almost impossible for him to devise an ethic in which God's judgment is a positive norm for that ethic. Yet Barth does have a "primary ethic" for acting and a "secondary ethic." [106] The primary ethic is the more fundamental, characterized by "sanctification": humankind presents itself to God as a sacrifice without conditions and lets God's grace possess and direct its existence and action. Therefore, the problem of political ethics is connected at once with the problem of dogmatics, that is, humankind must belong to the gracious God in order to legitimate his existence. [107] Humankind can demonstrate God's will and honor in its acting, but God's will remains sovereign and independent of its acting and praise.

The secondary ethic is related to the primary one and is characterized by making concrete the love and justice of God. That is, whilst the primary ethic is a re-formation of our thinking and knowledge about God, the secondary ethic is acting in light of this re-formation (Umdenken).

> Ethos muss sich durch Logos so gut wie Logos durch Ethos an den Ursprung, an das Problem der Existentialität seiner Akte erinnern lassen. [108] (Ethos must be reminded of its source--the problem of its existentiality--by logos, just as logos must be by ethos.)

This acting is grounded ultimately in Christ,

> the living kernel of the new world . . . (which he) uses as the basis on which a new humanity will be built and who already has His eye on (Christians) as members of a growing organism, as foundation stones of this rising (entsteheden) house. [109]

The effect of this ambivalence on Barth's concept of political praxis in the state will be examined critically later. It does remain a constant thread throughout his writings.

The time in Safenwil as pastor in which Barth's embrace of social democracy and even some phases of Socialism through his supporting the radical wing of the Swiss Social Democratic Party, [110] activated him to continue to search out the grounds for legitimation of a theological ethics and praxis, which meant implicitly a political theological ethic. Barth always felt compelled to "correct" some of the misunderstandings of the nineteenth-century pietistic Protestant churches in this field. As he wrote in the article, "Jesus Christ and the Social Movement,"

> For 1800 years the Christian Church has, over against the social needs, always referred to the spirit, to the inner life, to heaven. It preached, converted, comforted, but it did not help. Indeed, it recommended in all times help for the social needs, as a good work of Christian love, but that help itself is a good work; that the Church did not dare to say. [111]

Barth felt that such help could be partially demonstrated by joining a working class political party because Christ Himself was the model for such help. He repeated again and again in this article: "Jesus is the social movement and the social movement is Jesus in the present time." [112] Such an emphasis became more apparent in the second edition of **Romans**, which he finished just as he took up his new appointment as Professor of Reformed Theology in Göttingen in 1921, and which he felt corrected many of the mistakes and misunderstandings about his theological ethic emerging from critics' appraisals of **Romans**(1). The manuscript was published in 1922, the effect of which on the theological world was described by Barth himself as "fast schicksalhaft entscheidend, [113] ("decisively fraught with destiny"). Indeed, in his preface to the English translation of the sixth edition of **Romans**(2), Barth apologized, saying:

> When, however, I look back at the book (1919) it seems to have been written by another man to meet a situation belonging to a past epoch. Those who read it . . . ought therefore to remember that they have in their hands what is, in fact, the beginning of a development. They ought not to bind the Professor at Bonn too tightly to the Pastor of Safenwil. [114]

The Second Volcano of Romans

In the second rewritten edition, Barth makes two significant revisions: first, the distance and strangeness of God over against humankind is stressed in an even more radical way through his emphasis on God's wrath, and secondly, there is a decided deemphasizing of the concept of revolution as a method of political restructuring and change in human society. As Barth wrote in his exegesis of Romans 8:24, in **Romans(2):**

> By hope we are saved--in as much as in Jesus Christ the Wholly Other, unapproachable, unknown eternal power and divinity (1:20) of God has entered into our world. . . . For hope that is seen is not hope. Direct communication from God is no divine communication. If Christianity is not altogether restless eschatology, there remains in it no relationship whatsoever with Christ. . . . All that is not hope is wooden, hobbledehoy, blunt-edged, and sharp-pointed, like the word "Reality". There is no freedom, only imprisonment; no grace, but only condemnation and corruption, no divine guidance, but only fate; no God, but only a minor of unredeemed humanity. And this is so, be there never (sic) so much progress of social reform. . . . Redemption is invisible, inaccessible, and impossible, for it meets us only in hope. [**115**]

Human society stands under God's judgment in **Romans(2)** as in **Romans(1)**, but whereas God's No conceals His Yes which was revealed in Christ in the first edition, in the second edition, God's wrath is totally negative. In the first edition humankind can come to know God directly as an impossible possibility, provided that it is seized by Christ and thereby put into a position by God to acknowledge His Yes. In the second edition "the protest pronounced always and everywhere against the course of the world" is always accompanying man's society. [**116**] Even man's effort to affirm God is in fact negation:

> That which we, apart from faith in the resurrection, name "God" is also a final consequence of the divine wrath. But the God who, contradicting His own name, affirms the course of this world, is God--God in His own wrath, God who sorrows on our behalf, God who can only turn Himself from us and say "No". . . . The whole world is the footprint of God; yes, but in so far as we choose scandal rather than faith, the footprint in the vast riddle of the world is the footprint of his wrath. . . . The wrath of God is the righteousness of God--apart from and without Christ. [**117**]

Thus our fundamental relationship to God is "ungodly" and a contradiction of our intended being; this relationship indeed casts its shadow across all human institutions, since in begetting and perpetuating these institutions, we seek to eternalize human society and ourselves. We confuse the temporal and passing with God's eternal, and the permanent, with God's distance:

> God Himself is not acknowledged as God and what is called "God" is in fact man. By living to ourselves, we serve the "No-God". [118]

The second edition of **Romans** makes no provision for Christians as mirrors of God's action in the world. They too stand under God's wrath. We erect various institutions like "civil religion" or "family" or "nation" or "church" or "father-land", hoping to reduce this distance, but we only succeed in creating idols:

> It is not merely that the world exists side by side with God; it has taken His place, and has itself become God, and demands the same devotion which the old-fashioned believer offered to his God. (F. Strauss) Contradictions within the deified world--Nature and Civilization, Materialism and Idealism, Capitalism and Socialism, Secularism and Ecclesiasticism, Imperialism and Democracy. . . . Such contradictions are contradictions within the world and there is for them no paradox, no negation, no eternity. [119]

Because of this unrighteous negation which shadows all of society, God has provided the law as a reminder, as a pointer to God's revelation which has been twisted and corrupted by humankind:

> The law is . . . a heap of clinkers marking a fiery miracle which has taken place, a burnt-out crater disclosing the place where God has spoken, a solemn reminder of the humiliation through which some men have been compelled to pass. . . . They are stamped with the impress of the true and unknown God, because they possess the form of traditional and inherited religion. . . . Consequently they have in their midst the sign-post which points them to God, to the Krisis of human experience, to the new world, which is set at the barrier of this world. [120]

The law guides and teaches us of God's coming Kingdom. As such in spite of the hiddenness and inaccessibility of God, the law functions as a witness to God in society:

> Through the law, therefore, attention is directed towards God and by it He is displayed as the Judge. This is the

> positive relation between God and man, which is disclosed
> to men when they perceive the utter separation between
> here and there, and become aware of the only possible
> presence of God in the world. [121]

Yet God is not bound by law; He acts and reveals Himself where there is no law as well as where there is law. This is the unlimited divine freedom. [122]

There is also a different emphasis on the character and function of the state/society/world in the two editions of the **Romans**. In **Romans**(1), the world is the living and temporal space for man, both for the redeemed (the Christians) and those resisting redemption. It was in this space that Christians could act to prepare for God's revolution. [123] In **Romans**(2) the society/state/world is a realm which is totally conditioned by sin so that the goodness of God is hidden from them. There is no Heilsgeschichte (which comes out of the Revolution Gottes) in **Romans**(2).

> In this world, on this earth, and under this heaven, there
> is no redemption, no direct life. Redemption can be only
> through redemption. But redemption can only take place
> at the coming Day, when there shall be a new heaven
> and a new earth. [124]

Because of this, ethics is seen primarily as acting, but acting within the realization that man's being is evil and therefore is to be consoled in light of such knowledge. [125] Ethics assumes part of the function which the Christians had in **Romans**(1): it is to direct humankind toward grace, toward the eschatological, toward its institutions becoming a sacrifice to God and thereby sanctified to God. [126]

Barth eventually returns to the theme of sanctification as the inner meaning of ethics in his **Church Dogmatics.** [127] Sanctification means our surrendering our historical existence and our society to God alone. The problem of ethics is the problem of dogmatics: "soli Dei gloria." [128] Consequently there are political acts which may be understood as a token indication of the new, of the divine:

> There are actions from which the light of sacrifice shines,
> actions where men are offered up, not in order that
> a new human achievement, positive or negative, may
> be brought to view, but that the peculiarity of God,
> His particular will and power and might, may be disclosed,
> and that He may be known as Lord. It is this enlightenment
> which disturbs men, whether they be formed according
> to the idealism of a Ludendorf and a Lenin or of a Foerster

and a Ragaz. This enlightenment is an assault upon all men. [129]

The character of ethics is that of protest, hence even a minority may take an action which will be disturbing to the "many", since such an action may also reflect the disturbance of God in man's world. [130] A prophet can wear political clothing and even a minority within the society may do a political act which can point to "the truth of the Coming World, to the truth of the One in the 'All'." [131] This is the criterion by which one should judge the political or social disharmony.

It would appear that Barth legitimates theologically on-going revolution as a possible bearer of truth by the few for the many. But he draws back from such a legitimation, at least as directly as he did in **Romans**(1). Indeed he moves back from an endorsement of revolution altogether and is more cautious. [132]

> These powers demand recognition and obedience. . . . If we admit their authority, we concede quite clearly the principle of Legitimism; if, on the other hand, we reject it, we are bound to accept the principle of Revolution. Being, however, concerned to demonstrate the honour of God, we do not . . . concede the principle of Legitimism. But, on the other hand, neither do we . . . concede the principle of Revolution. On the contrary, for reasons which will appear later, we find in the Epistle a direct denial of Revolution. We have, however, already suggested that we find in it also a denial of Legitimism. [133]

Barth defends this understanding because he is sensitive to the possibility that on the basis of his first edition, the reader could trace an almost anarchistic, anti-state, anti-authority attitude in him, which could be used to justify political radicalism:

> For the honour of God we have to bring the revolutionary within the orbit of sacrifice, and his sacrifice is a sacrifice of quite peculiar dignity. [134]

Barth relativizes political ordinances, even those promoted by democratic governments, warning that even when "the right of the Many really has become the right of the One," all legality is fundamentally structured upon sin and therefore illegal. [135] It is the revolutionary who acutely perceives the structural evil of society and political institutions and rebels against them for this reason. ("The revolutionary Titan is far more godless, far more dangerous, than his reactionary counterpart--because he is so much nearer to the truth.") [136] But in so doing he confuses his intentions with those of what Barth calls the "One" -

> ... the subject of the freedom which he so earnestly
> desires ... he is not the Christ who stands before the
> Grand Inquisitor, but is contrariwise, the Grand Inquisitor
> encountered by the Christ. ... He, too, usurps a position
> which is not due to him, a legality which is fundamentally
> illegal, an authority which--as we have grimly experienced
> in Bolshevism ... soon displays its essential tyranny. [137]

The danger with the revolutionary is that though he recognizes
the No to the existing order and rebels against the No perpetuated
in the societal institutions, his revolution tends to take on the
character of deity and thus an absolutism. "With his 'No' he stands
so strangely near to God." [138] He tends to confuse his relative
revolution with the eternal one: the "impossible possibility,"
the forgiveness of sin, the resurrection of the dead, i.e., Jesus
Christ. In point of fact, the revolutionary simply strengthens
the reactionary powers and forces. The revolutionary, so close
and yet so far from the command of God, can best obey the command: "overcome evil with good", that is returning to the original
root of "not-doing", not assaulting, not demolishing:

> It is God who wishes to be recognized as He that over-
> cometh the unrighteousness of the existing order. This
> is the meaning of the commandment. [139]

In point of fact the existing order merely retreats and withdraws
from the assaults of revolutions and usually re-emerges in a different form; thus ironically the revolutionary stands on the side
of the existing order. [140]

> No-revolution is the best preparation for the true Revolu-
> tion; but even no-revolution is no safe recipe. To be
> in subjection is, when rightly understood, an action void
> of purpose, an action, that is to say, which can spring
> only from obedience to God. Its meaning is that men
> have encountered God and are thereby compelled to
> leave the judgment to Him. The actual occurrence of
> this judgment cannot be identified with the purpose or
> with the secret reckoning of the man of this world. [141]

Hence revolutionary praxis and society fall under what
Barth calls the "negative possibility". This can be countered with
what he calls the "positive possibility," which is love. This is
an act which can be exercised by all, both redeemed and unredeemed:

> It is not permitted to us to excuse ourselves for the
> absence of love by saying that, since we live in the
> shadowy region of evil, we can only bear witness to
> the Coming World by "not-doing". Even in the world

> of shadows, love must come into active prominence,
> for it does not stand under the law of evil. Love of
> one another ought to be undertaken as the protest against
> the course of this world, and it ought to continue without
> interruption. We remember that human conduct is positively
> ethical when it is not conformed to this world (xii.2),
> when, within the framework of this world and in complete
> secrecy, it bears witness to the strangeness of God. [142]

To love is therefore a political act, which in turn can be an overthrowing force of the existing structures and institutions. It is,
in fact, the presupposition of all human acting in much the same
way that the revolution of God was the presupposition and end
of all revolution in **Romans**(1):

> No impossibility of my not doing good in the realm of
> evil--the only realm we know!--can rid me of the duty
> to love. . . . This is the relentless, impelling, earnestness
> of the command of love; and--therefore love is the ful-
> filling of the law. [143]

Love is the force which can overcome evil in society in even
its institutionalized forms.

Barth's insistence on the relativity of political movements
and institutions also has another function: their concreteness
and not their abstractness is considered crucial as is their power
to claim obedience from and authority over citizens. That is,
political institutions can also establish a horizontal relationship
between fellow humans. [144] Marquardt calls this "Christian
radicality" because it puts all systems under God's judgment and
under the norm of the revolution or Kingdom of God, i.e., an
eschatological norm. Revolutions, as well as "the system", are
examined by Barth with the same critical eye. He seeks to erect
a theological method for discrediting political utopianism or at
least its tendency to identify itself with the will and kingdom
of God.

> In a differentiated field of left-wing orientation (Linksver-
> weisung) the Barthian Christian operates: from religious
> socialism to Social Democracy--to Bolshevik revolution--to
> anti-authoritarian/anarchistic critique--to the Kingdom of
> God. This outward possibility, however, provides the basis
> for the components and differences of all the others.
> The Christian can choose between them in time. They
> are all socialistic possibilities. The time is an important
> factor in his choice. The criterion: the revolution of
> God, God as revolutionary. [145]

Summary

In trying to show how Barth understands the link between ethics and dogmatics and therefore the relationship between acting and God's command in scripture, this chapter has sought to demonstrate how Barth began to develop his methodology for such a link in some of his early writings and particularly in the two editions of **Romans.** The ongoing motor of that link was initially an eschatological one. This eventually, in the **Dogmatics,** took on a christological character, since Jesus Christ established in Himself and His life the link between God's Word, obedience to that Word, and the political implications of that obedience in man's world.

Young Barth, through his exegesis of **Romans,** would characterize man's world and state as a necessary evil, filled with evil at all levels in all its institutions. Even though the state existed under God's wrath, God's concern for that world, whilst not having the full affirmation that Barth declared many years later, in his lecture, "The Humanity of God", nevertheless, was evident in **Romans.** That is, even under God's No to our world and our sin, there is a stress on God's Yes. This is the embryo of Christ as the redeemer of our society and as the participant in our political and social praxis. The eschatological element which impels the Christian to be subject unto the state takes on different forms in the young Barth's writings: Ursprung, totaliter aliter, Revolution Gottes, even the resurrection. It is full knowledge of this fact that the Christian can therefore be consoled in being active in the affairs of state.

At no point does Barth counsel abandonment of political involvement, although he does pour abuse upon the state/society. And at each point he tries to measure the praxis of human institutions and society against his interpretation of God's command as established in scripture and the Word of God. It is this unwillingness to allow theology or dogmatics to become too narrow and esoteric by not concerning itself with real or actual existence and his equal unwillingness to allow utopias and devised "better" societies to become identified with the Kingdom of God that drives Barth to test both God's Word and man's word, even though he recognizes the infinitive qualitative difference between them. The fact that the kingdom has not come and that evil and the "old man" still exist means that the Christian is obligated to be active politically, since politics, in its widest sense along with economics, shapes the destinies and character of society and our relationships with each other. As Barth noted in his praise of Schleiermacher on this point:

And is not also Christian doctrine ethical doctrine? Of course. . . . The Kingdom of God on earth is nothing but the Christian way of life which must always reveal itself in action. [146]

Chapter Three

THEOLOGICAL FOUNDATIONS OF THE STATE AND SOCIETY

In this chapter Barth's understanding of the relationship between society (and the world) and the reconciling work of Jesus Christ will be examined. That is, there will be undertaken an analysis of Barth's explication of reconciliation as an operating principle in political and economic praxis in order to demonstrate the necessary relationship between christology and political praxis. This is a consequence of the emerging model already evident in **Romans,** except that the eschatological and negative categories characterizing the model and the theological foundations undergirding that model now give way to more deliberate christological categories.

Methodologically, one can speak of an "inner shell" of the state and an "outer shell" of the state in Barth. The "inner shell" includes what can be described as the "unredeemed society" and the "redeemed society". Both of these forms of societies yield up contrasting political and social institutions and actions. The "outer shell" of the state includes what might be described as the ontological foundation of the state.

Gerrit C. Berkouwer in his book, **The Triumph of Grace in Karl Barth,** reminds us that to say Karl Barth is to mean simultaneously "christocentricism", especially in reference to Barth's deliberate reversal in the **Dogmatics** in 1932. That is, the use of christology as a modus operandi for ethics and political praxis must be looked at differently after what Barth himself called his "well-known false start". [1] But even Berkouwer, who criticizes Barth for underplaying the demonic effects and influences of evil through his emphasis on grace, admits that Barth's "Christocentricism" has epistemological, as well as ethical implications quite different from those found in other theologians. Observes Berkouwer:

> . . . Barth underscores with increasing emphasis that
> all knowledge of God is exclusively determined by and

> is dependent upon the knowledge of Jesus Christ, and
> that this is not simply a matter of our epistomology,
> but that it is directly related to the nature of God in
> Jesus Christ who is the dominant and all-controlling central
> factor in the doctrine of election, creation, and reconcilia-
> tion. Only in Jesus Christ do we meet the true and decisive
> revelation of God. [2]

What will be explored first, therefore, will be an explication of what Barth calls the "civil community" (Bürgergemeinde),
i.e., the state and the shape of society within the state, as contrasted with what he describes as the "Christian community"
(Christengemeinde), i.e., the Church, with particular attention
given to the "redeemed" and "unredeemed" character of the civil
community in light of Jesus Christ. Secondly, I shall demonstrate
how these two aspects of civil society are related to Barth's
understanding of political and economic institutions and praxis.

At the outset, I am by-passing deliberately the polemical
period of young Barth's understanding of culture and the state,
particularly as they were perceived in the **Römerbrief** days (1919-
1922), which was the Barth introduced to most of the English-
speaking world by Douglas Horton (**The Word of God and the Word
of Man**) in 1928, [3] Strathearn McNab (**The Christian Life**) in
1930, [4] Wilhelm Pauck (**Karl Barth: Prophet of a New Christianity?**) in 1931, [5] not to mention Edwyn Hoskyn's translation
of the **Epistle to the Romans** in 1933. [6] I would suggest that
the Barth of the **Römerbrief** period and the Barth of the calmer,
more reflective post-Römerbrief days ought possibly be remembered
in much the same way that the poster, nailed to the wall of the
Sorbonne during the heady days of 1968, admonished onlookers
about confusing love with revolution: both are made, but their
charms are entirely different. So it is with Barth, when examining
his understanding of culture, although there is some danger in
making such a by-pass in light of Prof. Friedrich Marquardt's
able demonstration of Barth's early socialist/social democratic
period. Prof. Marquardt persuasively, if not completely convincingly,
shows the influence of this period in the shaping of Barth's theological views of the state and political and economic institutions. [7]
Also the recently translated work of Eberhard Busch's **Karl Barths
Lebenslauf**, [8] reveals for English-speaking readers some very
important clues to the relationship between Barth's early political
activism and his theological views, particularly during his days
as pastor in the industrial village of Safenwil (1911-1921). [9] Yet
Barth himself points out that his aim during these polemical days
was to do battle primarily with Kulturprotestantismus and with
his former teachers, Wilhelm Hermann and Adolf von Harnack.
As he wrote some forty years later, he felt summoned to take
a polemical stance because the God who had so freely given Himself
to man and had so freely given man a history and a hope was

being reduced "to a pious notion, a mystical expression and symbol of a current alternating between man and man's own heights or depths". [10] Also during this period there occurred what some have described as the watershed in Barth's theological development, namely, his series of lectures on St. Anselm whilst he was Professor of Systematic Theology at the University of Münster in 1930, an event which Barth describes as providing "a vital key, if not the key" to a major reversal in his theological method and direction. [11] Hence, one can justifiably begin to analyze Barth's christological basis of society after this initial, albeit important, polemical period.

The External Foundations of the State

To begin to understand Barth's theological analysis of the civil community, one has to start, first, with the "outer basis" or ontological foundations of the phenomenon called the state; that is, how it came to be, and, secondly, with the "inner basis" or internal character of the state as civil community; that is, how it looks and functions. In 1938, Barth wrote an essay entitled, **Rechtfertigung und Recht,** [12] whose contents are revealing, considering the fact that it was written some five years after Barth had seen the Nazis dissolve the SPD political party of which he was a loyal member, as well as occupy the administrative offices of the Prussian Evangelical Church in Berlin. Its content was also shaped by the events in 1934 when Hitler had personally summoned Barth's friend, Pastor Martin Niemöller (1892-1984), and other Church leaders to the Chancellery, where he admonished them that the care and guidance of the state and its institutions were exclusively the dominion of the Führer, whereby the Evangelical bishops declared that they were "unconditionally loyal" to Hitler and the Third Reich. One also ought to remember that in 1935 Barth had been fined in the courts for refusing to make the Hitler salute at the beginning of his lectures, which led to his subsequent dismissal from the university by the Reichkulturminister, Bernhard Rust. [13]

Barth maintains in this essay that the Church's understanding of its relationship to the state has to be seen in light of the model established by Jesus Christ shortly before his execution as He confronted the authority of the state, i.e., Pontius Pilate. Pilate reminds Jesus in John 19:2 that he, as an instrument of the state has the power of life and death over Him and all subjects of the state. This passage, suggests Barth, does not insist that power in and of itself is evil, corrupt, or even demonic; indeed Jesus recognizes the power of the state over Him and over the religious community and does not suggest that the nature of that power is evil or demonic. But Jesus does remind Pilate that God Himself has provided both him and the state with this power.

Nonetheless, Jesus accepts the power of the state to pronounce and execute judgment through laws and statutes. [14]

How, therefore, asks Barth, is one to understand the nature of the authority and power of the state in light of Pilate performing what seems to Christians to be an unjust act, namely, the crucifixion of Jesus rather than His release? Does this mean that in exercising his power, Pilate, under the cloak of legality, willingly allows injustice to rule? Dare one suggest that this is the true nature of the state? No, replies Barth,

> . . . even at the moment when Pilate (still under the garb of justice! and in the exercise of the power given him by God) allowed injustice to run its course, he was the humanly created Instrument of that justification of sinful man that was completed once for all time through that very crucifixion. [15]

Pilate "became the involuntary agent and herald of divine justification" [16] and as a Roman governor "became the virtual founder of the Church". [17] That is, even through the doing of the unjust, the state might nevertheless still render service to furthering the cause of the just. Hence, the honor due to the state as a created earthly institution holding a mandate from God Himself, as established in Rom. 13:1-7 and I Pet. 2:17, cannot be dismissed lightly or ignored by Christians. This is the relationship between the two communities which commands support and service by the Church and at the same time which has the seeds for constant tension between the two since both the civil and the religious community carry out divine mandates:

> Certainly in deflecting the course of justice, (Pilate) became the involuntary agent and herald of divine justification; yet at the same time he makes it clear that real human justice, a real exposure of the true face of the state, would inevitably have meant the recognition of the right to proclaim divine justification, the Kingdom of Christ which is not of this world, freely and deliberately. [18]

What is the nature of the divine mandate possessed and exercised by the political entity called the state? Barth's understanding of the foundation of the state is to be found in his angelology, curiously enough, since the temptation of all states to make themselves absolute can be traced to the angelic powers mentioned in the New Testament which threaten to demonize the state. [19] Col. 2:15 reminds us that Jesus Christ defeated and overwhelmed the angelic powers; ("He disarmed the principalities and powers and made a public example of them, triumphing over them in him") as does I Pet. 3:22 (Who is gone into heaven and is on the right hand of God; angels and authorities and powers being subject to him"). This view also reappears later in the **Church Dogmatics**. [20] These angelic powers were understood in the New Testament to be demonic and they shaped the state. The New Testament does not say that these angelic powers were annihilated by Christ, but rather, through His resurrection and parousia they were "forced into the service and glorification of Christ, and through Him, of God." [21] Thus, as the result of this triumph of Jesus Christ,

> . . . the State as such, belongs originally and ultimately to Jesus Christ; that in its comparatively independent substance, in its dignity, its function, and its purposes, it should serve the Person and Work of Jesus Christ and therefore the justification of the sinner. [22]

Subsequently, when the state does become demonic and assumes theonomous pretentions, it is not so much due to its true character as to the renunciation of its true dignity, function, authority, and purpose. Such a betrayal may reflect itself in Caesar worship or Führer worship or in cultic myths about the state and the natural superiority of a particular nation or race. This emphasis on the betrayal of its true ontological character by the state is an important emphasis for Barth because later in his **Church Dogmatics** he attacks natural theology and its use as a guarantee for the authority and internal order of a nation. [23] Rather, insists Barth, the foundation of the state cannot lie in the Schöpfungsordnung, as natural theology would have to maintain, but in the Bundesordnung, that is, the realm of the covenant. [24] Thus, as Eckhard Lessing quite rightly points out, Barth is always impatient with using natural law or natural theology as a foundation for the state and its authority. Instead, he insists that the state is a part of the creaturely history of God in His relationship with mankind. [25] Otherwise, there is no biblical or theological basis for Christians to see and criticize the dangers of such ideologies of fascism and nationalism, which are manifestations of the state claiming absoluteness and theonomy. [26]

As part of the Bundesordnung the state comes under the aegis of God and its ontological grounding as well as its historical development in man's culture under the power of God, as Jesus indeed reminds Pilate. Barth's leading idea in describing the relationship between creation and the covenant is to establish that God is faithful to His creation and remains faithful to His creature in spite of the creature's turning away from God in sin. Thus, suggests Lessing, the extension of this relationship to the political organs of man must be seen in light of what Barth calls the covenant of grace (Bund der Gnade). [27] The intention of creation is historicalness and concreteness, not abstraction. Hence, creation always leads to praxis and particularity:

68

> The execution of this (covenantal) activity is history. What is meant is the history of the covenant of grace instituted by God between Himself and man; the sequence of events in which God concludes and executes this covenant with man, carrying it to its goal, and thus validating in the sphere of the creature that which from all eternity He has determined in Himself; the sequence of events for the sake of which God has patience with the creature and with its creation gives it time--time which acquires content through these events and which is finally to be "fulfilled" and made ripe for its end by their conclusion. This history is from the theological standpoint <u>the</u> history. [28]

Therefore, the internal basis of creation is history as demonstrated in the covenant, and creation itself belongs to God's history. But at the same time, creation initiates history and hence God is both historical and a-historical.

> As Jesus Christ Himself is eternal as God and stands as Lord above all times, but is also concretely temporal and in this way the real Lord of the world and His community, so it is with creation. Those who regard God's creation as an eternal but timeless relation of creature and its existence can certainly boast of a very deep and pious conviction, but they cannot believe it in the Christian and biblical sense. . . . That we can understand our creaturely existence as such as the gift of the divine grace depends--if "grace" is not just a pious word--on the fact that its creation and preservation is a concrete act of God and therefore a historical reality fulfilling time. Then and only then does our creaturely existence as such already stand in connexion with the organising centre of all God's acts, with the reality of Jesus Christ. [29]

One consequence of this understanding of the covenant and history being the internal basis of creation, as Barth phrases it, is that man's time, which is characterized by sinfulness and isolation from God, becomes under the covenant of grace God's time. That is, man's time is made anew through grace: " . . . there is initiated with God's acceptance of man in grace the new time which God has for us and which, now that we have lost the time loaned to us, He wills to give us again as the time of grace." [30] Only this time has a new content, namely, Jesus Christ:

> As the time of the Creator, whose concept cannot be confused by any blunder on the part of the creature, it is a genuine temporal present with a genuine temporal past and future. If the Word of God had not become temporal, it would not have become flesh. [31]

Thus, there is no time in which man's time is without the content of grace, even though we may not recognize [it] or refuse to accept this time of grace:

> When man lost the time loaned to him, he received it back again in Jesus Christ, i.e., in the history, commencing immediately after creation, of the covenant of grace which was fulfilled in His death and resurrection. From the beginning his lost time was surrounded and enclosed by the time of the divine covenant of grace directly continuing the time of creation. [32]

Another consequence of this understanding of the "co-temporality" of divine history and creaturely history in Jesus Christ is that history has both a "non-historical" and a genuine "historical" character. It is "non-historical" in that it is "pre-historical" history, that is, God is its content and thus cannot be perceived and comprehended simply as history with a beginning, present, and end. [33] The vehicle through which this "pre-history" is communicated to us is through saga, which includes both poetry (the emergence of the divine vision as witnessed and passed on by the poet) and divination (the vision of the historical development in which "historical history" occurs). [34] The "historical" character of history means that which is a creaturely event preceding or following other creaturely events which can be interpreted and compared on the basis of other similar events. [35] It is in light of these two directions of "history" that one has to understand the ontological beginnings of the state, since it is an entity which has both a historical character (such as the monarchy, the democratic state, etc.) and a non-historical character (such as the divine mandate for authority mentioned in the New Testament). But it is also in light of these two directions of "history" that this ontological foundation of the state must be understood to be rooted in christology:

> The Christian conscience does demand that they should submit to authority (Rom. 13). Clearly this is because in this authority we are dealing indirectly, but in reality, with the authority of Jesus Christ. [36]

As mentioned previously, Barth is most concerned to refute any kind of "natural" justification of the state which does not begin with scripture and with Jesus Christ. Barth thinks this particularly to be a tendency in Roman Catholic thought, which maintains that the state is a product of man's sin and fallen existence, thus coming into existence as a kind of "emergency relief measure" so that the creaturely order could be maintained. Contrary to this, says Barth, the Christian must insist that the state is provided for by God in His providence and governance of the world:

> It is an order of divine grace, inasmuch as in relation
> to sinful man as such, in relation to the world that still
> needs redeeming, the grace of God is always the patience
> of God. It is the sign that mankind, in its total ignorance
> and darkness, which is still, or has again become, a prey
> to sin and therefore subject to the wrath of God, is
> yet not forsaken but preserved and sustained by God.
> It serves to protect man from the invasion of chaos
> and therefore to give him time. . . . It is, according
> to the New Testament, one of the "powers" created
> through Him and in Him and which subsists in Him (Col.
> 1:16f). [37]

Having grounded the authority of the state in the divine
mandate (Bonhoeffer), Christians must raise the question about
their own role and relationship to the state in light of I Pet.
2:15, but also in light of such fascist and totalitarian states which
have developed from time to time. Barth maintains that the freedom
of the Church to preach the message of justification, and therefore
the reconciliation of the world to God in Jesus Christ means
that the Church's freedom is intrinsically bound up with that
model of the state which guarantees and legitimizes such an internal
order permitting this proclamation to take place. This becomes
the important criterion for the Christian. And as the state, carrying
out its divine mandate, guarantees this freedom of the Church,
so the Church, in turn, should guarantee the existence of that
state. [38] As such the responsible Christian is as much of a
political being as a "religious" being. Christian service and responsibility in the state means understanding political concern and activity
as a bounden duty:

> It makes one thing impossible, however: a Christian
> decision to be indifferent, a non-political Christianity.
> The Church can in no case be indifferent or neutral
> towards this manifestation of an order so clearly related
> to its own mission. Such indifference would be equivalent
> to the opposition to what is said in Rom. 13:2 that it
> is a rebellion against the ordinance of God--and rebels
> secure their own condemnation. [39]

The Internal Foundations of the State

Having examined the "outer shell" or "external basis"
of the state, one must now move to the "inner character" or
"internal basis" of the state. Barth already has forewarned us
that the Christian cannot seek to establish a so-called "Christian"
state, that is, a civil duplication of the Church and its message. [40]
The state is temporal and provisional, a creaturely instrument
"which as such (does) not bear the distinctive mark of revelation . . .

and can therefore not lay any claim to belief," at least in the theological sense of ultimate commitment and divine justification. [41]

> . . . the Church cannot itself become a State, and the State on the other hand, cannot become a Church. The Church gathers its members through free individual decisions, behind which stands the quite different free choice of God, and in this age, it will never have to reckon with gathering all men within itself. . . . But the State has always assembled within itself all men living within its boundaries, and it holds them together, as such, through its order, which is established and maintained by force. The State as State knows nothing of the Spirit, nothing of love, nothing of forgiveness. The State bears the sword. [42]

The constitutive character of the state is power (Gewalt), whereas the constitutive character of the religious community is justice and freedom; the state has the obligation of hindering and checking evil and violence; the Church has the function of supporting the state in carrying out this mandate. [43]

> The "subjection" (Rom. 13) can in no case mean that the Church and its members will approve, and wish of their own free will to further the claims and undertakings of the State, if once the State power is turned not to the protection, but to the suppression of the preaching of justification. Even then, Christians will never fail to grant that which is indispensable to the State power as guardian of the public law, as an ordained power--tribute to whom tribute is due, custom to whom custom, fear to whom fear, honour to whom (as representative and bearer of exousia) honour--even if the State abuses this exousia and demonstrates its opposition, as a demonic power, to the Lord of lords. [44]

"Unredeemed" Society and Its Political Character

To understand the inner character of the state, one must examine what can be called the "unredeemed" and the "redeemed" parts of the civil community, particularly as the tension between these two constitutive parts of the civil community can provide clues and functions about political phenomena and praxis within and between states. These are two directions within the same community, which means that it is not possible to speak of some states as being totally unredeemed and others being totally redeemed. As Jesus Christ Himself reminds us, says Barth, with His recognition of the power of Pilate in the confrontation between them, the power of the state can be used demonically or beneficially without losing its divine character. [45]

> The very state which is "demonic" may will evil, and yet in an outstanding way, may be constrained to do good. The State, even in this "demonic" form, cannot help rendering the service it is meant to render. It can no more evade it in the incident recorded by Luke 13:1-5, where the same Pilate, the murderer of young Galileans, becomes at the same time the instrument of the call to repentance. . . . This is why the State cannot lose the honour that is its due. [46]

Indeed the state can be said to have a role to play in guaranteeing the freedom for preaching and executing the divine summons to redemption: "Pontius Pilate now belongs not only to the Creed but to its second article in particular." [47]

One may say that generally Barth's understanding of the "unredeemed" society is related to his doctrine of providence, where the content of conservatio has to do with being preserved by God against chaos, a phenomenon which Barth defined as simply being that which God did not will or choose, "that which as Creator He passed over, that which, according to the account in Gen. 1:2, He set behind Him as chaos, not giving it existence or being." [48] Thus, the content of chaos is negativity, but negativity which is allotted it by the Creator. This does not mean that it does not have actuality or force or power, for within the sphere of chaos are the demonic, evil, sin, and death, which are very actual and powerful in man's world. Chaos is always a continued menace to creation, but it is a menace which has been overpowered and overcome by God. It is that which is not, alluded to in Gen. 1:3-9 when God marks off the light from the darkness, separates the waters below from the waters above, delineates the cosmos from chaos. Paul Tillich might call this the threat of non-being, which carries with it the threat of evil as a cause and a constitutive element of self-destruction. [49] Barth enlarges the context even more:

> What makes non-being a menace, an enemy which is superior to created being, a threatened destroyer, is obviously not its mere character of non-being, but the fact that it is not elected and willed by God the Creator, but rather rejected and excluded. It is that to which God said No when He said Yes to the creature. And that is chaos according to the biblical term and concept. [50]

Therefore, the thrust and effect of this threat in society is negative and negating. In a picturesque way Barth describes its power and attractiveness to the creature as being similar to that of a single minus which is put before a bracket in an algebraic equation that cannot be removed or lessened by any plus sign within the brackets. [51]

The negation of the "unredeemed" society has spiritual, political, and economic consequences which must be examined. First, spiritually, it means that the creature wants to become his own judge, that is, he establishes his own right over against God:

> He measures himself by this right; he thinks that measuring himself by this right he can pronounce himself free and righteous. . . . All sin has its being and origin in the fact that man wants to be his own judge. And in wanting to be that, and thinking and acting accordingly, he and his whole world is in conflict with God. It is an unreconciled world, and therefore a suffering world, a world given up to destruction. [52]

Under God's judgment, that is, His No, the creature cannot but promulgate further spiritual negation. God's judgment is revealed in the "enfleshing" of the Word:

> . . . the incarnation of the Word means the judgment, the judgment of rejection and condemnation, which is passed on all flesh. Not all men commit all sins, but all men commit this sin which is the essence and root of all other sins. There is not one who can boast that he does not commit it. And this is what is revealed and rejected and condemned as an act of wrong-doing by the coming of the Son of God. This is what makes His coming a coming to judgment and His office as Saviour His office as our Judge. [53]

The political effects of the "unredeemed" society can be seen in the phenomenon of war, an effect which is not made any milder by theological justifications for Christian participation in and support of war, such as the Augustinian idea of "the just war". This does not mean that when a state goes to war the necessary component of war, namely, killing, can be denied or rejected by Christians as though there could be war without killing. But because war and killing are intricately interwoven, neither does it mean that Christians can be neutral about war or assume that war is an inherent part of the state's divinely given authority and function, such as Barth's former professor, Wilhelm Herrmann, attempted to maintain during World War I. Barth criticizes Herrmann's statement about war being "neither Christian nor un-Christian, neither moral nor immoral." [54] Such a position simply provides cover for any kind of theological sanctioning and moral support for aggression and imperialism. Such a position can also imply that war is a natural and proper function of statecraft according to the Christian view of the state. [55] The Christian has to remind the state that war is a manifestation of the "unre-deemed" society within the state and that the state's "normal task is to fashion peace in such a way that life is served and war is kept at bay." [56] Thus, the Christian cannot be at home either with the absolute pacifists or with the militarists.

Pacifism errs in its abstract negation of all war without considering the context or circumstances preceding it. The pacifists fail to consider both the political and the economic circumstances leading up to war. It is during the time before the explosion of war that the community and individual citizens alike should act to form both a national and an international climate in which war will be abnormal rather than normal. [57]

> Neither rearmament nor disarmament can be a first con-cern, but the restoration of an order of life which is meaningful and just. When this is so, the two slogans will not disappear. They will have their proper place. . . . But they will necessarily lose their fanatical tone, since far more ugent concerns will be up for discussion. And there can always be the hope that some day both will prove to be irrelevant. [58]

The militarists, on the other hand, err in thinking that war is the normal task of the state and that killing can be a legiti-mate part of foreign policy. The Church does indeed accept the fact that the state is called upon to exercise power, but it cannot justify the exercise of that power through war as the political opus proprium of the state. The Christian must always point out to the state that the annihilation of life is not a necessary corollary to nourishing and fostering life.

> Pacifists and militarists are usually agreed in the fact that for them the fashioning of peace as the fashioning of the state for democracy, and of democracy for social democracy, is a secondary concern as compared with rearmament or disarmament. It is for this reason that Christian ethics must be opposed to both. [59]

Theologically, war recalls the chaos threatening society and penetrating society at a very basic level. It demonstrates man's inability to be both his own judge and master; it shows man's ability to be his own destroyer. War demonstrates the truth of God's judgment on man as he submits to chaos:

> Do we possess the power to live, or does it possess us? So long as it possesses us, war will always be inevitable. Si vis pacem, para bellum, says the old Roman proverb.

But a wiser version would be: si non vis bellum, para pacem. [60]

Yet there is a dialectical tension for the Christian, says Barth, because modern war, nourished and planned with very advanced technology and scientific tools in military hands, means "no more and no less than killing" instead of simply neutralizing the enemy. [61] Nor is war any longer simply the task of a group of professional officers and soldiers. The entire nation, directly and indirectly, is involved when that particular nation is engaged in war. That is, the entire nation is engaged either in the killing itself, in preparing for killing, or in supporting killing. This is done both by those wanting the killing and by those--even those who are silent--who permit the killing. [62] This means that war, together with its essential component of killing, shapes consciously and unconsciously the national morality.

> To kill effectively, and in connexion therewith, must not those who wage war steal, rob, commit arson, lie, deceive, slander, and unfortunately to a large extent fornicate, not to speak of the almost inevitable repression of all the finer and weightier forms of obedience? . . . The fact is that war is for most people a trial for which they are no match, and from the consequences of which they can never recover. Since all this is incontestable, can it and should it be nevertheless defended and ventured? [63]

And as the civil community "is not God, nor can it command as He does," [64] the Christian, obedient to the imperative of the Sixth Commandment, cannot be content to adopt simply a civil ethic or endorse civil expediency with respect to killing. Thus, whilst the absolute pacifist position too easily slights some of the circumstances leading up to and encouraging the continuation of war in the society, nevertheless the Christian has to make some allowance for the claims of pacifism because pacifism can act as a conscience both within the unredeemed community and within the religious community. It reminds both of the imperativeness and relevance of the Sixth Commandment. [65] Consequently, it is not unlikely that even as a loyal member of the civil community, the Christian will find himself compelled under the command of God to move in opposition to the government in matters of war and conscription and even be disloyal when war is a component of a foreign policy. [66]

Economically, the "unredeemed" society manifests the power and influence of chaos through the privatization of one's existence in society and one's possessions. Lessing comments that for Barth this privatizing of existence and being in the civil community, which means the exclusion of the "I-Thou" component of true humanity, a component revealed at the creation itself, is an even harsher example of the "unredeemed" community than war. [67] As early as 1928, Barth suggested in some lectures that the chief characteristic of the "unredeemed" society is Aneignung, that is, appropriation or usurpation of possessions and existence of individuals, as contrasted with Enteignung, which is expropriation usually by the state. Aneignung is more personal and means that the individual lives in such a manner and style that he grabs after this or that solely for the satisfaction of his own needs or pleasures or for exercising power over and to the exclusion of the other. [68] This attitude and action, in turn, defines the circumstances and frame of reference in which one thinks and fashions one's relations and actions towards others. In that one lives unto oneself and for oneself, one necessarily lives against the neighbor. To live as such is to live under ontic and noetic estrangement. [69] This position of Barth's has to be recalled when reading some twenty-three years later his elucidation of humanity in the **Church Dogmatics:**

> Humanity, the characteristic and essential mode of man's being, is in its root fellow-humanity. Humanity which is not fellow humanity is inhumanity. [70]

Barth extends his idea of Aneignung into socio-economic areas as well. Sociologically, Aneignung means that Europeans and whites in general seek to enjoy and claim all possible material and intellectual advantages as being inherent to the superior intelligence of Europeans and a testimony to the disadvantages of other non-European races and states. [71] Economically, Aneignung means that egoism, which is the root of privatization, is not only veiled under ruthless economic competition, called capitalism, but also is legitimized and approved through laws and statutes. "I take only my interest (in shares and investments), I take only what belongs to me by God and by right" is the motto of economic Aneignung without concern for the nations, peoples, and workers upon whose backs the investments and wealth have been accumulated. [72] When this Aneignung is also made into a national myth and legitimized in social mores, then it institutionalizes itself in what Barth calls "Kampf ums Dasein," that is, "indem ich für mich lebe, lebe ich notwendig gegen Andere." [73]

This process concreticizes itself most clearly in "property" (Eigentum), which includes both material and spiritual values that exclude cooperation with others. [74] Thus, private property by its very nature and development is founded upon such an exclusion. This means that the Christian cannot simply interpret the commandment forbidding stealing as summoning one to respect private property. Rather, says Barth, the commandment ought to make the property owner ask himself whether the legal protection provided by society under which he holds his property is not itself a concept transgressing this commandment in that the lives and labor of others have been upset and exploited so that he could maintain his private property. [75]

> This reversal (of interpretation) is not an evil or communistic discovery; rather, it is the most serious radical sense of the commandment: "Thou shalt not" because this commandment is not man's but God's. [76]

This is the foundation of capitalism which, according to Barth, reinforces the alienation of the creature from creation in the "unredeemed" society. This Kampf ums Dasein in which private ownership becomes the basis for one's values and status in society takes on a particularly sinful character when communal and collective concerns are excluded, as is often the case in capitalistic societies. Here, when there is often a conflict between private property and communal concerns, private property is given priority,--a tendency and practice which are challenged in the German idiom, Eigentum ist Diebstahl.

Private property and the privatizing of values and human relations which in turn are institutionalized in capitalistic society also determine the shape of the domestic and foreign policy of such a state. "It is when interest-bearing capital rather than man is the object whose maintenance and increase are the meaning and goal of the political order that the mechanism is already set going which one day will send men to kill and be killed." [77] Indeed, the pursuit of markets and products in other lands shape both foreign and domestic policy as does the armaments industry in western countries. Thus, suggests Barth, in the capitalistic society there is a necessary interrelatedness between foreign policy, economics, military aims, and industrial power:

> Even though we may constantly forget it, we have no good reason not to recognize that modern war, especially between great nations and national groups, is primarily and basically a struggle for coal, potash, ore, oil, and rubber, for markets and communications, for more stable frontiers and spheres of influence as bases from which to deploy power for the acquisition of more power, more particularly of an economic kind. . . . This means, however, that in a way very different from previous generations we can and should realize that the real issue in war, and an effective impulse towards it, is much less than man himself and his vital needs than the economic power. . . . [78]

A consequence of the "privatizing" and "individualizing" of social relations is the corruption and fundamental alteration of the divinely ordered and commanded task of labor or work.

Barth understands labor to be more than simply earning money to satisfy material needs. Work is a gift of man's existence as a creature and as God's covenant partner:

> God in Jesus Christ wills not only the election, call, justification and sanctification of man, and for the attestation of this work the service of the Christian community, but in order that all this may take place, in it and for the sake of it, He wills man himself and his existence as a creature. Similarly, man cannot will only to believe, to hope and to love . . . but in order to do all this, to be an acting subject as well as an object in relation to the coming of God's kingdom, he is summoned to continue in existence as a human creature. . . . [79]

Labor is man's active testimony and affirmation of his creatureliness giving service to God as He claims and summons man both as creature and as partner. This is the distinguishing feature of man's creatureliness as contrasted with animal creatureliness. [80] This does not make man a second God, nor does it mean a completion of God's work on the part of man. Labor is simply a form of man's obedience to God's command and his fulfillment as a human creature.

> We may certainly maintain that when human work takes place in the service and under the blessing of God, it is a proof of the goodness of God's creation and a confirmation of the wisdom of His providence. But we cannot possibly maintain that the creation and the providence of God need this proof. For only of the free and superabundant grace of God can man prove himself and therefore the works of God and the divine goodness and wisdom. [81]

As such, says Barth, labor has the goal of preserving, safeguarding, developing and shaping human life in order that that life may be a witness to the kingdom of God. Labor aims to do this in three directions: 1) the subjective determining of certain goals on the part of the individual and the attempt to achieve these goals, [82] 2) the objective promotion of certain universal goals and conditions in society which are important for the workingman's situation, [83] 3) the undertaking of cooperative ventures on the part of workers which will move toward strengthening solidarity with others. [84] Capitalism both perverts and corrupts such endeavors in that it 1) is based on the idea of the individual working only for his own ends and needs under the category of what Barth calls "thoughtlessness" [85] and 2) excites and nourishes individual claims and individual inordinate desires to the exclusion of fellow-humanity. [86] It is the extension of this "thoughtlessness", that is, the deliberate neglect or denial of the social and therefore cooperative character of labor, that is the motor for capitalism. Capitalism thrives, therefore, on

> . . . the lust for possessions which will not be used even perhaps for the purpose of luxury, but are desired only as a security and pledge against future use, or perhaps only for the sake of the idea of possession, as if this were a guarantee of life; (on) the lust for an artificially extended area of power over man and things in the form of artificial instruments. [87]

As such, labor in a capitalist society is organized on a basis of dependency and dominance: those not controlling the "means of production" are dependent on those who do for opportunities or work and reward and those who own the means of production dominate and exploit those who work. Barth disallows the Marxist idea that a capitalist is ipso facto an exploiter and oppressor. Nevertheless, he remarks,

> it can hardly be denied that on the whole, at least in the West, the modern industrial process does, in fact, rest on the principle of the exploitation of some by others, or, to put it less dramatically, on the aiming and obtaining of a profit which accrues to the economically stronger, i.e., to the owners of the means of production, in virtue of the fact that they can turn to their own advantage the contract of labor with the economically weaker who are dependent on them, i.e., those who have nothing to offer but their time and ability. [88]

This is Barth's most serious indictment of the economic forces at work in the "unredeemed" society, a situation, he points out, which has been improved somewhat by the empowering of the working class through the efforts of the unions, socialists, and the Marxists. [89] But even these efforts have not ended exploitation, and because of this the Church in the West must render service under the command of God by being advocates and supporters of the exploited. That is, the Church must usually stand to the left politically:

> Christianity in the West has its main work cut out to comprehend the disorder in the decisive form still current in the West, to remember and to assert the command of God in face of this form, and to keep to the "left" in opposition to its champions, i.e., to confess that it is fundamentally on the side of the victims of this disorder and to espouse their cause. [90]

In order to understand the need and importance of its task, the Christian community must, therefore, grasp the fact that the "unredeemed" society as reflected in the capitalistic socio-economic organization of society 1) hinders the emergence of the social and cooperative quality of working class life in society, 2) does not liberate either the employer or the employee, but rather enslaves them to individualization and privatization of needs, personal claims, and goals, 3) cannot resolve the fundamental exploitation of workers, which Barth describes as "the injustice of the treatment of one man by another merely as a means to his own ends, as a mere instrument", [91] and 4) remains basically unfree as long as capital is the modus operandi for determining and shaping the economic values and relations between various classes in that society. The Church is summoned to support various social programs aimed toward progress in removing these injustices and even if such move is toward a socialist society. It does so, however, whilst realizing that all reforms and revolutions thus far still have not destroyed the basic problem in the "unredeemed" society, namely, the exploitation of man by man in ever-changing forms:

> Its decisive work cannot consist in the proclamation of social progress or socialism. It can consist only in the proclamation of the revolution of God against all ungodliness and unrighteousness of man (Rom. 1:18), i.e., in the proclamation of His kingdom as it has already come and comes. [92]

"Redeemed" Society and Its Political Character

The other direction of civil society, as I interpret it, is what Barth might call "redeemed" society. This is that part of the state which understands itself as existing under the hope and eschatological promise of Jesus Christ. This "redeemed" society was advanced by Barth as early as 1926 in a lecture given in Amsterdam after his appointment as professor at the University in Münster. [93] In that lecture, Barth defined culture theologically as "the promise originally given to man of what he is to become." [94] Culture is a historical and institutionalized witness to the fact and promise that the alienation of man from God has, in fact, been overcome:

> Reconciliation in Christ is the restoration of the lost promise. It renews the status of the creation with its great "Yes" to man, with its reasonableness of reason. It gives man again insight into the meaning of his activity. It gives him the courage to understand that even the broken relation in which he stands and acts toward God is still a relation and to take it seriously. [95]

But this culture is neither a Schleiermachian nor a Hegelian model, that is, an idealized form of Prussian culture and society, warns Barth. It simply means that in the redeemed society social and political structures and achievements can illuminate the promise and fact of reconciliation--something which the unredeemed society cannot do. The redeemed or reconciled society has, therefore, a primary eschatological significance which allows the Christian to envision and to work for political and social aims in light of the telos toward which all society is striving. As Barth so characteristically puts it in an exposition of the concept, Das Spiel:

> With this eschatological anticipation, the Church confronts
> society. . . . Not as a spoilsport, but in the knowledge
> that art and society, business and politics, techniques
> and education are really a Spiel (game or play)--a serious
> Spiel, but a Spiel, and Spiel means an imitative and ulti-
> mately ineffective activity--the significance of which
> lies not in its attainable goal, but in what it signifies. . . .
> Our earnestness could not be impaired by making clear
> to ourselves that the Spiel can never be ultimately serious,
> and never is; that the right and possibility of being wholly
> in earnest is God's alone. [96]

It is as the forma Dei in the grace of God becomes the forma servi in the sinful "far country" of man that the reconcilica- tion of man's world and society to God occurs. [97] But the recon- ciliation occurs not only to the world but in the world, it not only affects it from without but determines it from within. [98]

> God takes it to Himself, entering into the sphere of it
> as the true God, causing His kingdom to come on earth
> as in heaven, becoming Himself truly ours, man, flesh,
> in order to overcome sin where it has its dominion, in
> the flesh, to take away in His own person the ensuing
> curse where it is operative, in the creaturely world. [99]

Barth maintains that to say less than this is to give credence to the modalistic and subordinationist interpretations of Christ's deity. [100] The reconciling work of God in the world affects both Christian and non-Christian alike, and this is universal, whether or not the non-Christian admits to it or experiences it. [101] The historical character of the life and work of Jesus Christ has shown the overcoming of all human resistance and indifference. The promise of the spirit affects all mankind. [102]

> In his dying, the dying which awaits us in the near or
> distant future was already comprehended and completed,
> so that we no longer die to ourselves . . . but only in
> Him, enclosed in His death. We died: the totality of
> all sinful men, those living, those long dead, and those
> still to be born. Christians who necessarily know and

> proclaim it, but also Jews and heathen, whether they
> hear and receive the news or whether they tried and
> still try to escape it. [103]

Barth also wishes to emphasize a second point when pointing to the reconciling of the creaturely world with the Creator, namely, a criticism of natural theology which conceives the state to be a part of the natural or created order (Schöpfungsordnung) rather than the state being a part of the covenantal order of things (Bundesordnung). [104] Natural theology understands the state to be an instrument which is a reaction to man's sinfulness and a means of keeping man's sinfulness under control in order that community may be established. But to do this, says Barth, means the state as evidence of God's wrath is separated from the state being an instrument of God's grace:

> (The state) is God's ordinance for the security of the
> collective life of man even where the latter provides
> no scope for grace. . . . But divine wrath does not really
> exist apart from grace. That God's grace prevails here
> in the form of His anger is shown by the fact that the
> political order is the order of the sword, of compulsion,
> and of fear. [105]

Understood in this light, the hidden mission of the state is to provide time for man and his culture to receive grace. Hence, where this grace is not known, there can reign only the sword, compulsion, and fear. God summons the Christians to participate fully in the political order, not so much to abandon this waiting as promised and revealed in Jesus Christ for the sake of civil expediency or civil pragmatism, but rather because of their political participation as a witness to the eschatological waiting.

> In so doing they as little compromise with the form of
> this world as does God Himself who appoints this order
> for humanity as it is entangled in the form of this world.
> For He does not do this in order to confirm this form,
> which has been overcome and abolished in Jesus Christ,
> but to prepare its final and total dissolution. It is in
> this sense that Christians must adapt and subordinate
> themselves to the temporal order. [106]

Thus, remarks Barth, Christians cannot be indifferent or a-political with regard to political praxis. To do or be so would be an abandonment of their summons to proclaim the Word of God and to do it. Political activity is what Barth describes as the Christians' "reasonable service". [107] The Christians must be aware that it is often in what appears to be the gracelessness of the state or society that they can recognize the graciousness of God.

There is yet another danger, according to Barth, in establishing the foundation of the state within the order of creation instead of the order of the covenant. Such a foundation would provide a false basis for political praxis on the part of Christians in society. The state may well move and act on the basis of an appeal to "natural law", by which Barth means that which is regarded as "universally right and wrong as necessary, permissible, and forbidden 'by nature'," [108] and what is thought to be a rational and natural apprehension of God's revelation apart from God initiating that apprehension. But were the Christian community to use this as a basis for political action in the civil community, it would, in fact, be adopting and would be determined by the norms and methods of the pagan, indifferent state, thereby relinquishing its particular and unique service in the civil community. The norm for Christian political action must be the promised kingdom of God:

> It is the rule of God in the redeemed world. In the Kingdom of God the outward is annulled by the inward, the relative by the absolute, the provisional by the final. In the Kingdom of God, there is no legislature, no executive, no legal administration. For in the Kingdom of God there is no sin to be reproved, no chaos to be feared and checked. [109]

Yet at the same time the state, as a pluralistic institution, may have social aims and ideals based on natural law; hence it ought to reject any attempt by the Church to make it into an earthly kingdom of God. [110]

What are the implications of this redeemed society for political praxis? Paralleling the three categories mentioned under the unredeemed society, i.e., spiritual, political, and economical, one may say that spiritually the redeemed society testifies to the obedience of Jesus Christ to the command of God as being the model for the religious community. The reconciliation or redemption of the world with God means that the power of wrath manifested in so many of the state's institutions and actions as well as "world-time" have been given a new character and significance:

> The "for us" of His death on the cross includes and encloses this terrible "against us". Without this terrible "against us" it would not be the divine and holy and redemptive and effectively helpful "for us" in which the conversion of man and the world to God has become an event. . . . . It is a completed fact, to which nothing can be added by us in time or in eternity, and from which nothing can be taken away by us in time and in eternity. [111]

Barth suggests that the spiritual implications of the redeemed society can best be illustrated by contrasting the disorder
of human society with the divine order of grace as manifested
in his christology. [112] First, when we claim that in Jesus Christ
the Word became flesh, man is revealed as someone who wants
to become God, that is, he exalts himself and in so doing exceeds
his intended creatureness. [113]

> The speech of the famous serpent in Gen. 3:1f, like all
> bad theology--of which this speech is the original--is
> itself only an interpretation of human existence which
> does not explicitly express but only implies a call to
> disobedience. . . . The serpent's speech simply showed
> the existence of man to be formally autonomous, self-
> governing and self-sufficient. It simply laid down the
> possibility that man might see his own needs and satisfy
> those needs by his own efforts. [114]

In choosing to be autonomous, man chooses self-alienation, for
man was created for partnership--partnership with God and partnership with his fellowman. [115]

> For neither as an individual nor in society was he created
> to be placed alone, to be self-controlling and self-sufficient,
> to be self-centered, to rotate around himself. [116]

Secondly, when we use the christological model of the
Lord becoming a servant, man is revealed as the servant who
wants to become lord. That is, he exalts himself in order to control
his society and his fellowman as well as God. [117]

> Wanting to act the lord in relation to God, man will
> desire and grasp at lordship over other men, and on
> the same presupposition other men will meet him with
> the same desiring and grasping. The struggle for power--the
> power of the sexes (did not this begin with the prominence
> of the woman in Gen. 3:2f?), the power of individuals,
> nations, classes, and ranks--is bound to follow, and it
> will be accompanied by the execution of a mutual judgment
> which is a judgment without grace, for where is the
> grace to come from? [118]

Such a move is really megalomania, notes Barth, and is a model
which was particularly encouraged in western society of the nineteenth century as industrialism was so dominant in shaping and
influencing the internal social life of the various western nations.
[119]

Thirdly, when the work of Jesus Christ is considered,
a further christological model is revealed, namely, that of God

as Judge becoming the judged who was judged in man's place. That is, as Barth puts it so aptly:

> He pronounced sentence on us by taking our place, by unreservedly allowing that God is in the right against Himself--Himself as the bearer of our guilt. He was the divine Judge and fulfilled the divine judgment in such a way that He caused Himself to be judged, so that we should not suffer what we deserved, so that we should be those who are judged in His person. [120]

Yet, under the light of this model, man is shown to be desirous of being his own judge. In choosing to be his own judge, man become "unfree". [121] "He is a free man when he thinks and decides and acts at peace with God, when his decision is simply and exclusively a repetition of the divine decision." [122] In wanting to be his own judge, man is not protected from the evil of chaos and thus does that which is evil. This doing of evil is reflected in his breaking the fellowship between himself and others through his desire and acting to privatize all things in the civil community:

> I am already choosing wrong when I think that I know and ought to decide what is right, and I am doing wrong when I try to accomplish that which I have chosen as right. I am already putting myself in the wrong with others, and doing them wrong. . . . For when I do this I divide myself and I break the fellowship between myself and others. I can only live at unity with myself, and we can only live in fellowship with one another, when I and we subject ourselves to the right which does not dwell in us . . . but which is over me and us as the right of God. . . . [123]

Finally, when the reconciling work of Jesus Christ is examined alongside the being and activity of humankind, it should be noted that man thinks his salvation rests in "self-help". [124] That is, man claims to have a right to be autonomous, to determine his relationship to his neighbor and his neighbor's relationship to him on the basis of his own needs and goals. [125] Man is indeed expected to affirm his creatureliness by assuming responsibility for his actions, but he has to make this claim within the freedom given him by God. Man is free to the extent that he understands his freedom within the free and gracious grace of God. To do otherwise is not only to alienate oneself from God, but also from one's intended self:

> Man sets out to be his own helped and that is what he has to be. He is left to himself, to his phantasy, his self-will, his projects and constructions and crafts, his natural capacities and powers in the service of the

> hopeless task of helping himself. And this is pure helpless-
> ness: to be without grace is to be without help. [126]

It is when man accepts his creatureliness, which is revealed and demonstrated in the being and work of Jesus Christ, that he becomes concerned with providing for a better environment and society for himself and his fellowman. This is what Barth calls the "active life" in his **Dogmatics.** [127] This "active life" includes change and production, a chief ingredient of which is labor (Arbeit). In spite of its limitations, Reformation ethics about work was headed in the proper direction as a way of interpreting God's summons to the active life in contrast to an over-emphasis on the contemplative life of medieval catholicism:

> And in its suspicion that the vita contemplativa has perhaps
> far too much in common with the indolence condemned
> in Scripture, it was historically right to the extent that
> in the monastic ideal of the perfect life there was un-
> doubtedly at work an ancient Greek and Stoic view accord-
> ing to which the perfect man belongs to the higher classes
> and has the leisure to fashion himself physically, intellectu-
> ally and aesthetically into a harmonious being, whereas
> the rest, the real working classes, exist only to procure
> for the aristocrat, who is occupied with himself and
> therefore with real living, the basis of existence which
> he too requires. [128]

What is the character of labor? Barth broadens this term to include more than the satisfaction of material or even spiritual needs. Its character is to be seen in service:

> Human life participates in the freedom of all God's crea-
> tures to the extent that it does not have its aim in
> itself and cannot therefore be lived in self-concentration
> and self-centredness, but only in a relationship which
> moves outwards and upwards to another. [129]

Politically, Barth sees the redeemed society taking on the form of what is usually understood as democracy, although he conditions and limits this form of government with regard to the command of God. Early Barth embraced democracy as a justified political extension of the New Testament's understanding of the state much more passionately than later Barth. Even in 1938, Barth could exclaim:

> When I consider the deepest and most central content
> of the New Testament exhortation, I should say that
> we are justified, from the point of view of exegesis,
> in regarding the "democratic conception of the State"
> as a justifiable expansion of the thought of the New
> Testament. [130]

The democratic state is a better alternative to what he called the "Pilate" state, that is, a state whose very fabric is based on injustice. [131] The democratic state is more likely to provide the Church with the freedom to proclaim its message of "divine justification". [132] To this extent the totalitarian state is a falsification of the New Testament's understanding of the state to which Christians can subject themselves, although, Barth cautions, Christians ought not to forget that even in a democracy they are "foreigners" in terms of the eschatological claims of scripture:

> The democratic state might as well recognize that it can expect no truer or more complete fulfillment of duty than that of the citizens of the realm that is so foreign to it as a State--the Church founded on divine justification. [133]

When this freedom is recognized and granted, then this is a just and legitimate state, and this more often than not occurs within a democracy:

> . . . Tyranny on the one hand, and anarchy on the other, Fascism and Bolshevism alike, will be dethroned; and the true order of human affairs--the justice, wisdom and peace, equity and care for human welfare which are necessary for that true order--will arise. Not as heaven (not even as a miniature heaven) on earth! No, this "true order" will be able to arise only upon this earth and within the present age, but this will take place really and truly, already upon this earth, and in this present age, in this world of sin and sinners. [134]

However, by 1941, Barth was less enthusiastic about democracy, at least as developed in western models and societies. Professor Helmut Gollwitzer points out that Barth had early on actually tended to identify the kingdom of God with socialism. [135] He suggests that this tendency was related to Barth's disappointment with the support of the European Social Democratic parties for the First World War as well as his disappointment with his formerly admired university professors who supported the war aims of Germany. But in his famous letter to an American churchman, [136] Barth begins to caution about the Church identifying any state as a "Christian" state. [137] Barth's disappointment with western democracy may also have been related to his fears about the origins of the cold war after 1945. In 1946, Barth wrote that the granting of freedom to the Church to proclaim its message of divine justification might occur under a monarchy or an aristocracy or even a dictatorship. [138] Whilst the Christian view would seem to support the democratic state and find an affinity with the democratic ideology of the "rule of the people"; "no democracy is protected as such from failing in many or all of the points we have enumerated and denegrating not only into anarchy, but also into tyranny and thereby becoming a bad state." [139] Barth does not support the cold-war theology of a godly west and a godless east. As he wrote in 1958:

> Anti means against. God is not against man, rather he is for man. The Communists are also men. God is also for the Communists. Thus, a Christian cannot be against Communists, only for them. To be for the Communists does not mean to be for Communism. [140]

Democracy signifies for Barth not so much a particular cultural possession and wisdom in the west or in any other geographic region as a Weltanschauung which is built upon "humanity, freedom and justice". [141]

Economically, Barth traces the strengths of the redeemed society to the different character given labor, a difference which he finds very much akin to the character of labor under what he calls "true" socialism. This means labor without the exploitation, which seems necessary under capitalism. But neither is it the concept of labor under "state socialism" of the eastern European countries:

> . . . although the letter of the Marxist programme means that there can be no more exploiters and exploited, it does not settle the matter that there is no more private ownership of the means of production or free enterprise, or that the direction of the labour process has been transferred to the hands of the state. The injustice of one man by another merely as a means to his own ends, as a mere instrument, once rested on a foundation of private capital, and still does in the West. Yet it is by no means impossible . . . that this injustice can perpetuate itself in a different form on a different basis, namely, on that of state socialism which is, in fact, directed by a ruling and benefit-deriving group. [142]

As mentioned earlier, it is against all forms of exploitation, and most especially economic exploitation, that the "revolution of God" is to be proclaimed by the Church. [143] In the redeemed society labor takes on the aspect of true freedom, that is, a freedom to serve. But this freedom in the redeemed society really has as a goal that which prevents man from exploiting himself and his fellowman, namely, the recognition that labor does not mean that good works are able to create the kingdom of God on earth or to earn one a right to the kingdom of God. It is the recognition that labor has its limits.

> God certainly demands that man should work. He also demands, however, that he should rest, that there should

be in his life a place which is free for God and therefore for himself, in order that he may thus be protected against himself and the overwhelming power which his work, and the prospect of its reward, its aims and its objectivity, might gain over him. . . . If it is done aright and in obedience, it allows itself to be characterized as a restricted activity. [**144**]

Barth sees a democratized socialism or a socialized democracy as the model within redeemed society reflecting the command of God. It is a model which enhances both freedom and true justice, both individual worth and fellow-humanity. In the East, according to Barth, there is the problem between how to achieve freedom with an already achieved economic justice; in the West it is the question of how to reconcile achieved freedom with not yet achieved economic justice. [**145**] Democracy as propagated in the West is often only a formal democracy, whose alleged superiority is depicted by going into voting booths, being able to express contrary opinions, and having independent newspapers and mass media. But these attributes, important as they are for enhancing freedom, do not determine a democracy alone, since private capital and managers who control the means of production and the newspapers have a great deal of influence over what is read and often what is voted upon.

. . . so long as there is in the West, "freedom" to start economic crises, "freedom" to throw grain in the sea, even though people were hungering in (Russia), so long should we as Christians refuse to speak an unconditional No to the East. We accuse it of its inhumane methods not without some justification. But we do not forget that they can accuse us of an inhumanity, namely, an inhumanity shown in our deathly respect for material values which in a fundamental way corrupts our thinking and doing. [**146**]

Perhaps the most telling model of the state toward which the Christian community serving the civil community should work is suggested in Barth's letter to America in 1942:

Der von den Kirchen heute wie morgen zu vertretende christliche Begriff des rechten Staates hat zweifellos eine bestimmte Grenze und eine bestimmte Richtung. Indem er auf Ordnung zielt, widerspricht und widersteht er aller politischen, sozialen und wirtschaftlichen Tyrannie und Arnarchie. Und indem er das gemeinsame Recht und die persönliche Verantwortlichkeit zum Massstab der Ordnung macht, liegt die Demokratie mehr in seiner Linie als eine aristokratische oder monarchische Diktatur, der Sozialismus mehr als die ungebundene Wirtschaft und das auf sie begründete Gesellschafts= und Erwerbssystem,

eine Föderation freier (auch von Nationalitätenprinzip
möglich freier!) Staaten mehr als das Nebeneinander unab-
hängiger und unkontrolliert konkurrierender Nationalstaaten.
[**147**]

Chapter Four

JESUS CHRIST AS SERVANT, LORD, AND WITNESS

Karl Barth's christology is found appropriately enough under his doctrine of reconciliation, for, whilst God's deity and sovereignty is fully and completely a matter for God alone, He chose to be God in partnership with man. That choice was revealed most profoundly and primordially in Jesus Christ, who revealed and was the reconciling act between a faithful God and faithless man. But also, Jesus Christ revealed that God elected sinful man as well as electing Himself for the partnership. Reviewing his arrival at this point from the dark polemic of **Römerbrief** period, Barth said in a lecture given in 1956, which startled the English-speaking world because of its de-emphasis on the gulf and distance between man and God:

> . . . It was pre-eminently the image and concept of a "wholly other" that fascinated us and which we, though not without examination, had dared to identify with the deity of Him who in the Bible is called Yahweh-Kyrios. We viewed this "wholly other" in isolation, abstracted and absolutized, and set it over against man, this miserable wretch--not to say boxed his ears with it--in such fashion that it continually showed greater similarity to the God of the philosophers than to the deity of the God of Abraham, Isaac, and Jacob. [1]

Barth insisted that the togetherness of this electing God and the elected man reveals most clearly God's humanity as well as His deity. To speak of God's deity is to speak thus of His humanity. To speak of God's humanity is to speak christologically, for God cannot be perceived apart from the Christ.

> Rather, in Him we encounter the history, the dialogue, in which God and man meet together and are together, the reality of the covenant mutually constructed, preserved, and fulfilled by them. . . . He is the Word spoken from

91

> the loftiest, most luminous transcendent and likewise
> the Word heard in the deepest, darkest immanence. [2]

It is Jesus Christ who certifies and attests to God's grace, who is in fact God's grace, but who, at the same time, certifies and attests to man's gratefulness. In Jesus Christ, God demonstrates that He has chosen not to be against man, but supremely to be for him as his redeemer and reconciler:

> This gift, this humanity, is not blotted out through the fall of man, nor is its goodness diminished. . . . He is elected through God's grace alone. He is elected, however, as the being especially endowed by God. . . . Above all, however, (this election) is shown in the fact that from the beginning he is constituted, bound, and obligated as a fellowman. [3]

Whilst this chapter will examine Barth's "christological" foundation of God's relationship to us and our society, one ought to be cautious about separating his christology from other doctrines of his thinking. Christology, as is understood above, penetrates all of theological and dogmatic reflection. According to Barth:

> . . . thinking is christological only when it consists in the perception, comprehension, understanding, and estimation of the reality of the living person of Jesus Christ as attested in Holy Scripture, in attentiveness to the range and significance of His existence, in openness to His self-disclosure, in consistency in following Him as is demanded. . . . We are not dealing with a Christ-principle, but Jesus Christ Himself as attested by Holy Scripture. . . . Within theological thinking generally unconditional priority must be given to thinking which is attentive to the existence of the living person of Jesus Christ . . . so that per definitionem christological thinking forms the unconditional basis for all other theological thinking, even that which deals with the relationship between God and evil. [4]

Barth uses the vehicle of the covenant as the uniting link between the Old and New Testaments, as well as establishing the "basis for the relationship between God and man." The content of the covenantal theology is dealt with in his volumes on creation. [5] One might summarize Barth's understanding of the covenant by saying that the covenant provides both the form and the content of the most fundamental contractual relationship between God and man in which both recognize their claims and responsibilities. It also provides the context for understanding the person, mission, and efficacy of Jesus Christ as God and as man. The concept of the covenant distinguishes the biblical understanding of God from a philosophical concept of God in that it establishes an event in which one knows God as <u>acting</u>, not a condition in which one knows God as <u>existing</u>. But the covenant also establishes the <u>modus operandi</u> for witnessing and testifying about man:

> A report about ourselves is included in that report about God. . . . To put it in the simplest way, what unites God and us men is that He does not will to be God without us, that He creates us rather to share with us and therefore with our being and life and act . . . that He does not allow His history to be His and ours ours, but causes them to take place as a common history. [6]

Briefly, the Old Testament idea of covenant has a threefold significance for the partnership between God and man. First, there is the covenant in embryo as witnessed in Genesis 9:1-17. This covenant established Yahweh's commitment not only to Israel, but to the larger community of humankind. [7] This was the Noachic covenant which provided the background against which the Fall and all its subsequent results have to be considered. [8] But even this covenant with Israel's patriarchs presupposed and established God's relationship with all nations. Thus from the very beginning of ancient Israel's history, there was already a universalism about God's care and providence.

> Those who come from outside (the Noachic covenant) do not come from a vacuum, but from the sphere of a relationship of God to man which is also in its own way effective--not generally and naturally, but historically, in virtue of a particular divine act. . . . In the last days it will be wonderfully shown that the covenant of Yahweh with Israel was not an end in itself, but that it had a provisional and a provisionally representative significance. Israel had and has a mission--that is the meaning of the covenant with it. [9]

Secondly, the covenant reminds us that the historical unfaithfulness of Israel is overruled by the promise of redemption, particularly in the light of the Servant Songs (Isaiah 52:13-53:12). This is the witness to the permanent and continuing Yes of God to humankind and the promise of fulfillment of that Yes:

> (The texts) also connect the salvation which is the final goal of the history of Israel with the salvation of the Assyrians and the Egyptians and all nations, and in such a way that the special existence of Israel is an instrument by which God finally manifests and accomplishes salvation for the nations. . . . By these strangely complimentary aspects on the borders of the Old Testament we are not merely enabled, but summoned, to take even the most elusive thing which it speaks, the covenant relationship

> between Yahweh and Israel, which is the presupposition
> of everything that takes place in the relations between
> these two partners, and, to understand it inclusively,
> as that which points to a covenant which was there
> in the beginning and which will be there at the end
> of the covenant of God with all men. [10]

Thirdly, the covenant between these two partners in the Old Testament is promised renewal because of the sinfulness of Israel and as promised in Jeremiah 31:34. [11] But it is not an abrogation of the old covenant for it does not negate the faithfulness of God. This faithfulness was not absent from the old covenant and only visible in the new; it was simply "hidden." [12]

> Jeremiah 31 is the final word in matters of the divine
> covenant with Israel. In the light of the last days it
> describes it as the covenant of the free but effective
> grace of God. But at the same time it is also the first
> word in these matters. And this description is an indication
> of what the divine covenant with Israel has been in
> substance from the very first. [13]

The content and meaning of this new covenant is Jesus Christ Himself, "the servant of God who stands before God." [14] "the representative of all nations" who is also the representative of God. This new covenant is the "covenant of grace", [15] which is a relationship characterized by God freely becoming man for the sake of man. It is man's ingratitude for this act by God which continues to scandalize Barth in his christology and he feels driven to discover why this is the case.

> By deciding for us God has decided concerning us. We
> are therefore prevented from thinking otherwise about
> ourselves, from seeing or understanding or explaining
> man in any other way, than as the being engaged and
> covenanted to God, and therefore simply but strictly
> engaged and covenanted to thanks. . . . In freedom he
> can only choose to be the man of God, i.e., to be thankful
> to God. [16]

To choose otherwise is for us to negate and betray our own true humanity, which, for Barth, means a reflection of true humanity as shown by Jesus Christ.

This covenant of grace has two implications for God's creation and for our creatureliness. If the basis of the old covenant is God's pro nobis, and if this is the internal basis of creation itself, then Jesus Christ as the new creation and as the content of the new covenant means that He is not simply the highest form of the covenant relationship; rather he is that which predetermined that relationship as it was intended with the creation of Adam. Jesus Christ is therefore the Adam preceding the first Adam and that Adam coming after the first Adam. [17]

How is this possible in light of the claim that Jesus Christ is the second Person in the Trinity who also is God become man in man's time? Barth simply says that God in His own freedom and graciousness made the decision, behind which we cannot go. [18] Jesus Christ as the Word of God and as the fulfillment of that Word is God's decision to be a partner for all of humankind: therefore Jesus Christ is a reality which precedes and undergirds all of reality--something which Paul Tillich might describe as "the ground of being". [19] Yet Barth extends the pre-temporal reality of Jesus Christ a bit further. If He is the first-born of all things as well as the sustainer of all things, then the decision of God to be Emmanuel or Deus pro nobis does not rest entirely on the Noachic covenant. Rather that decision rests on the fact that Jesus Christ as the preexistent subject and fulfillment of the covenant provides the basis both for the beginning and the shaping of the covenant:

> He and He alone is very God and very man in a temporal fulfillment of God's eternal will to be the true God of man and to let the man who belongs to Him become and be true man. Ultimately, therefore, Jesus Christ alone is the content of the eternal will of God, the eternal covenant between God and man. He is this as the Word of God to us and the work of God for us, and therefore in a way quite different from and not to be compared with anything we may become as hearers of this Word. [20]

The persistent question is what does this kind of analysis do for the claim that the covenant of biblical faith was established within historical time and fulfilled within historical time? Does the preexistence of Jesus Christ as the matrix establishing and shaping the covenant relationship give truth to Berkouwer's claim that grace in Barth triumphs in such a way as to lessen the content of history and historical events? [21] That is, what is the relationship between the eternal election preceding the creation and the covenant established between God and man as an historical event? What is the meaning of humankind's faithlessness if the faithfulness of grace has already been assured prior to the covenant which was a vehicle reminding man of his responsibilities and needs to be faithful?

Barth is obviously bothered by this issue because he returns to it again and again in other doctrines. [22] He maintains that the covenant is the historical content of and witness to the eternal election of God to be a partner with man:

> It consists in the fact that He causes the promise and
> command of the covenant: "I will be your God and
> ye shall be my people", to become historical event in
> the person of Jesus Christ. It consists, therefore, in the
> fact that God keeps faith in time with Himself and with
> man, with all men in this one man. [23]

Once God freely decided to participate in time, the character of that relationship with man was altered by man's breaking of the covenant through his sin. Barth's christology, in a sense, has to do with various actions related to and initiated by the event and person of Jesus Christ which are aimed at restoring us to our true humanity and at removing the cause of that sinning once and forever.

> If he breaks the covenant, he is lost as a creature, and
> if he is lost as a creature, the promise of the covenant
> cannot hold good for him. But the divine loving in the
> form of the sending of the Son is the confirmation of
> the will of God not to acquiesce in this but to cause
> man to have the eternal life which he has forfeited
> with his right to exist as a creature. It is His will not
> merely to rescue, but to save. . . . And He does not
> allow Himself to be foiled even in this far-reaching purpose
> for man by the opposition of man. [24]

That overcoming is the center of the restored relationship with God which was accomplished through an exchange advanced by God Himself as mentioned in II Corinthians 5:18-21. One part of that exchange is God's taking on human sin, accepting "a complete solidarity with sinners." [25] The other part of this exchange is that we are put into a righteous relationship with God because Christ takes on our sin. This means that man's world is also converted to God in Christ. [26] Barth spells out the nature of this exchange and those actions of man and his world responsible for the breaking of the partnership as well as the conversion of these hindrances under three headings: "Jesus Christ the Lord as Servant" (IV/1, 157-642); "Jesus Christ, the Servant as Lord" (IV/2, 3-613); and "Jesus Christ, the True Witness" (IV/3.1, IV/3.2, 481-680). The exchange carries within it a dialectic of the No of man's sin, on the one hand (pride, sloth, falsehood), and the Yes of God's triumph over that sin with the resulting consequences for man (his justification, sanctification, vocation).

In seeking to trace the movement of the dialectic of the exchange and thus the reconciling work of Jesus Christ, Barth is not happy with the traditional separation between the person and work of Christ. [27] He opposes this separation because it allows for abstractions about Jesus Christ:

> If this is the way of it, an abstract doctrine of the work
> of Christ will always tend secretly in a direction where
> some kind of Arianism or Pelagianism lies in wait. What
> is needed in this matter is nothing more or less than
> the removal of the distinction between the two basic
> sections of classical Christology, or positively, the restora-
> tion of the hyphen which always connects them and
> makes them one in the New Testament. Not to the detri-
> ment of either the one or the other . . . but to give
> a proper place to them both. [28]

He is equally cautious about speaking of the two states
of Jesus Christ or His two natures, [29] insisting that although
it is important to affirm vere Deus vere homo, such conceptions
might move toward an autonomous being separated from the divine
action in the being and work of Christ.

> As with God who humbles Himself and therefore reconciles
> man with Himself, and as the man exalted by God and
> therefore reconciled with Him, as the One who is very
> God and very man in this concrete sense, Jesus Christ
> Himself is one. He is the "God-man". . . . [30]

There is a dynamic in Barth's christology which consists
of a single movement with two actions. One action is the negation
of opposites through a radical transformation of the negation.
The other action is a movement which links the negation of the
opposites from above with that coming from below and from below
to that from above. [31] This two-fold dynamic characterizes
the life and ministry of Jesus Christ as the God-man. We shall
first examine the dynamic as it is viewed under the rubrics of
the three parts of Barth's christology mentioned above. Then
the dynamic of the dialectic as it is shown in the action of man
under the rubrics of the various forms of sin will be reviewed.

Jesus Christ as Servant

Under the first part of his christology, the Lord who
became a servant, Barth finds the metaphor of the Prodigal Son
going into the far country useful for illustrating the journey of
God into the sinful world of man. [32] This capacity to condescend
to man's world without becoming less than God is a particular
character of the biblical God:

> God is not proud. In His high majesty He is humble. It
> is in this high humility that He speaks and acts as the
> God who reconciled the world to himself. [33]

God chose freely the path of obedience in Jesus Christ for the sake of the other half of the partnership, namely mankind. What is the nature of this obedience? asks Barth. It is characterized in the New Testament in various ways: "emptying himself" and becoming a servant (Phil. 2:7), "humbling himself" and going to the cross (Phil. 2:8), "suffering" (Heb. 5:8), taking on the sinful flesh of man. [34] But this New Testament witness must be seen in light of the Old Testament; otherwise Docetism is always a lurking possibility when the two testaments are separated. That is, it is urgent that it be remembered that Jesus Christ was Jewish flesh:

> In its bracketing with the Old Testament the New closes the door against every kind of Docetism, however crude or subtle, by positing the man who was and is the Son of God in his singularity and at the same time in the relevance of His existence for every man of every place, by setting the happening of the redemption history between God and man in world history, at a cosmic place, a place on earth. [35]

But obedience also has to include the risk of God alienating Himself from His own command as the God-man when undertaking the journey into the far country; otherwise there is the danger of a Deus ex machina:

> He does not merely go into lowliness, into the far country, to be Himself there, as He did in His turning to Israel. But now he Himself becomes lowly. He Himself is the man who is His Son. He Himself has become a stranger in Him. [36]

The obeying Lord takes on the character and sinfulness of the disobeying creature in order to overcome and triumph over that disobedience and rebellion. The obeying Lord is at the same time the obeying servant.

In taking on the human condition, Jesus Christ reveals two things about the "flesh". First, to be in the flesh means to be sinful and therefore under the wrath of God. This is what Barth calls the "deity of Christ", [37] but this "deity of Christ" is an act of God who remains God even when humiliated. The "deity of Christ" means the obedience of the Son as well as the humiliation of the Son, but God did not cease or surrender His character as a sovereign God. [38] This is Barth's disagreement with the kenosis theologians, using a rather bold phrase to emphasize his point of view: God dared to be "God against God." [39]

Secondly, to be in the flesh means to be in contradiction to oneself. In Jesus Christ God makes man's contradiction His own without being in disunity with Himself. As Barth puts it in a poignant sentence: "God gives Himself, but He does not give Himself away." [40] All of this is the "outer" mystery of the "deity of Christ." [41]

But one must also understand the inner content of this mystery, that is, to understand the fact that obedience is a part of the Godhead itself. Barth is aware of the dangers implicit in trying to move human concepts inside the Godhead, [42] but he persists, remarking that if the New Testament witness about God being the acting subject in reconciliation and His being for the world rather than against it or far from it is to have credibility, then very much depends on this effort to grasp the inner dynamics of this divine mystery.

In order to be liberated enough for this pursuit, Barth forewarns that some conditions which hinder our thinking about the Godhead must be given up. First, one must stop assuming that unity is necessarily single in character and enclosed:

> (God's unity) is a unity which is open and free and active in itself--a unity in more than one mode of being, a unity of the One with Another, of a first with a second, an above with a below, an origin and its consequences. It is a dynamic and living unity, not a dead and static one. [43]

Secondly, one must give up the idea that the above description somehow lessens or cheapens God's sovereignty. If the biblical witness about Jesus' obedience is true,

> we have to draw the no less astonishing deduction that in equal Godhead the one God is, in fact, the One and also Another, that He is indeed a First and a Second, One who rules and commands in majesty and One who obeys in humility. [44]

Yet as God, He is able to maintain fellowship within the Godhead, which means that there is also a third relationship within the Godhead. [45] This is what the biblical witness means by Jesus Christ being the Son of God who became man and yet also remained at one with the Father, both equal in deity, and who is affirmed and loved by the Holy Spirit. [46] These are not the traditional persons of the Trinity, Barth insists. That term persona carries too much baggage of linguistic confusion and misunderstanding with it. Rather these terms, Father, Son, Holy Spirit, speak to the interconnection and interrelatedness within the Godhead. But how is all of this related to the question as to whether the obedience of Jesus Christ reflects the inner nature of the Godhead? Barth suggests the fact that Jesus Christ freely obeyed demonstrated not only His difference from all other men, although He was fully and completely human; it also demonstrated the lordship of God through His obedience even unto suffering and death. "In rendering obedience as He does, He does something which, as in the case of that lordship, only God can do." [47]

The ministry which revealed this obedience was Jesus being willing to be placed on the docket as the judged one in place of sinful man. [48] By "judge" Barth is thinking biblically of the Old Testament judges:

> . . . men awakened by God and their main office is to be helpers and saviours in the recurrent sufferings of the people. . . . Similarly in the New Testament . . . the coming of the Judge means basically the coming of the Redeemer and Saviour. [49]

As Judge, God is the measure of all righteousness and renders judgment accordingly. The problem with us is that we want to be our own judge, which puts us in conflict with God. Under the power of sin, we seek justification not from God, but from our own world. God became man in order to judge the sin of the world. But He judges it

> in order . . . to show His grace in the execution of His judgment, to pronounce us free in passing sentence, to free us by imprisoning us, to ground our life on our death, to redeem and save us by our destruction. That is how God actually judged us in Jesus Christ. [50]

That was God's "kingly freedom" as Judge who let Himself be judged.

What is the content of this judgeship and what role does it play in the reconciliation between God and man? First, according to Barth, a judge is one who has the power to pronounce judgment because of his knowledge of what is good and what is evil. The crux of man's desire as sinner is wanting to be his own judge even though he was created and sustained by God as Judge. Man wants to pronounce himself always righteous and not guilty. [51] Jesus Christ as the judge who takes our place as a would-be judge has two implications for our existence.

One is that man is deposed as judged by God in the flesh. [52] The other is that Jesus Christ liberates man from his arrogation of judging himself and others, thereby freeing him for true service to God and true humanity. [53]

Secondly, this divine judgeship means that as Jesus Christ took our place in the docket as the judged, so he also took on the sin which shapes our case in the courtroom before God. [54] As Barth states it:

> He can conduct the case of God against us in such a way that He takes from us our own evil case, taking our place and compromising and burdening Himself with it. And as He does that, it ceases to be our sin. [55]

To ask why God chose to do this is simply to point to the mystery of God's mercy, which at the same time is also the "mystery of His righteousness." [56]

As the judge who takes on man's sinfulness, Jesus Christ reveals three things about man's sin. One is that only in Jesus Christ can man know the serious dimensions of his sin. [57] The second is that as man's representative, Jesus Christ answers for us. This does not mean that man is no longer sinner, rather it points to man being a sinner constantly in need of the support of God's gracious forgiveness. [58] The third is that as man's judge and representative Christ redeemed us. Man can only repent; there is no going back. [59]

Jesus Christ not only takes our place as judge and our place as the judged, he also takes our judgment, our sentencing through His suffering, crucifixion and death. [60] God becomes both the subject and the object being acted upon in Jesus Christ. But this is not simply the suffering of a "great man" cautions Barth.

> . . . If we are not to turn the "What" into something else, but answer it with a plain "This", then we must not be afraid to take the true statement that in the passion of Jesus Christ we have to do with God's act for us, and to put it in a slightly different form, that it is in the passion of Jesus Christ that we have to do with the act of God for us. [61]

Finally, as Judge, the judged, and the one taking on the judgment, Jesus acted justly, for He reflects and authenticates God's justice. [62]

> The suffering and death of Jesus Christ are the No of God in and with which He again takes up and asserts in man's space and time the Yes to man which He has determined and pronounced in eternity . . . Cur Deus homo? Because God, who became man in His Son, willed in this His Yes to do this work of His, but His human work, and therefore this work for the reconciliation of the world which is effective for us men. [63]

This is the clue to God's justice as done by Jesus Christ: that "he acted justly in that He did not refuse to do what they would not do." [64] Thus, the "for us" of His death on the cross also included God's terrible "against us".

> Without this terrible "against us" it would not be the divine and holy and redemptive and effectively helpful "for us" in which the conversion of man and the world to God has become an event. [65]

Jesus Christ as Lord

The second part of Barth's christology has to do with Jesus Christ as the Son of Man just as the first part had to do with Him as the Son of God. Whereas the first part deals with the condescension and humiliation of God in making man's sin and therefore his existence His own in Jesus Christ, the second part deals with man being exalted and lifted up to true fellowship with God. Just as Jesus Christ is the model for the reconciling God, so He is also the model for the reconciled man. This direction of the reconciling event adheres to the second part of the dynamism in his christology in which the negation of opposites takes place from below upwards. This is an examination of true humanity as witnessed to and lived out by Christ. [66]

Here Barth would seem to complicate still further the dialectic involving the "flesh". Whereas in the first part of the christology, flesh is identified with that which is sinful, in this part of the dialectic "flesh" (according to Barth's rendering of John 1:14) signifies a statement about God the Word and the "word" indicates a statement about man in the flesh:

> The reconstitution and renewal of the covenant between God and man consists in the exchange--the exinanitio, the abasement of God, and the exaltatio; the exaltation of man. It was God who went into the far country, and it was man who returns home. Both took place in the one Jesus Christ. [67]

Man's way back to God is seen by Barth to be analogous to the return of the prodigal son and the father's welcome of that son. But Barth warns that even that is only a copy and not strictly a quid pro quo comparison. [68] Jesus Christ makes the same journey as He shares man's humanitas in its creaturely and sinful form. Yet He is not exhausted by this complete identification with sinful and creaturely man:

> He is decisively and totally different from us in the fact that in His human existence, in the history in which

> He became and is man, and suffers and acts as man,
> there took place an exaltation of the humanity which
> as His and ours is the same. . . . Exaltation does not
> mean a destruction or alteration of His humanity. It does
> not abolish His likeness with us, emptying it out of its
> substance. . . . It means the history of the placing of
> the humanity common to Him and us on such a higher
> level, on which it becomes and is completely unlike ours
> even in its complete likeness. . . . [69]

The basis of Christ's humanitas is 1) God's choice to reconcile Himself with us in Jesus Christ made before creation, [70] 2) the historical boundaries of the incarnation, [71] and 3) the revelation of true humanity in the resurrection and ascension of Jesus Christ. [72] This choice to be humiliated, based on the intent of God to be at one with man, corresponds to the first part of Barth's christology in which God is depicted as going into a "far country". That is, Jesus Christ as the Son of God became the Son of Man via the incarnation. And in so doing, man was exalted. But man's exaltation in the incarnation cannot be separated from God's humiliation in Jesus Christ. The important emphasis about the incarnation is that God became man. Jesus Christ took on that humanity (humanum) which identifies Him as a creature and at the same time distinguishes Him from other creatures of creation.

> In Jesus Christ it is not merely one man, but the humanum
> of all men, which is posited and exalted as such to unity
> with God. [73]

Barth understands this unity to be the clue to the traditional rendering of the hypostatic union, for "the existence of the Son of man became and is the existence of a man." [74] But this unity has to be understood possibly via negativa. 1) It is not a unio coessentialis, but a unity of the Son of God with the humanum of man. Yet this is not a unity of two equals. "The divine humanity of Jesus Christ is . . . the work of the mercy of God turning in inconceivable condescension to very dissimilar man." [75] 2) It is not a unio essentialis, but a unity which preserves the difference between God and the world. There is no pantheistic identity here. "Even this union and unity cannot therefore be compared or exchanged with the unio personalis in Jesus Christ." [76] 3) This is not analogous with a union even between two close friends or between man and wife; rather it is a one-sided act of mercy initiated by God aimed at overcoming the antithesis between Creator and creature. [77] 4) This is not a complementary or completing unity understood to mean that the Son of God needs humanity as form needs matter or spirit needs nature. "He is not like Hegel's absolute spirit who can develop to a synthesis only in thesis and antithesis. He is actual in Himself--the One

who is originally and properly actual." [78] 5) It is not a unity
analogous even to the intimate unity between body and soul, for
whilst the divine nature in Jesus Christ is indispensable for the
human nature, the human nature is not indispensable to the divine.

This careful delineation of what this unity does not consist
of allows Barth to press further in an effort to describe what
the unity is. Upon doing this he sees the dialectic and the dynamic
of that dialectic at its highest level fulfilled in Christ, namely,
that in Him that is united (divinity and humanity) which by definition cannot be united. [79] This unity, however, simply reflects
the a posteriori/a priori character of the Godhead itself:

> He in His divine essence takes part in human essence--so
> radical and total a part that He causes His existence
> to become and be also the existence of the man Jesus of
> Nazareth. Again, He gives to the human essence of Jesus
> of Nazareth a part in His own divine essence as the
> eternal Son who is co-equal with the Father and the
> Holy Spirit. . . . Hence it is "from above to below",
> and only then . . . "from below to above." [80]

It is the awesomeness of this act and its consequences for man's
reconciliation with God for which man ought to be grateful. It
is this awesomeness which is so important that it is safeguarded
against the excesses of Alexandrian theology in the first part
of the Chalcedonian formula. [81] This unity affects all of human
nature as well as all of humanity. Against the excesses of Antioch-
ian theology, Barth feels it important to stress that there is no
element of human essence unaffected by this unity or excluded
from it. Nor are there any instances in this unity in which Jesus
Christ is less than divine. Both the humiliation of the divine and
the exaltation of the human are a single event occurring within
a single being. [82]

But the question persists, if Jesus Christ is as truly human
as He is divine, can one claim to be truly human and not sin?
Barth suggests that Jesus Christ did in fact bear sin and fully
shared man's sinful existence, but He did not sin, that is, He
did not transgress His true humanity as established in God:

> He bore an alien guilt, our guilt, the guilt of all men,
> without any guilt of His own. He made our human essence
> His own, even in its corruption, but He did not repeat
> or affirm its inward contradiction. . . . He overcame
> it in His own person when He became man. . . . The
> sinlessness of Jesus was not a condition of His being
> as man, but the human act of His life working itself
> out in this way from its origin. [83]

Through His obedience to God's command, Jesus Christ demonstrated both true humanity and true human freedom.

> As the Son of God He goes into the far country. As the Son of Man he returns home. . . . As He adopts it, making it His own existence in His divine nature, He does not deify it, but He exalts it into the consortium divinitatis, into an inward and indestructible fellowship with His Godhead. [84]

To speak of something being "natural" for us in light of this event can only mean speaking of categories which are separated from God, since there is no knowledge of God apart from and through Jesus Christ. Thus, the antithesis of "natural" is not "revealed", but rather true human nature which has once and for all been exalted in Jesus Christ. [85] Barth, hence, seeks to correct the idea of some of the Fathers that God became man in order that man might become more like God; rather God became man in order that man might come to God. [86] This is what Barth means by the unten nach oben movement. The event of the Christ is at the same time the reality of the Christ:

> He acts as God when He acts as man, and as man when He acts as God, not in the state but in the event of the coordination of the two predicates. The word God-man obscures again the event, the novum of the act of God in which Jesus Christ actualizes Himself and is actual. [87]

Barth pursues the movement of the above/below, humiliation/exaltation theme to the last concluding events in Jesus' life, namely, the resurrection and the ascension. These two events are important, says Barth, because they determine the authenticity of the apostolic or New Testament witness to the revelation of God in Jesus Christ. They are both distinct, but again also inseparable movements within the same event:

> In the pre-Easter history and existence of Jesus Christ, fulfilled in His death on the cross, it was a matter of the exaltation and majesty of this man in His unity with the Son of God. And in the resurrection and ascension of Jesus Christ it was and is a matter of the revelation of the exaltation and majesty of this man in His unity with the Son of God. What is revealed is that in His identity with the Son of God this man was the Lord. [88]

These two events draw the above/below dynamic to an historic close, for they reveal that Jesus Christ goes to the origin of divine power and grace, identified in the New Testament as "heaven". [89] In these two events God reveals the dialectical pattern of transfiguring opposites, which by definition cannot be united: life is given to One who was dead, a servant becomes lord, a rejected and despised one is elected.

But what can be said about the historical content of this Son of Man who was also the Son of God? Barth depicts the character of Jesus' life and ministry under the Calvinist doctrine of the three-fold ministry, which he characteristically alters somewhat: the kingly office is to be examined under the rubric of "the royal man", the priestly office under "servanthood", and the prophetic office under that of His being a "true witness".

God chose Jesus Christ as an obedient servant to endure humiliation in order to reassert His Lordship. This servanthood was witnessed in four ways in Jesus Christ. First, there was the negation: he was ignored, despised, and forgotten for His kingdom was not accompanied by pomp, His power showed no visible strength at the time, and His glory seemed to be cloaked under lowliness. [90] Secondly, He did not fit the customary role model: He ignored the rich for the poor, the high and mighty were overlooked for the sake of the lowly and humiliated, thereby establishing

> the transvaluation of all values, acknowledging those who (without necessarily being better) are in different ways poor men as this world counts poverty. [91]

Thirdly, He reversed the relationships in his world, bringing a sense of krisis to all human relationships.

> Jesus was not in any sense a reformer championing new orders against the old ones, contesting the latter in order to replace them by the former. He did not represent or defend or champion any programme--whether political, economic, moral or religious, whether conservative or progressive. . . . He set all programmes and principles in question . . . a remarkable freedom which again we can only describe as royal. [92]

The radicality of Jesus was His freedom in light of the Kingdom of God to disclose that all human conditions and relationships as well as institutions are vulnerable. Fourthly, Jesus Christ was able to be for man and not against him, this in spite of man's own estrangement and alienation from God.

> The divine Yes echoed by the royal man Jesus is the divine Word of comfort for this very misery, and only as such, and working back as it were from it, for the human corruption which is the basis of it. God grapples with sin as He has mercy on the men who suffer in this way as sinners. [93]

It is under the rubrics of Christ's royal character that Barth has much to say about human political, social, and economic relationships as well as religious ones. Indeed it was because of the radicality of Jesus' obedience to the Kingdom of God and thus His exercise of true freedom that He was free to show what Barth calls "passive conservatism", that is, the capacity to accept various institutions of His day without feeling compromised, such as the temple, the family, the law, and even existing political institutions and relationships. [94]

> Jesus acknowledged them and reckoned with them and subjected Himself to them and advised His disciples to do the same; but He was always superior to them. And it was inevitable that this superiority, the freedom of the Kingdom of God, should occasionally find concrete expression in His words and actions, that an occasional creaking should be unmistakably heard to be in the timbers. [95]

Jesus, for example, accepted the temple, but He reminded the Pharisees that there was something much greater than the temple. He acknowledged the family as an institution, but He also often urged the separation from family for the sake of the kingdom. The cultic use of the law was recognized, but He also insisted at times that one could breach the law as well as some of the economic and political relationships. Behind all of this was an eschatologically-based questioning of man's presupposition that his order and institutions were permanent. He reversed the existing values and relationships as the Son of Man. [96]

> For Jesus, and as seen in the light of Jesus, there can be no doubt that all human orders are this old garment (Mk. 2:21f) or old bottles, which are in the last resort quite incompatible with the new cloth and the new wine of the Kingdom of God. The new cloth can only destroy the old garment and the old bottles can only burst when the new wine of the Kingdom of God is poured into them. [97]

Barth also sees the various beatitudes as a vehicle for making judgment on man's social institutions and values, that is, groups of words or sayings addressed to people which declare them blessed by virtue of their particular situation. These beatitudes, the makarisms, fall under God's being for man and are hence addressed to differing circumstances of man's life in society. One group emphasizes faith and the hearing of that faith, such as Mt. 13:16, Mt. 5:7-9, and Luke 14:14. [98] A second group is addressed to situations in which people find themselves unwillingly, such as the poor, the mourners, the meek, the hungry and destitute, as seen, for instance in Mt. 5:3f. They are promised renewal by Jesus in the form of a reversal of their present situations.

> Like the contrast of the rich man in hell with poor Lazarus on Abraham's bosom, it is simply a declaration that they are to be pitied because the nearness of the Kingdom of God, the presence of Jesus, cannot be seen in their lives. Conversely, the sufferers of this world cannot pride themselves on the fact that their lives have this transparency, that the kingdom, Jesus, is in fact near to them. . . . To them, too, the new thing is said when they are called blessed in relation to their misery. [99]

There is yet a third group addressed, namely, the religiously persecuted and scorned. They find themselves in a situation which depends on their relationship and confession of that relationship with Jesus Christ. They are counted blessed because they are witnesses to the kingdom. [100]

Jesus Christ as Witness

Having looked at the priestly office (the servant who became Lord in His humiliation under the sinful conditions of man) and at the royal office (the servant who in God's exaltation of man became Lord), Barth insists that the third aspect of christology is the prophetic office of Jesus, an office which was rediscovered primarily by John Calvin and the Reformed tradition. [101] Barth prefers to describe this office as that of "the true witness". It is that office which provides for verification of the reconciling act and without which would always be the danger of that reconciling act being interpreted totally subjectively and thus being dependent on the limitation of human verification. This is the munus Christi propheticum. [102]

Barth seems to rule out any methodology for getting to this witness which begins with any kind of division between general and special revelation as a modus operandi. One must begin with Jesus Christ who lives as God and as man. He points to five aspects of this office of Christ's person and ministry, which he calls the "light of life", i.e., "the light which life itself radiates because it is itself light." [103]

1) Jesus Christ is His own light which provides light to humankind and its world.

2) Jesus Christ in His declaration of Himself and His mission tells us the character of His own existence.

3) His life and history show the history of God's purpose as that purpose moves toward a goal.

4) His mission is so recognizable that one ignoring or denying it can only live under the anxiety of falsehood.

5) His life is also His ministry, that is, there is no dualism between theory and praxis in Christ. [104]

Barth compares the prophetic functions of the Old Testament prophets with the prophetic office of Christ, noticing certain similarities, but also certain major differences.

1) Christ does not acquire the prophetic role subsequent to His being chosen; His life itself is prophecy. that is, a witness to God's grace, judgment, and salvation. [105]

2) He not only speaks to Israel; He is a prophet addressing the whole world beyond Israel. [106]

3) Christ is the fulfillment of the covenant which the Old Testament prophets proclaimed but did not see fulfilled. Therefore, the contradictions of Israel as she contravened the covenant do not lie in front of Christ; rather they lie behind Him. [107]

4) Christ in His own person and life removed the opposition between Israel and Yahweh which the Old Testament prophets were unable to do. [108]

> According to Romans 12:6, the Christian prophets mentioned in the New Testament are bound to the analogia tes pisteos. This means that they are secondary witnesses of the first and true witness. In other words they are witnesses of Christ. To try to speak in abstractions from His coming and work in the style of Elijah, Amos, Isaiah, or Jeremiah, is to be a false prophet post Christum. . . . Prophetic (preaching) only in the Old Testament sense is false prophecy. Nor can even the most powerful preaching of the Law in abstraction, whether directed to individual, social or political concerns, escape the same verdict. [109]

Yet there are certain common features existing between Christ as prophet and the Old Testament prophets.

1) Both occur within the history of the Word of God.

2) Both are intended to enlighten sinful humanity.

3) Both witness to God's activism in man's world as well as beyond man's world.

4) Both mediate between God and man's world. [110]

This anticipation of the fulfillment of the covenant is called by Barth "pre-history". [111]

> It is not a new or different covenant which is established and proclaimed in the history of Jesus Christ. It is the one covenant in a new reality which is only now fulfilled in this form . . . because it is only now immediately and directly conformable to its basis, content and goal as the reality of this Messiah Jesus latent in what came before, in the history of Israel and Its prophecy. It is He who, as the electing God and elected man in one person, is the basis, content and goal of the covenant of God with man. [112]

Barth seems to understand the claim of Jesus Christ being the light of the world as synonymous with the claim that Jesus Christ is the Word of God. He recognizes the inherent problems in such a claim. Intellectually, it sounds very restrictive in terms of allowing one to remain open to new fields and new words which may bring new light for man. Morally, it would seem to block off communication between Christians and non-Christians having opposing ideas. Politically, such a claim would seem to encourage the intolerance and persecution which has so often accompanied the spread of the Christian faith, particularly as the faith had to deal with the idea of freedom of conscience and the role of those who thought differently in a Christian society. [113] But Barth is prepared to support such a claim in spite of these problems:

> It looks away from non-Christian and Christian alike to the One who sovereignly confronts and precedes both as the Prophet. As Jesus Christ is its content, the one who confesses it in no sense marks himself off from those who do not. . . . He is in solidarity with them. [114]

The Old Testament prophets were also aware of surrounding ideologies and religions which differed from their faith, but that did not lead them to insist on a "plurality of divine revelations" which might be used as a norm for measuring the revelation of Yahweh and His relationship to Israel. [115] Such competing claims cannot claim obedience either from ancient Israel or from the Christian community. To make such a claim about Christ does not mean that there are not other notable words. Nor should it be understood to mean that other words spoken outside the Bible or outside the Church are necessarily false words and prophets.

Rather this claim about Christ simply means that Jesus Christ as the one and only Word of God limits all other words demanding obedience from the Christian. Repeating the opening words of the Barmen Declaration of 1934, Barth states: The Church rejects as false the teaching that events and sources outside this one Word of God can be a source of proclamation and obedience. [116]

To press the implications of this claim even further, Barth states that Christ as the Word means also that He is a complete declaration of God, not to be completed either by man or by historical processes or philosophical categories.

> To be sure, the Word meets opposition in the world and also . . . in the Church. To be sure, its light is resisted by darkness in the many forms of sinister powers, all of which are connected with the sin of man, all empowered and unleashed by his falsehood, all to be taken seriously as opponents of the one Word of God. [117]

But His truth and prophecy cannot be combined with some other system and still make the same claim for obedience, although Christ does make use of other witnesses. Attempted synthesis, conjunctions, and unions between Christ as the Light and Word of God and other systems "imply a control over Him to which none of us has any right." [118]

Nonetheless, how does all of this relate to the pluralistic society in which competing claims have their own truths and allegiances as well as needed insights? What of the claims of modern technology and sociology, to mention but a few "words" in the pluralistic society, not to mention competing political "words"? Barth points out that the various claims to truth in a pluralistic society may indeed bear some resemblance to the claims of Jesus Christ and thus ought to be respected and listened to. And one needs to test these claims against the claim that Jesus Christ alone for the Christian should demand his loyalty and allegiance.

There are three aspects to be used for testing this claim about Christ against other ones. First, such other "words" ought to conform to the one Word of God, i.e., Jesus Christ. [119] Secondly, they ought to confirm the truth of the one Word of God. Thirdly, they can claim truth only as their witness has been acknowledged by God as Lord. [120] The dangers of the Christian not heeding these criteria are always present in the modern pluralistic society, particularly as that society becomes more and more secularized, remarks Barth. But even within secularized societies, there are different forms which the Christian must consider when trying to determine his loyalty to and obedience in that society. One form of secularism is that which makes absolute claims that deny God and His Gospel. This kind of secularism may well be hostile to the Gospel, but the Christian ought to be cautious about assuming an inflexible attitude toward such a secularism.

> No Prometheanism can be effectively maintained against Jesus Christ. As the One who suffered and conquered on the cross, He has destroyed it once and for all in all its forms. But this means that in the world reconciled by God in Jesus Christ there is no secular sphere abandoned by Him or withdrawn from His control, even where from the human standpoint it seems to approximate most dangerously to the pure and absolute form of utter godlessness. . . . Even from the mouth of Balaam the well-known voice of the Good Shepherd may sound, and it is not to be ignored in spite of its sinister origin. [121]

Another form of secularism might be a mixed form which allows itself to be questioned by the Gospel and thus open itself to possible modification and added illumination because of the Gospel. [122] Barth insists that both of these forms of secularism ought not to be regarded as alien territory by the Christian, but rather as signs and guideposts pointing to the lordship of the one Word.

> . . . In no case must (our fears and suspicions) be stronger than the readiness to hear, and to test whether what is heard is perhaps a true word which Christianity cannot ignore as such, as though Jesus Christ were bound to its own task and promise, as though this task and promise were a possession behind which it could and should conceal itself with closely stopped ears. [123]

What then are the criteria for testing or attesting the "trueness" of other words?

1) The word ought to agree with the witness of scripture. [124] That is, its message ought to be illuminated by that witness as found in Jesus Christ. "It will not lead its hearers away from Scripture, but more deeply into it." [125]

2) It ought to agree with the witness of the dogmas and confessions of the Church, i.e., the tradition. [126] This does mean that there is always the possibility and necessity that the Church has to hear new things and learn new methods. " . . . They will guide it, not to break continuity with the insights of the preceding fathers and brethren, but in obedience to the one Lord of the Church and in the discipleship on the basis of better instruction." [127]

3) It ought to have some relation to "world-occurrence", that is, some interaction with the secular world surrounding the community. [128]

4) It ought to have some significance for the life of the community, i.e., the Church and for its activity. [129]

> We may recognize its truth by the fact that it concerns and activates Christians as Christians and the community as the community in this two-fold sense. A word which merely pacified and confirmed, or unsettled and shattered, would by its very nature reveal that it had nothing whatever to do with the one truth of Jesus Christ, that it was not then a true Word, and that it should not therefore be heard. [130]

But Barth also admits that often the Christian Church as an institution can receive some illumination from particular other words spoken or heard in "world-occurrences":

> There are words which need decades and even centuries to be finally, and even then only approximately, heard and recognized throughout Christendom. [131]

He admits to the legitimacy of what he calls the world's "own lights". [132] These are witnesses which are not diminished by man's corruption of his relationship to the Word of God. Rather through the true Light of Christ they are exposed as light and words within the created cosmos and, whilst limited, not destroyed.

> As the divine work of reconciliation does not negate the divine work of creation, nor deprive it of meaning, so it does not take from it its lights and language, nor tear asunder the· original connexion between creaturely esse and creaturely nosse. [133]

Our world is a **real** world in that it speaks and has authoritative words which point to something lasting and constant even amidst change. [134] In light of this the world and its institutions cannot be considered an alien place. One cannot live without acting in the society, for to deny or ignore action is to deny oneself. "He has good cause to be grateful for the shining of this light, even though it is not the eternal light." [135]

What then is the relationship between the Word of God and the words in man's world? Barth considers that there are at least three. First, God in His Word binds Himself to the man who hears it and at the same time binds the hearing man to Himself. God establishes him on a new course. Creaturely words do not bind man nor do they judge his existence. They often simply enlighten him and then leave him to his own devices. [136] Secondly, the Word of God is a unity needing no completion or emulation, whilst this is not so with creaturely words. [137] Thirdly,

God's Word is a final word not subject to qualification or condition-ing. It determines its own criteria of truth.

> The only serious distinction between us men is that in the one case, as among believing Christians gathered in the community, it is knowledge which is predominant and ignorance is giving ground, whereas in the other, as among the theoretical and practical ungodly or idolatrous of every type, it is ignorance which is predominant and knowledge is held in check. [138]

The Word of God also has a liberating effect on the hearing man in relation to the other creaturely words. On the one hand, it attacks our world, giving us the knowledge that our sin is outmoded and overtaken. On the other hand, the Word gives us the knowledge that the future has already been realized, already established.

> Since the enslaved man who was can be no longer, all that is needed is that he should now be the man he is. It is just as though a newly tailored and ornamented garment were ready and we had only to put it on, with no possibility of delay since the old one has already gone to the ragman and is no longer available. [139]

The liberating consequences of this knowledge for us are several. For one thing, it indicates that one is now free to live and act with greater imagination in his world. [140] For another, one is now free to move into new situations with some abandon, having an assurance of God's grace and love. "It demonstrates itself at once in cheerful thoughts and words and actions." [141] For yet another, one is now free to act in solidarity with other human beings as "companions in the partnership of reconciliation, as brothers and sisters in the fulfilled covenant of God." [142] One acts on behalf of others as a given in light of Christ's reconciling act in the Word.

> (Man) can only be a lord as in his own place and manner he is a servant. This is his future as a new man as now disclosed--and not just proposed or prophesied to him by the Word of grace. This is the given and only future intimated to him. [143]

The strangeness of this Word is that it does not say that man will be this new man, remarks Barth. It says that he already is. It is strange exactly because it is not man's word. It is the Word of God spoken in Jesus Christ which speaks of the end of the old man in the cross and the coming of the new man in the resurrection.

This Word of God also appears strange to man because it attacks his presumption about himself--a presumption which relies on his wanting to know himself and his future completely. [144] Barth in scathing terms compares this presumption which he calls a "something" in man (as it resists the grace of God) to a wild beast:

> The wild beast does not even need to switch its tail to remove the threatened danger. It has simply to act as if the danger were not there. It has simply to continue in error, in stupidity, in wickedness, without love, according to the course of the world. [145]

This "something" tries to protect its own self-interests and fend off challenges by adopting various world-views (Weltanschauungen) as counter-truths. Barth thus continues to display a mistrust of Christians trying to "christianize" any and all ideologies even when elements of those ideologies bear a close resemblance to the Christian faith and visions of society. All ideologies must be measured under the light of the witness and prophecy of Christ. Barth further warns that all ideologies bear a common trait in that they all give man a central place. This has several results. First, they provide man with an apparatus aimed at controlling things from a distance so that the author cannot be threatened from a too-near proximity. Secondly, they give their author, i.e., man, the central place allowing the author to escape what for him becomes

> the oppressive atmosphere of this triangle of God, fellow-man and oneself. . . . [146]

Thirdly, they absolutize and abstract reality so that it is seen as a truth which is everywhere and always the same, whereas the Word of God speaks of the uniqueness and particularity of events which bear on particular things that may then lead to general truths. World-views tend to relativize this method by coordinating one event with all other events, which would apply to the Word of God as well.

Fourthly, a world-view of ideology is usually arrived at deductively as the concluding summation of particular events, whereas the Word of grace comes in a declaration, a summons from which particular events take their meaning and to which one is summoned to obedience. Finally, an ideology or a world-view is an endeavor on the part of man to examine himself from within as a means of coming to terms with himself, but he remains the supreme master and is not offended by his ideology. The Word of grace calls man himself into question and may even offend him. [147]

Nevertheless, Jesus Christ as Witness is also victor over this "something" within man in its various manifestations which resist God's word of grace. What allows one to say this with any certainty? asks Barth.

1) Jesus Christ is the Word of God, that is, He not only speaks the Word; He effectively can take the offensive because to know Jesus is to know God.

> It is to know His nature and existence, His power and mercy, His will which is done and His lordship which is established among us. . . . God in person enters the battlefield in the living Jesus Christ and His prophetic work. It is not any light which shines in darkness, but the eternal light. [148]

2) He is the claim of a God who has made man's cause His own and who stands in conflict with the resisting "something" in man. Barth sees this as evidence enough to allow him to expect God's triumph in all situations with an absolute certainty:

> There can be no doubt that where we have on the one side the Word of the act of God, of this act of reconciliation (and the living Jesus Christ is this Word in His prophecy), and on the other empty word of falsehood (and this is the weapon and power of the resisting element in man), the relation between aggressor and defender in this conflict is so unequal that in relation to it there can and must be the fullest certainty of victory, and it would be sheer folly not to find a place for it. [149]

3) The prophecy appeals to the **real** man, by-passing the resisting element in man--"the man whom God created and whose divinely created nature has not perished even in the alienation in which he now exists, the man who in this reality of his is still the nearest and most direct object of the move of His Creator." [150] As Barth puts it rather forcefully:

> Reconciliation is God's solemn non-recognition of the incident which separates Himself from man and man from Himself. [151]

Christology and Anthropology

Having departed from the traditional method of dogmatics by starting with Christ rather than with sin in formulating his christology, Barth then considers his anthropology in the light of his christology. He maintains that one can only understand man and his condition by first looking at the person and ministry of Christ:

> That man is evil, that he is at odds with God and with his neighbour, and therefore with himself, is something which he cannot know of himself, by communing with himself, or by conversation with his fellowmen, any more than he can know in this way that he is justified and comforted by God. Anything that he accepts in this matter which is not from God, but from communing with himself and his fellows . . . may well be the inner tension between a relative Yes and a relative No, between becoming and perishing. . . . But it is not as such the evil which makes man the enemy of God and his neighbour and himself, puts him in need of atonement, of conversion to God. In itself and as such it belongs rather to the nature of man as God created it good. [152]

Man may well come to some conclusions about his malaise and the problematic nature of his existence, but this will not lead to a knowledge of the cause of it, i.e., sin, since he can only see, think, and know in a limited way in relation to a crooked existence. [153] Even should he come to have knowledge of God, man may only learn of His presence without knowing of His relationship to him. To understand God's relationship with man in its fullest sense, one must understand Jesus Christ, who plunges man's existence into crisis and question.

> To affirm evil as such (being independent of and preceding Christology) it is forced to have a standard of good and to apply that standard. But independently of Christology what standard can there be other than a normative concept constructed from philosophical or biblical materials or a combination of the two. [154]

In addition to using philosophical ideas for a knowledge of man, many theologians portray a kind of misleading biblical methodology by "returning" to scripture, as did the seventeenth-century protestants under the rubric of a "verbal inspiration of Holy Scripture." [155] This idea attempted to use direct knowledge as a kind of biblically founded rationalism, divorcing the word of the printed text from the living Lord. Jesus Christ was no longer the controlling norm but rather one source and subject amongst others, even if they considered Him the chief source. The danger with all of this was that sin which conditions man's existence did not cause a crisis; it tended to become something non-threatening and manageable. [156] There was the tendency to seek a continuity between man and God rather than a confrontation:

> The grace of God and the sin of man must be approached
> as states on the one level, in a relationship which--if
> it has been disturbed--cannot be really jeopardised or
> broken, and therefore at bottom does not have to be
> renewed. [157]

Barth maintains that a particular source for this understanding of man's condition and existence can be traced to several
of the giants of nineteenth-century thought, especially Hegel
and Schleiermacher. Hegel understood sin as a doctrine which
precedes the God-man and the atonement. Sin is only a necessary
moment within the history of the finite spirit as that spirit moves
within the Hegelian dialectic. [158] As the finite spirit raises
itself from mere volition to cognition and conceptionalizing,
it becomes conscious of an antithesis which has to do with the
contradiction within itself that leads eventually to the phenomenon
of evil. It is when spirit posits itself as evil, as that which it
ought not to be, that the spirit begins the process of reconciliation.
But it is reconciliation with itself. That is, the source of evil
is also the source of reconciliation in Hegel. [159] That is, says
Barth, since this finite spirit is only a moment in the movement
of the absolute spirit, which is God, this continuity is sanctioned
and guaranteed by God Himself:

> In short, there is an unbroken continuity between creation
> and sin, and sin and atonement. [160]

For Schleiermacher, sin came about when man's God-
consciousness limited and relativized his self-consciousness. Whilst
it is the God-consciousness which makes man aware of sin, there
can be no consciousness of God without a correlative consciousness
of sin and redemption. Sin is that opposing element in man's
consciousness which accuses man and renders him guilty. It is
negated by God's grace, but this negation does not occur when
man is confronted by Jesus Christ. Rather, it occurs in man's
consciousness of God, which is not necessarily dependent on the
God-man in history. God simply sees to it that this consciousness
arises without it having been revealed or overcome in Jesus
Christ. [161]

> It is as we have a consciousness of our redemption--and
> in it a consciousness of the original unity of our existence
> and of a future overcoming of the discord--that we
> are aware of the discord as such, of our sinfulness
> and guilt. Hence, the definition of sin as the ineffective-
> ness, the contradiction, the limitation, the shrinking
> of our God-consciousness. [162]

Sin for Schleiermacher, according to Barth, would seem
to have a positive character since it can only be conceived in

relation to redemption and God. This raises the more serious question, however, as to whether this is the biblical understanding of sin and grace, for where there is no confrontation as in scripture, there is hardly likely to be a great division between the two. [163] This is a problem both of nineteenth-century and twentieth-century liberalism. They both fail to realize that only when Jesus Christ is seen as revealing what man is like can the man of sin be known and can the true character of sin be known. [164] The verdict of the Father declared in the crucifixion and resurrection of Jesus Christ reveals the old man, the man of sin, who is everyone.

> Jesus Christ suffered and died in our place, in solidarity with this old man and therefore with us, without any clever reservation in respect of a secret innocence or freedom or capacity for redemption which might be maintained and ascribed to this man and therefore to us . . . without any control over the grace of God. . . . [165]

Jesus Christ has significance in revealing the truth about man in the following ways. First, it is in His existence that we see human sin in all its ramifications. This witness is seen in the New Testament, where man is shown to be an opponent of Jesus Christ and therefore of God. [166] Secondly, Jesus Christ as Judge reveals the corruption of man which diseases his existence. But as Judge, He also reveals Himself as man's eternal brother and as the archetype of every man. [167] Thirdly, Jesus Christ reveals sin to be that which is characteristic of human existence and activity. [168] Fourthly, the knowledge of Jesus Christ leads to the knowledge of sin and its dimensions. [169] Sin has no positive basis in God or in relation to God:

> Sin is that which is absurd, man's absurd choice and decision. . . . We say too much even if we say that this event may take place according to the divine will and appointment. We must not go beyond the negative statement. [170]

Thus, unlike nineteenth and twentieth-century liberalism, Jesus Christ reveals that there is a great antithesis between sin and God which is a menace to God's creation.

Human Sin: Pride and Unbelief

Barth now asks the question, what is the nature of this sin which alienated us from God and from ourselves? How is it to be identified? He replies that sin at its most fundamental level is pride. [171] This can also be called unbelief. [172] This is our rejection of God's goodness, our apostasy from God's free grace, and thus our unbelief. Man can obey God if he believes, but he cannot obey because he does not believe. How, then, is this form of sin manifested?

First, it is shown in the fact that man wants to be God. [173] This is concealed from him and can only be communicated to him by the Word of God. Man does not wish to be responsible to or for anyone else nor disturbed by any claims on his existence or conscience. Man does not think that he is denying God in all of this; indeed he may well think that he is being humble, that it is "natural" wanting only to be by himself. [174] Barth traces this attitude back to the serpent in Gen. 3:1f:

> The serpent's speech simply showed the existence of man to be formerly autonomous, self-governing and self-sufficient. It simply laid down the possibility that man might see his own needs and satisfy those needs by his own efforts. It simply safeguarded human autonomy. [175]

But there are three mistakes concealed in this attitude.

1) Man thinks he can will and determine his own being and selfhood and thus be true man. [176] He overlooks the fact that he was not created for or unto himself, but for the glory of God and for others. In choosing to be self-controlling, man really chooses to be non-human--se se propter se ipsum maxime.

2) Caught in this error about himself, man thinks he can be supreme and therefore like God. Even if he is powerless to become like God, his attempt to do so must be taken seriously-- diligere propter se ipsum. [177]

3) Man wants to be a caricature of God in that he wants to be self-contained, self-centered, forgetting that God as God is supremely pro nobis on behalf of man. Man, in ignoring the grace of God, tries to make God into a solitary glory. [178]

Man's unbelief is also shown in the fact that he acts in opposition to Jesus Christ as the servant wanting to be Lord and master:

> He thinks and acts only as a shadow of himself, as though he had it. Like the sergeant-major in Schiller's Wallenstein, he can only act as though he were a field-marshal. He can only play the lord. [179]

This aspect of his sin is also concealed, allowing him to perceive it as a virtue.

> In effect--the serpent does not need to say it but man
> can and will deduce it for himself--it is time for man
> to be enlightened and to come of age. It is time for
> him to appeal from a Deus male informatus to a Deus
> melius informandus, to do a little demythologising, to
> pass from the decision of the obedience of God to that
> of his own choice, from service in the garden to rule. [180]

1) Man conceals this aspect of pride by disregarding his servant relationship with God, namely, that of being below where God is sovereign. [181]

2) Man errs by calling this his true development, but it is really rebellion, for it disturbs and makes chaotic the relationship between God and man. The below appears to be above and the first appears to be second. Barth sees this as being related to the beginnings of power struggles and wars between nations and peoples:

> The struggle for power--the power of the sexes (did
> not this begin with the prominence of the woman in
> Gen 3:2f), the power of individuals, nations, classes, and
> ranks--is bound to follow, and it will be accomplished
> by the execution of a mutual judgment which is a judgment
> without grace, for where is the grace to come from? [182]

3) Man, in fact, misunderstands the relationship, for God is not the grand overlord, but the lord who condescends to be at one with man and who Himself became a servant. [183]

Thirdly, God in Jesus Christ judges ' man and accuses him, but also allows Himself to be judged and indeed took the judgment upon Himself on behalf of man. Yet man wants to be his own judge and thus to set himself in the right. [184] Most individuals spend a life-time searching for standards by which they can judge their own affairs and those of others according to their own standards, which, according to Barth, is a source of conflict and misunderstanding between people in society.

> Again, human life in society whether on a small scale
> or a large, means the emergence and conflict, the more
> or less tolerable harmony and conjunction, of the different
> judges with their different rights, the battle of the ideas
> formed and the principles affirmed and the standpoints
> adopted and the various universal or individual systems,
> in which at bottom no one understands the language
> of the others because he is too much convinced of the
> soundness of his own. . . . [185]

This produces a self-righteousness which is also concealed in the following forms:

1) Man misunderstands himself and therefore confounds himself about his own role as judge. Man is given the freedom to make a choice in knowing and judging things, but it is a choice which has to be made in light of his relationship to God as His obedient servant. Man desires to make the ultimate choice between light and chaos, darkness and light, good and evil, ignoring the fact that God has already made this decision for him. [186]

2) In thinking that he is sovereign enough to judge between good and evil, man in fact does that which is evil because he does not have a standard for that which is good. In all of this there is a strong communal component for Barth:

> I am already putting myself in the wrong with others, and doing them wrong, when . . . I confront them as the one who is right, wanting to break over them as the great crisis. For when I do this I divide myself and I break the fellowship between myself and others. I can only live at unity with myself, and we can only live in fellowship with one another when I and we subject ourselves to the right which does not dwell in us and is not manifest by us, but which is over me and us as the right of God above. . . . [187]

This must lead to war, whether an active one or a "cold" one because man, who thinks he is the sole judge of what is good and evil, will seek to impose this standard on others for his own benefit. [188]

3) Man, in his self-righteousness, misunderstands the nature of God. Sinful man conceives of God as a Judge who sits on a divine throne indifferent and inapproachable. He tries to imitate this image of God, which is a false image. God is not indifferent to man, says Barth. "He places Himself between us and nothingness." [189]

Finally, the human sin of pride and therefore unbelief can be characterized by man's idea that he can help himself and in so doing can count on God's help. [190] Man can and should help himself, says Barth, but he does not have the power to liberate himself. He can only be liberated by the fact that God is his living helper, his provider, his elector. [191] Man wants a supreme being as a helper, but not one who will call his ideas and existence into question.

Yet, like the other aspects of pride, this aspect also conceals itself.

1) It is not so much a question of self-affirmation and autonomy toward God and our neighbor as it is a question of man wanting to be independent and wishing to help himself alone. [192] When man exceeds the limit of dependence on God's free grace, he contradicts himself, for he forgets that he exists because of God's graciousness and his expressing gratitude for that graciousness. When he rejects this, he loses himself. "He is free to the extent that he knows himself to be free by the grace of God and continually allows himself to be made free by it." [193]

2) In setting out to be his own helper, man is left to his own phantasy and constructions, his own "natural" capacities and needs in trying to help himself. This means that he is no longer confronted either by the gracious God who confronts him as helpless man or by his fellowman, who properly confronts him only as a fellow-human in God. [194] Thus, he isolates himself from his neighbor.

3) Once again, man misunderstands God. He assumes that God is a despot, which He is not. God wills to be a partner with man, even sinful man.

Consequence as Sinner: the Fall

Having examined the nature of the sin committed by man, Barth now moves to examine the nature of man as sinner or what Barth calls "the man in the character which is proper to him as such, the man of sin." [195] This man is fallen man--a characterization which must be seen christologically so that one does not interpret the fall to mean that man is totally lost to God.

> He cannot really escape God. His godlessness may be very strong, but it cannot make God a "manless" God. Man in his fall cannot cease to be the creature and covenant-partner of God. [196]

Whilst the covenant with God has been violated by man through the fall, from God's side and intention, it has not been reversed or destroyed by this act of man. "God does not allow Himself to be diverted by the sin of man from addressing His Yes to him." [197] God reconciles even this fallen man to Himself. What then is the character of this sinful man who does not deserve, but still is the recipient of, God's great Nevertheless?

First, fallen humanity is in debt to God. It is a debt which can only be repaid by God's forgiveness.

> He does not do so without any ground or basis. . . . Nor
> does He forgive man in a good nature which treats the
> sin of man lightly. Nor does He forgive man simply because
> he is not in a position to make payment or restitution.
> [198]

Man is forgiven by God simply because His forgiveness alone
is the proper restitution for the debt. Man is not forced to become
the debtor. He chooses to do so by repudiating God's grace.
God's forgiveness repels chaos and closes the gulf which threatens
man as the result of his repudiation. [199] Barth is aware that
he departs from Anselm at this point, for Anselm insisted on
God demanding satisfaction for the injury done. God does not
forgive unconditionally and man cannot fulfill the condition for
divine forgiveness--hence the necessity of the incarnation. But,
says Barth, Anselm fails to get to why man cannot liberate himself:

> The dreadful nature of the transgression committed by
> sinful man derives from the character of the obligation
> which he has broken. But how are we to see the quality
> of human guilt and the character of human obligation
> except in the light of the fact that God's answer and
> reaction is simply and unequivocally His forgiveness in
> sheer mercy? [200]

God forgives man without being untrue to Himself, asking not
that man be something different, only that he be what he is--as
one who is loved and addressed by God. The relationship is already
there. Man does not have to create it or invent it. [201] But
man absurdly transgresses this relationship and thus incurs the
wrath of God, which Barth describes as "the lordship of God
on the left hand" that is, the threat of divine rejection. [202]

A second point about fallen humanity is that his corruption
is total and radical. [203] The sin of man extends itself to man's
total existence, but again, this does not mean that man is entirely
lost or has ceased to be a partner of God:

> The Bible accuses man as a sinner from head to foot,
> but it does not dispute to man his full and unchanged
> humanity, his nature as God created it good, the possession
> and use of all the faculties which God has given him.
> He still has his determination for God, his being as the
> soul of a body, his being in his time. [204]

Man may repudiate and abuse the covenant relationship, but
he cannot step out of it. He contradicts his true humanity, and
thus in a paradoxical fashion, "he lives out his own death." [205]
Many theologians like to speak of a relic in man, but Barth says

that the only relic in the light of the total corruption of man is God's own gracious will. [206]

An implication of all this is that there never was a time when man was not a transgressor and thus guiltless before God. There was never a "golden age" of innocence. [207] Jesus Christ obediently died for sinful man in order to overcome and set aside this false beginning so that man might be born again.

But at the same time there was never a sphere of man's activity or existence which did or does not stand under the grace of God. [208] It is this connection which leads Barth to quarrel with the expression "hereditary sin" (Erbsünde). Barth thinks this traditional term obscures the totality of the sin of man as well as the effects of its imprisonment of man. An inheritance is something, he says, which is given to someone and he accepts it simply as an heir. "Heir" can confuse the meaning of "sin" in this connection, especially since "hereditary sin" suggests naturalism and a determinism. [209] Therefore, Barth pleads for Ursünde (original sin), which is a stricter translation of the Early Church's term peccatum originale. [210] This carries with it the idea of choice on the part of man in terms of his corruption.

Still a third statement concerning the nature of humanity's corruption is that all are placed under a verdict and sentence. [211] There are two parts to this verdict: one is God's mercy which embraces humanity for the future, shown by the Son of God coming into the far country of sin in order to seek out man; the other is God's sentence which embraces humanity in the past and which is co-extensive with God's mercy. But this old humanity has been set aside.

> What we have had to say concerning him can only be put in the perfect or even the pluperfect tense. In the light of this present he is the one that we were, or had been, not the one that we can be or will be again. . . The Old Testament is the indispensable lens by which we can read in the mirror of the obedience of the Son of God who and what we were before Him and without Him--men of sin and disobedience and pride, and therefore fallen men guilty before God and radically and totally corrupt. [212]

The generic name, **Adam**, tells us neither to think of some past nor future perfection, rather the name reveals the truth about us before God.

Jesus Christ as the Victorious Servant

But there is a second part to the ministry of Christ, which Barth has called the humiliation of Christ or the servant who became Lord. This, too, is a summons and a judgment on sinful man, who is now examined in light of this second aspect. Since God has humbled Himself to become man, man's hitherto existence can no longer be man's imprisonment. He has been exalted by God, and as Barth puts it: "He is no longer unfree to let himself be exalted and to exalt himself." [213] Jesus Christ, in exalting mankind, revealed man's shame, but also his immobility:

> We are ashamed because our own human essence meets us in Him in a form in which it completely surpasses and transcends the form which we gave it. In Him we are not encountered by an angel, or a being which is superior and alien to our own nature, so that it is easy to excuse ourselves if we fail to measure up to it. We are confronted by a man like ourselves, with whom we are quite comparable. [214]

To test this claim after examining some incidents in the Gospels, [215] Barth poses some control questions as a means of getting at the character of this shame. First, he asks, does this sense of shame in the light of the lordship of Jesus Christ have some universal significance for all people? Might not there be exceptions to this rule and might not there be people as exalted in their own right as Christ? No, replies Barth, Jesus Christ as a man of history summons the Christian to recognize both himself and others in Him. [216] It is primarily in Christ that one is able to recognize all others.

Secondly, Barth asks, is this mediocrity really to be understood as shame? Ought it not be considered as something which is basically normal for the average man? No, Barth replies, Christ lived, died, and rose again in solidarity for all of humankind. This is a critical point for Christians since non-Christians, even with lofty moral principles, often defend themselves and others by citing their ordinariness and mediocrity as evidence that all men are good morally. [217] Christ did not isolate Himself, but took the place of Christian and non-Christian alike in order to lift us up out of this mediocrity. But he also showed that to be ordinary and mediocre in the light of His exalting of human-kind is to be in sin. [218] And related to this is the fact known by Christians that all people try to rationalize or justify their being and conduct, which, in fact, is a shame.

Finally, Barth poses the control question: how much ought one to relate this shame to the individual? Is it only a function of his human nature? Might not one confess to sinning without declaring oneself a sinner? No, replies Barth again, Jesus Christ does not permit us to reserve a portion of the human being as untouched by sin and evil.

> In the very One in whom the Christian sees himself quali-
> fied and exalted, he has also to see that he is disqualified
> and abased. . . . This one confesses in toto those who
> are shamed by Him, but only these. Hence no one can
> confess Him, and therefore be a Christian, unless he
> confesses that he is totally ashamed by Him. [219]

But, asks Barth, might it not be that all of the previous answers are a part of a dialectic which is characteristic of man's existence in which his abasement and sin are part of a nexus through which he actually affirms himself and his world? Might it not be that in the long run he does not die unto sin but lives because of it in harmony with Jesus Christ? Might not all of this really be a part of a tale in which "they all live happily ever after"? No, insists Barth, the old man died in Christ and with that death the power of sin over man's existence and being also was overcome. Jesus Christ established a discontinuity between the old man of sin and the new man of reconciliation through the crucifixion. God allowed His own glory to be called into question for the sake of sinful man. [220]

Human Sin: Sloth and Stupidity

Just as Barth's analysis of the nature of human sin under the lordship of Jesus Christ led him to label that aspect of sin "pride", so under the servanthood of Christ as Lord he finds sin to be "sloth". By this he means the inaction and tardiness of humanity in responding to the graciousness of God's grace. [221]

> In its form as man's tardiness and failure, sloth expresses
> much more clearly than pride the positive and aggressive
> ingratitude which repays good with evil. It consists in the
> fact, not only that man does not trust God, but beyond
> this that he does not love Him, i.e., that he will not
> know and have Him, that he will not have dealings with
> Him, as the One who first loved him, for all eternity. [222]

Barth calls even this inaction an action which expresses hate, for if one does not love God or is indifferent to Him, it is in fact a hate of Him. The pride of man, consisting of his wanting to be like God is really a perverse love of God. The sloth of man begins with the statement; "There is no God." [223]

Man initiates this action because he does not want to

be bothered either by God or by his neighbor. He wants to deny his freedom given him in Jesus Christ because that freedom implicitly is linked to his neighbor. [224]

> In the freedom of the man Jesus it seems that we have a renewal and exaltation from servitude to lordship. But this is exacting and dangerous business if it necessarily means that we acquire and have in Jesus a Lord, and if His lordship involves that we are demanded to leave our burdensome but comfortable and secure life as slaves and assume responsibility as lords. [225]

It is sin because it is a rejection, an avoidance of God's grace. This refusal affects four human relationships: man's relationship to God, to neighbor, to creation, and to his historical situation. [226]

Barth then uses a christological modus operandi to examine each of these relationships and their connection to sloth. First, man's relationship to God is injured by his refusing to acknowledge the event of the Word becoming flesh. Under the aspect of pride, this injury was shown in man's usurpation; [227] under the aspect of sloth this damage is seen in man's stupidity:

> He does actually will not to know God as he might and should know Him, thanks to the freedom in which the man Jesus does so for him, in the bright light of the existence of this Fellow and Brother. . . . Yet he does will it, and in this will which is opposed to the good will of God, he creates a fact and lives in it. He does not live as a wise man, but as a stupid fool. [228]

This is a conscious act of evil, which, in fact, is his inaction, his refusal to accept the summons of God in Jesus Christ. Man assumes that he can attain his true nature and mission apart from the Word of God even though he knows what that Word entails. [229] And like pride, this sin of sloth is also concealed.

First, it is concealed under man's inhumanity, that is, a rupture of his relationship with his fellowman which is the basis of his humanity. [230] Since it is God who guarantees this relationship, a rejection of God also endangers this relationship. Secondly, it is concealed under a dualistic understanding of the emotional and physical components of man's being, the old matter versus spirit dualism. [231] It is God who guarantees this unity and without it, man lives alternatively sometimes in the life of the spirit and sometimes in the life of the flesh. He allows himself to be ruled by his head at times and by his appetites at others, only to find himself in a state of perpetual flux and unrest. Thirdly, it is concealed under a misapprehended understanding of his limited temporality. [232] God guarantees the fulfillment of time and the right relationship of man's time to His time, which is the foundation of all historicity--the story of man being in time existing under the limitations of time. When man abandons this by his inaction, he becomes disoriented.

The second part of the disturbed relationships through sloth is that of man's relationship with his neighbor. "In Him (man) does not live only in fellowship with God, but in so doing he also lives in fellowship with other men." [233] But man resists this activity by his inactivity, thereby resulting in what Barth calls "inhumanity", that is, we choose to live in isolation from or in hostility to others. [234]

> Nor can anything alter the fact that in Him all men, even the most deformed and unnatural, are elected and created and determined for fellow-humanity, for neighbourly love, for brotherhood. . . . In this respect, too, I can refuse to be the new and neighbourly man that I am already in this One. In this respect, too, we can involve ourselves in self-contradiction. [235]

To be without one's fellow-human is to be inhuman. This inhumanity also has practical consequences because when man is set against his neighbor, he is prepared to violate his neighbor's dignity and rights, eventually resulting in robbery, murder, and war. [236]

This inhumanity is also concealed. One form of concealment is hypocrisy, [237] whereby one tries to persuade oneself, others, and even God that one really is human. This persuasion is often executed under the guise of philanthropy:

> Philanthropy is the focusing and concentrating of human will and action on the prosecution of one such anonymously human cause to a victorious and successful outcome. And there can be no doubt that the genuine humanity which is fellow-humanity does include philanthropy of this kind. The fact that there are always in human society questions and causes which claim the attention and loyalty of individuals and groups is in itself, because the ultimate concern is always man, a sign of the great inter-relatedness in which alone we men can be men. [238]

The difficulty is that such causes, noble as they may be, more often than not have a nameless, anonymous humanity attached, which really permits one to continue one's own activity for his own self-interest rather than for the cause of his fellowman. Barth thinks that the disguising of inhumanity under such social institutions as law to be particularly the situation in western societies. [239]

> Not least, the Church itself, the proclamation and hearing
> of the Word of God, the confession and doctrine and
> liturgy and order of the Church, and even its theology,
> offer a vast opportunity for philanthropic activity which
> is devoid of true humanity. All these things are "causes"
> which in their context do not lack the appearance of
> human justification, necessity, and value, which from
> some standpoint can and must also be the concern of
> the man who is directed to his fellowman. . . . But there
> is not one of them which does not leave open the question
> of how their promotion is going to affect the concrete
> man envisaged and embraced by them. [240]

A second form of concealment is the dissolution of the bond uniting men as brothers and sisters for the sake of one's own exploitation and ends. This is sheer stupidity which means that man is also inhuman when he does this, for whilst one's relationship to fellow human beings is not in itself a relationship with God, still God as the God of his fellows, as well as of himself, includes both:

> The former is the horizontal line to which the vertical
> is related and without which it would not be a vertical. . .
> I cannot know and honour and love God as my God if
> in the words of the Lord's Prayer, I do not do so as
> our God, as the God of the race which He has created. . .
> If I choose myself in my isolation from other men, eo
> ipso I enter the sphere of the even more terrible isolation
> in which God can no longer be my God. [241]

Still a third form of concealment is a collapse of the structure of one's human nature, i.e., the togetherness of body and soul. One withdraws to oneself and thus cuts oneself off from the thou of his fellowmen. Without his fellowmen, the I cannot really be authentic. He withers and dies as body and soul in psychical and physical isolation. [242] Fourthly, this sin is concealed under the loss of an historical perspective to which one's own existence is related. One has a history in relation to others and their experiences and collective lives. When that relationship is broken, one has little basis for historical identity or what could be called solidarity. [243]

The sin of sloth affects yet a third relationship--that of man to the created order. Barth calls this dissipation, a withdrawal into ourselves. [244] This means that man wills to be in disorder, disarray, and discord. [245] Body and soul become separated and one either spiritualizes or materializes his surroundings.

This relationship is also concealed in several ways: First,

in refusing the knowledge of God, we get involved in decline and disorder within our own being. As we become more and more disorderly, God becomes more and more of a stranger and eventually he becomes an enemy, for He is a God of order and peace. [246] Secondly, dissipation causes inhumanity:

> The destruction of the I in which we are involved necessarily means that there is a vacuum at the point where the other seeks a Thou to whom he can be an I. The dissipated man becomes a neutral, an It which is without personal activity and with which others cannot enter into a fruitful personal reciprocity. [247]

Thirdly, our assigned time of human existence becomes intolerable. We rebel against the limitation of time and become anxious about ourselves and our world. This is especially shown in anxiety about dying as evidence of our finitude:

> Carpe diem is the word of exhortation and comfort which the dissipated man addresses to himself. . . . But this is simply an expression of the panic. . . . Do we not always think that we are too late, sometimes even in youth, then in dangerous middle-age, and especially when we are old, and cannot conceal from ourselves the fact that in this or that respect we are indeed and finally too late, and we try to snatch the flowers that may be left, or surprisingly given, by the late autumn? [248]

The fourth guise for the sin of sloth is human care, or what the psychologists seem to mean by "paranoia", that is, man is overly worried and taxed about his finitude. [249]

> And it is this illusionary picture, the phantasy of a hopeless death, which with great definiteness and consistency dictates the law of his conduct. As he is anxious, he gives life to this phantasy, arming it with its illusory weapons and directing its illusory arm. Care is in fact existence from and to this death . . . [250]

This aspect also is concealed: First, in the west it might be concealed under the work ethic with its stress on activity, where success is the key to western man's anxiety about his security, whereas in the east it might be more passive. The latter may not be a slave to the work ethic, but he is a victim of sloth in that there is a disruption of his relationship to his temporal situation through his resignation, non-resistance, and contemplation. [251] More specifically, it is concealed under man's unwillingness to honor God as God who reminds us of the temporal limitations and meets us at the very limit of death. [252] Secondly, human fellowship is destroyed for man's cares about the threat of death isolate him from others:

> Even in society with others he secretly cherishes his own fears and desires. His decisive expectation from others is that they will help him against the threat under which he thinks he stands. [253]

Thirdly, it is concealed under the disintegration of man's unity as body and soul. The anxious man becomes so discontented with his finitude that he feels constantly menaced by the present, no longer ruling as a soul or serving as a body. [254]

Consequence as Sinner: the Misery

Just as the condition of humankind under the sin of pride was fallen humanity, so the condition of humankind under the sin of sloth is misery, says Barth, that is, misery induced by our being exiled from our true existence and thus imprisoned in a false existence. [255]

> Remaining behind instead of going up with Him, he is necessarily the one who is left behind in misery. He prefers his own life below to the divine life above. . . . This is what the older dogmatics called in its totality the status corruptionis. Our present term for it is the misery of man. [256]

This misery has three characteristics, but characteristics observed in the light of hope in Jesus Christ, not observed on the basis of any empirical evidence.

First, to liberate humankind from this misery, Jesus Christ took everything upon Himself and accomplished this liberation through His death. Man alone was unable to bear this misery, which Barth understands to be the equivalent of the New Testament's rendering and use of sarx in a negative sense--man's existence in the sphere dominated by sin which causes man's self-alienation and self-contradiction. [257]

Secondly, to liberate humankind from this misery, Jesus Christ died in order to initiate the new man through a new birth. [258] Thirdly, to liberate humankind from this misery, Jesus Christ exercised the royal freedom of providing man with a free will. Jesus Christ gave up his life freely for the sake of man's will. But free will does not mean free apart from Christ. Nor does it mean that man is free to decide that he no longer has a will. [259]

> Of the free man it has to be said: <u>non potest peccare.</u>
> His freedom excludes this. It excludes the possibility of
> sinning. He "cannot" sin in the capacity granted to him
> by God. In this capacity he can only believe and obey
> and give thanks and give to the faithfulness of God the
> response of his own loyalty. He can sin only as he re-
> nounces this capacity. [**260**]

The misery of man is in fact man acting as though he were not
free in Christ.

Human Sin: Lying and Untruth

A corollary of Barth's third part of his christology,
namely, Jesus Christ as Mediator and the Light of life, is a consideration of man's sin as falsehood or lying. [**261**] Through Christ
a knowledge of the covenant of grace has been communicated,
which means that sin and its nature is now known. [**262**]

> What characterizes it as sin, and makes it immeasurably
> dreadful and reprehensible, as an event which cannot
> be comprehended in its reality, is that it is the denial,
> perversion and falsification of what is said to man   as
> God's Word in Him, the Son of God and Man. [**263**]

Although pride is a form of falsehood in which man seeks to
usurp the place of God in contrast to Christ's humility, and although sloth is a form of falsehood in which man seeks to rid
himself of the dignity of his divinely given nature in contrast
to the majesty of the royal man, nevertheless, these are the
<u>works</u> of sin. The distinctive feature of falsehood is that it is
man's <u>word</u> of sin. [**264**]

To see the true character of falsehood, Barth first tries
to contrast it with real truth in Christ. He rules out, first of
all, that it is simply an idea or principle or a system:

> Indeed, falsehood loves to take the garb of doctrine,
> idea, principle, and systems. And the more divine an
> idea pretends to be, the more radically a principle is
> carried through and asserted . . . the more we have
> cause to suspect that what is trying to claim and enslave
> us is an idea, principle, system or doctrine of falsehood.
> [**265**]

Real truth must have the power of summoning and grasping man
for knowledge and obedience. Jesus Christ is also the truth and
the Lord of all truth who .is at the same time neither conditioned

nor limited by it. It is in His light as the true witness of the truth that man is unmasked as a creature of falsehood.

But neither is truth something which encounters man and is immediately pleasing, acceptable, and illuminating. [266] Real truth is unsettling, unwelcome. "It does not address us, it contradicts us and demands our contradiction." [267]

The true witness is the living Christ, needing no verification or replacement or supplementation by any other truth. His witness depends solely on His relationship to God and God's relationship to Him. The inner connection between these two relationships is that of freedom--the freedom to offer up His life and the freedom of God turning to Him.

What, then is the character of falsehood in the light of this true witness of Christ?

1) It has the character of avoiding Jesus Christ and His truth. [268] Man does not appear to be against the truth; in fact he appeals to it, setting up theoretical and practical systems of truth. But this is really evasion because man seeks to transform the truth into something he can control, "which is mastered by him instead of the truth which masters him." [269]

> The truth which He attests is the reconciliation of the world to God, but this reconciliation as effected in Him. It is the covenant between God and man, but this covenant as fulfilled in Him. . . . He attests this truth as He attests Himself. But He attests it as He attests Himself. We do not encounter Him without at once encountering this truth. But we do not encounter this truth without at once encountering Him. [270]

Man tries to change the truth of God because it shocks him or is offensive. It is man's evasion of true freedom. [271] He does this either by trying to coordinate God's truth with a system stressing the divine and the infinite, on the one side, or the human and finite on the other side. This is intended to neutralize (verharmlosen) the encounter, to relieve God's truth of all its tension and power.

2) It has the character of making man become a liar at every point of his existence:

> When and where, obviously in violent reaction against this voice, have society, business, states, their governments and parties, the classes and races (two terms of very doubtful origin), so boldly strutted across the stage with continually new and more refined and striking fictions

> than in world history post Christum? When and where
> has there been opened such a gigantic maw of lying
> as the so-called "press" which today . . . is the word
> which is drummed into the ears of all of us every day. . . .
> In it all the Christian churches in some way have a hand,
> at least in the sense that from their own standpoints
> they all accept as true the fictions spread abroad by
> these various authorities and help to pass them on to
> their members and the rest of the world with their blessing
> and in edifying garb. [272]

Thus, for Barth, the true witness also calls the nature and practices of the church into question as well as man, particularly when the social and political praxis of the church are so intertwined with cultural practices which in turn reinforce man's falsehood.

Consequence as Sinner: Condemnation

Again Barth asks the question: what is man's condition after having freely chosen this form of sin? The consequence of man's falsehood is his condemnation (Verdammnis). [273] Man is condemned because he tries to turn the truth of his liberation into its opposite. As a liar, man repudiates the free grace of God and as such stands under the threat of being damned. This results in man's aimlessness and not having a point of reference or orientation. [274]

And like the other forms of sin, this one also prevents co-existence with fellow-humans. He relates to his fellowhumans as though they were instruments for his purposes or as though they were his enemy. [275] Barth thinks this particularly affects the most important means of humans communicating truth and reality, namely, human speech:

> The painfulness of the situation is concentrated . . . in
> the problematic nature of human speech. . . . What should
> take place in human speaking and hearing is the utterance,
> declaration and revelation of human reality with a view
> to its indication, impartation, and communication to others
> and with the final purpose of the communion or fellowship
> of the one with the others. But when man not only
> resists the truth but changes it into untruth . . . human
> reality cannot be uttered or expressed or declared. . . .
> This is why fellowship in human reality, which must and
> may be the final goal of speech, is never attainable
> by man of himself, his speech serving rather to promote
> alienation and disunity between man and man, and there-
> fore inhumanity. [276]

Chapter Five

EFFECTS OF RECONCILIATION: OUR JUSTIFICATION, SANCTIFICATION, AND VOCATION

Having examined the effects of our alienation from God through the sin of pride which results in the fall, our alienation from each other through the sin of sloth which results in our misery, and our alienation from ourselves through the sin of falsehood with the result that we experience and know condemnation, Barth uses a method of correlation to demonstrate how Jesus Christ corrects these events of alienation. He does this by showing how the divine acts of justification, sanctification, and vocation not only restore our intended relationship with God, each other, and ourselves, but also how Jesus Christ as both the form and content of these acts is to be understood as the basis of human society in which the restoration is lived out. In a most profound way Barth understands Christian ethics to be founded on these three aspects of the reconciling act of God in Jesus Christ. Therefore this chapter will examine these three divine "corrections" and then look at the implications of these acts for Christian ethics.

One ought again to caution that these are not three separate acts, distinguishable from one another. They are in fact one act. They constitute the dynamic of, as well as the structure for our existence and therefore our society.

> What can and will become of the world now that God
> has reconciled it to Himself? In the light of the revelation
> of this divine action, and the alteration which has taken
> place in it, it is obvious that, since God has had mercy
> on it in Jesus Christ and corrected the situation between
> it and Himself, it is no longer a lost world. [1]

An entire new character is given to the world of humanity in which the antithesis is ended and a future is given to the human world. Indeed, this future has become the realized present. The resurrection of Jesus Christ proclaims already the dawning of realized eschatology in man's present world, says Barth:

> What came upon the world and man in the resurrection of the man Jesus, in His appearance in the glory of God, was this presence of its future salvation ordained as the fruit of its reconciliation. The news of the presence of this future, of this today of the last and first hour, of the dawn of the redemption and consummation, is the Easter message. And the presence of the future in this event is the new seed of life planted in world-occurrence on Easter Day. [2]

Therefore all models of human and societal existence must be viewed in the light of this new dynamic which has been implanted permanently through the resurrection.

But, cautions Barth, the fact that man's existence and his world have been reconciled and redeemed by Christ does not mean that it is a perfect world. One cannot overlook the goal of what could be called "unrealized" eschatology. [3] The declaration is not yet complete. Evil as well as the sins of pride, sloth, and falsehood still can attack--and do. The Christian existence as well as human society thus have a provisional character as they move toward a goal:

> Is the situation of Christians within the sphere of the conditions given to all really so very different from that of non-Christians? It would not be advisable, but false, dangerous and illegitimate, to try to contest that it is basically and factually different, that the difference between knowledge and ignorance of Jesus Christ as concerns the situation of man in his sphere is comparable only with the distinction between heaven and earth. [4]

Man in the light of Christ can indeed live with a new affirmation, but he dare not forget the "not yet". Though there is a difference in man's existence of which the Christian has knowledge, many live in ignorance of this difference and all, both Christian and non-Christian alike, live under the same threatening conditions:

> Everything depends upon our not reducing this difference to a mere peculiarity of thought, outlook and conduct, but recognising and maintaining that already here and now, in the sphere of the "still" and "not yet", the Christian exists as the creature of God which is good and reconciled, though not of course redeemed and perfected, but still threatened. [5]

This reconciling event occurred in the single dynamic

of God's No and God's Yes in the crucifixion and resurrection. These are the sources for the claim that there has been a permanent alteration and change in the very ontological structure of human society as well as in the goal (telos) of that society.

> According to the resurrection the death of Jesus Christ as the negative act of God took place with a positive intention. It had as its aim the turning of man to Himself, his positing afresh, his putting on a new life, his freeing for the future. And, according to the prior death of Jesus Christ, the resurrection has this negative presupposition in a radical turning of man from his old existence, in a total removing of man in his earlier form, in his absolute putting off, in his complete freeing from the past. [6]

Indeed, in light of the resurrection one can even speak of a co-temporality between man's time and the post-resurrection time. [7] This event affected all, even those who do not hear it or observe it, claims Barth. Christians particularly cannot avoid this knowledge nor live as though it had not taken place.

This is the time between the times, already alluded to above, a time "between the present manifestation of the alteration of the human situation and a future manifestation." [8] It is under the rubric of this altered situation initiated by Jesus Christ via the three processes of justification, sanctification, and vocation in Barth's christology that one has to consider the nature or character of the changed human situation. Barth understands this change to have individual consequences, hence the emphasis on the man of sin and the reconciling of that individual man to God, but most especially, social consequences and hence political and communal significance. Salvation almost always is its most profound for Barth when it includes fellow-humanity. As Barth states very clearly: Christians cannot renounce their solidarity with non-Christians without raising questions about the true character of their own salvation and without endangering their own being as Christians. [9]

Justification and Solidarity

Barth defines **justification** as God's pardon which separates man from his past and impels him toward a new future. [10] Already in this definition is the structural basis given for ending man's alienation and for altering his existence. Justification has both a "once for all" character as well as a "continuing" character. That is, the act of justification occurred once and for all, but the process set in motion by that act demands continued renewal in man's existence:

> There is no present in which the justification of man
> is not still this beginning of justification, and where if
> it is recognised it does not have to be continually recog-
> nised as such. There is no man justified by God who
> does not have to recognise and confess that he is still
> unrighteous, still the proud rebel before Him, who does
> not have to grant that God is always in the right against
> him and therefore that he is always in the wrong against
> God. [11]

What then is the significance of "forgiveness" if the
"new man" is really the "old man"? Barth suggests that forgiveness
of sin means that whilst God overlooks our sin and puts it behind
us--thus removing its sting as a determinative factor in man's
relationship to God--it nevertheless hangs about as a threat even
for the Christian. The instrument through which this forgiveness
is forever held before the converted or justified being but also
through which we renew our continued need to know this justification ever anew is **faith,** which Barth calls a legitimate "human"
work: [12]

> He will confess him, and therefore he will confess the
> judgment and pardon of God, the reality of that history,
> of that transition of man from his Yesterday to his To-day.
> In his own person? Yes, but in his own person in solidarity
> with all other men. [13]

How is this work related to the sin of pride which is
supposed to have been overturned by God's justification? How
does this work manifest itself in relation to this particular sin?
First, faith displays the bankruptcy of being proud, although
the attractions of that pride may still tempt and attract man:

> No, even in the believer we have to do with very vain-
> glorious man. The only thing is that--although he exercises
> vain-glory--he has acquired a distaste, a radical and
> total distaste for it. [14]

Man affirms his justification and opens the gate for his moving
toward God as an affirmation of the reconciliation already made
available by God in the cross and resurrection when he indeed
admits that he is bankrupt and acknowledges the limitations
of being unduly proud. [15]

Secondly, the work of faith calls for obedience, or,
what Barth calls an "obedience of humility". [16] This obedience
to humility excludes any cooperative works on the part of man,
for were it to base itself on any human action taking place before
faith or even in faith it would no longer be obedience. [17]

> What is the sola fide but a faint but necessary echo
> of the solus Christus? He alone is the One in whom man
> is justified and revealed to be justified. . . . And because
> faith is faith in Him, for that reason it is justifying faith
> only in that isolation. For that reason it spurns and rejects
> the rivalry and cooperation of any attempts of man to
> bring about his own conversion to God, to try to accomplish
> of himself the destruction of the old and the introduction
> of the new, of right and life, the evening of the past
> and the dawning of the future. [18]

It is in light of this two-pronged aspect of faith given in justification that man is both reassured and summoned to consider all of reality and existence as related to this movement between God and man as that movement has taken place and been revealed in and by Jesus Christ. This is liberation for man, for it is a freeing of man for venture and new visions which never cease. [19]

Sanctification and Solidarity

The second process/act is that of sanctification. Just as the act of justification has to be understood within the context of God allowing Himself to be humiliated, so the act of sanctification has to be understood in God's willingness to exalt humankind. Again, this is simply another aspect of the event of reconciliation. Whereas in justification God totally turns Himself to us, in sanctification God turns us to Himself. This process/act has been understood in the past under regeneration (regeneratio), renewal (renovatio), conversion (conversio), and even penitence (poenitentia) recollects Barth. He chooses to call it sanctification, however, because "it includes already, even verbally, the idea of the 'saint'," reminding us of the new character of redeemed man. [20]

Yet Barth cautions that sanctification has its own integrity in the salvation history between God and the world:

> Sanctification is not justification and does not merge
> into it. Thus, although the two belong indissolubly together,
> the one cannot be explained by the other. It is one thing
> that God turns in free grace to sinful man, and quite
> another that in the same free grace He converts man
> to Himself. [21]

The first act has to do with the forgiveness of sin and contrition, whilst the second has to do with discipleship. [22] And yet dialectically the two also belong together, for the forgiveness of sin is accompanied by liberating man from the inordinate desire to commit sin. And God's adoption of man into divine sonship is at the same time accompanied by man's service to his fellowman. [23] That is, justification also liberates man for service and new life in the service of God and for the service of others.

What, therefore, is sanctification? **Sanctification**, says Barth, is the act and process by which man, exalted by God, is converted to God and is deemed holy by Him. These are those,

> who in spite of their sin have the freedom which they have received from Him to live in it, to represent Him among all other men and to serve Him in what they are. [24]

Because this objective fact is not acknowledged by all in subjective consent does not mean it is any less of a reality.

> Only God Himself knows the extent of this people, and its members. The invitation to belong to it is extended to all. Certainly it is not co-extensive with the human race as such. Certainly it is a special people of special men who are marked off from all others because they are set aside by God from among all others. [25]

Yet, cautions Barth, this "marking off" de facto is in fact extended to all men de jure. It does separate those to whom it has come de facto as a holy people, but the possibility of this event encompassing all men is implicit. Certainly, all of human existence is affected by it. [26] Mankind, maintains Barth, consists already of "saints and sanctified because we are already sanctified, already saints in this One." [27]

What are the political consequences of this de jure theological fact? One might call it a solitary "tilt". That is, Barth's insistence on humanity always means that fellow-humanity is a presupposition of this sanctification. Sanctification carries within it both the seeds of the scandal of particularity in marking off a holy people, but at the same time the mantle of universality in that theologically all of mankind should be liberated to work on behalf of and for the social and political goals of a just society.

> As it creates the fact of the existence of these men, this people, within the world, their sanctification attests the great decision of God which in Jesus Christ has been made not only concerning them, but concerning all the men of every time and place. . . . It sets it in the larger sphere of the creation of God. It gives it a solidarity even with secular things with which it is contrasted. [28]

That is, the act/process of sanctification cannot be a private or an individual concern alone. There is a fundamental social and corporate component in it.

There is also a **theological** solidarity (Mitmenschlichkeit) in sanctification as well, namely, a reaffirmation of the Christian's solidarity with fellow sinners even though sanctified in Christ. The sanctified are what Barth describes as "disturbed sinners":

> They are still sinners--these saints, these recipients of the direction (Weisung) of the exalted man, of the Son of Man who is also the Son of God. They are still below. . . . What, then differentiates them from the world, from other men, from those who are not saints? . . . They are disturbed sinners. Their sleep as such is broken. . . . The unreconciled man, the man to whom the reconciliation of the world with God, which comprehends his own sanctification, is concealed, is an undisturbed sinner. [29]

As disturbed sinners, Christians are summoned to be witnesses in this world, having been startled out of their sloth and having had their existence and their frame of reference for what is reality fundamentally altered. [30]

> But even more true is the fact that as they lift up themselves they fulfill a movement in which their being-— however questionably they may fulfill it--becomes and is conformable to His being, the being oı their Lord. . . . The constitution of His people on earth takes place in the power of His drawing unto Himself. This drawing unto Himself is His kingly work fulfilled in divine power. It cannot then be called into question. [31]

This witness, however, is exercised by the Christian with the awareness that sanctification, and therefore the sainthood of mankind de jure, is only a foretaste, a penultimate reality, even in the altered human situation. There remains still the eschatological "not yet" aspect of human existence. [32]

The "work" of man in response to sanctification is theologically described by Barth in Bonhoeffer's phrase, "the call to discipleship". [33] This call is a direction which establishes a **personal** relationship between Christ and the individual, [34] a new beginning demonstrated in self-denial, and a radical determination to be of service in the present age. [35] As a result one knows real and true freedom in being able to provide new visions and forms of service to neighbor and to the society.

> The world which sighs under these powers must hear and receive and rejoice that their lordship is broken. But the declaration cannot be made by the existence of those who are merely free inwardly. If the message is to be given, the world must see and hear at least an indication, or sign, of what has taken placᵒ. The break made by God in Jesus must become history. [36]

The Christian is summoned to what Barth calls "God's revolution", which includes an "obligation to the godless and hostile orders already broken in Christ", that is, a continuing link and service to a world not wanting or able to acknowledge the word in Christ. [37] The "call to discipleship" for the advancement of "God's revolution" carries with it the obligation of action which indicates the break in and the brokenness of human society.

Barth mentions several concrete social and political consequences of this discipleship demonstrating both a break with the usual societal order and a brokenness within that order. One is the renunciation of the western attachment to and confidence in possessions. Barth claims that this is not a summons to monastic poverty. Rather, it is a summons to give of one's own to the person in need in the radical fashion mentioned in such Gospel imperatives as Lk. 6:35 or 6:19:

> The line along which all of this is said is obviously the same, although it cannot be reduced to a normative technical rule for dealing with possessions. . . . The drift of them all is clearly that Jesus' call to discipleship challenges and indeed cuts right across the self-evident attachment to that which we possess. The man to whom the call of Jesus comes does not only think and feel, but acts (here and now, in this particular encounter with his neighbour) as one who is freed from this attachment. [38]

Another social and political consequence of this discipleship has to do with a radical alteration in the conventional priorities given to fame and honor in society. This kind of discipleship speaks of humility and revilement or washing each other's feet. It challenges what constitutes social status and social values. It is intended to bring about what Barth calls a "transvaluation" of societal values in a radical fashion. [39]

Yet another instance of how discipleship furthers "God's revolution" in man's world can be seen in the questioning of the beneficial value of force and might. Christ's various admonitions and teachings against force are aimed at invalidating any kind of friend-foe, we-they relationship between fellow human beings.

> What the disciples are enjoined is that they should love their enemies (Mt. 5:44). This destroys the whole friend-foe relationship, for when we love our enemy he ceases to be our enemy. It thus abolishes the whole exercise of force which presupposes this relationship and has no meaning apart from it. . . . Once again there can be no question of a general rule, a Christian system confront-

> ing that of the world. . . . But we have to consider
> very closely whether, if we are called to discipleship,
> we can avoid being practical pacifists, or fail to be so. [40]

Barth is very careful to insist that the concreteness of one's action as a disciple depends very much on the situation, since this is also the model exhibited by Christ in the New Testament. Hence, in every instance "God's revolution" must be concretized in action in society politically and socially. This is the freedom restored in sanctification which allows the Christian to act in the given situation and not according to a fixed rule. [41]

Vocation and Solidarity

The third section of Barth's doctrine of reconciliation which exhibits human "works" as a response and an obedience to that reconciling act is vocation. Vocation is our "work" in response to God's overcoming our falsehood and condemnation. Just as justification and sanctification have a pre-historical and non-empirical foundation in Jesus Christ, so also vocation. By **vocation** Barth means that one is called and placed in actual fellowship with Jesus Christ in order to serve both God and other fellowmen. That is, as our response to God's justification is faith and to sanctification discipleship, our positive response to God's vocation is gratitude. [42] The basis of this vocation, which is initiated by God in Jesus Christ is our election by God. Barth describes election as a foreordination for and a predisposition to vocation already preordained in Jesus Christ. [43] Commenting on an interpretation of Mt. 22:14 in which Jesus tells the wedding guests, "many are called, but few are chosen," Barth observes that, whilst this passage seems to contradict all other passages having to do with calling by suggesting that the call has no presupposition in election, one must regard it simply as a **paradox** fundamental in the nature of vocation:

> Many are called, but there will only be few who in follow-
> ing the call will prove worthy of, and act in accordance
> with, the fact that as the called of God, they are His
> elect, predestined from all eternity for life with Him
> and for His service. [44]

As with justification and sanctification so is the component of solidarity between the Christian and all human beings to be emphasized in vocation. The first aspect of this solidarity with all of humankind, even non-Christians, is that the Christian remains open and sensitive to all situations and conditions in order not to restrict his service to all of mankind:

> . . . we cannot view any man only in the light of those
> factors, e.g., the corruption of his mode of life, the per-
> verted and evil nature of his actions, the untenability
> of the ideas and convictions expressed by him, which
> obviously seem to characterise, and in very many cases
> do actually characterise him as one who is not called,
> as non-Christian, unchristian, and even anti-Christian. [45]

A second aspect is that the Christian has to look on
every person as his own responsibility:

> The reference is not to a general moral or human responsi-
> bility which might be interpreted as man's obligation
> to his conscience or character or way. . . . It is to the
> fact that even man, as he co-exists as such with Jesus
> Christ, stands in the light of life, that the Word of God
> is directed to him too, that it comes to him, that he
> is to be called and that he is thus made responsible
> to the One who calls him. [46]

By his very existence the Christian reminds the non-Christian
of his roots, his source of being and his promised future.

Barth immediately recognizes the cultural and social
implications of such a Christian claim, particularly with regard
to non-western cultures and civilizations. One can legitimately
object to such a claim, he says, especially when recalling that
long before there was any development of Christianity, people
felt they had a vocation. In the West this has often meant being
socialized in a society shaped and influenced by Christianity
and therefore reared with an assumed superior consciousness
and sense of worth. Indeed, scolds Barth, western society and
western civilization have more or less become synonymous with
Christianity:

> Now obviously to be a Christian in this sense no vocation
> is required. All that is needed is to have, not a new,
> but a given and present attachment, implicitly and second-
> arily to Jesus Christ, but explicitly and primarily to a
> family, nature, culture and civilisation. All that is needed
> is some kind of fixed participation in the historical and
> intellectual context of the West. [47]

The political result of this is that pagans and others living outside
the western tradition are often viewed as in need of a special
vocation in order to become a Christian. [48]

Such a view especially was anchored in western ideology
during the Renaissance and the Reformation because it was based
on the thesis that a unity existed between the ancient Greek

and Roman cultures, various European cultures, and Christianity. But even in that romanticized view of society, there was no happy harmony between the sacerdotium and the imperium:

> In the so-called Renaissance, learning, art, social and individual ethos, and above all, political power, and in the Reformation and Counter-Reformation the Church, and increasingly within it the individual Christian, awakened to an awareness of their autonomy and particularity. If Christianity could not and would not deny its existence in connexion with non-Christian humanity, nor free itself from the problem of this humanity, just as this humanity rather strangely would not wholly or radically free itself from Christianity with a few well-known exceptions, the individual Christian found himself more and more compelled to consider his own specific characteristics and to set himself on his own feet. [49]

Thus, since one's Christianity can no longer be determined simply by the fact that one lives in a particular nation, one may argue that one's Christianity is either grounded in his vocation or it is illusionary. This means that one must try to examine the conception of Christianity in a pluralistic society. And when one looks at the New Testament, to be a Christian is to belong to Jesus Christ in a special way which is different from His universal claim on all of mankind. That special way is characterized by the Christian's existence being determined by his faith in Christ,-- a faith that is both liberating and binding, both freedom-bearing and obedience-laden.

Yet this existence is still a human existence, not an angelic one. It is a human existence shaped by the divine word, but it is nonetheless human:

> "I pray not that thou shouldest take them out of the world" (John 17:15). The new creation fulfilled in vocation (II Cor. 5:17) does not mean the cancellation or destruction of the old, but the investing of man, of the child of Adam, with the new clothing or armour of God of which Paul loved to speak of as the great transformation which has come to the Christian but which is also still to come on him without any grasping of his own. Christians are in no sense freed from their unity with humanity. [50]

If this be the case, then what is the particularity of the Christian existence amongst fellow-humans? First, the Christian is illuminated by the Word so that he has active knowledge of God and of his divinely shaped existence. This is what Barth calls the Christian's "awakening". That is, when awakened, the

Christian becomes a child of light amongst others as his Father Himself is light. [51]

> Like Christ, who sets them in fellowship with Him as their first-born Brother, they are the handiwork of this fatherly love of God. In this they are His new creation. In this consists their freedom in the glory which <u>hic et nunc</u> will be revealed to it. [52]

Secondly, as such the Christian's existence amongst humanity ought to reflect the fact not only that the Christian, like all of humankind, is elected for fellowship with Jesus Christ, but also that the Christian in counter-distinction to other humans is actually placed and set in that fellowship. [53] It is discipleship in the truest sense, a <u>vocatio unica</u> and a <u>vocatio continua</u>. [54] And whilst the Christian as a disciple believes in Jesus as his only Lord and obeys Him as his sovereign and confesses Him by being prepared to be a fool for His sake, the Christian does not merge into Christ or become a little Christ. Yet it is a true union.

> For it takes place and consists in a self-giving which for all the disparity is total on both sides. In this self-giving Christ and the Christian become and are a single total-ity . . . in which He is with His people. . . . Like His own unity of true deity and humanity, this unity is <u>hic et nunc</u> concealed. It may be known in faith but not in sight, not by direct vision. [55]

That is, Barth sees the union between Christ and the Christian being somewhat analogous to the hypostatic union of His deity and His humanity. The union cannot be characterized as concentric (living for himself) alone, but rather awakened to genuine humanity, he exists also eccentrically (living for others). This is the ruling principle which impels the existence of the Christian amongst his fellowmen. [56]

Thirdly, the Christian existence places the Christian in tension with the world, that is, he affirms within the world the possibility of his own non-worldly goal. The Christian is indeed called to a new order and orientation. Yet

> as soon as the Christian ethos is divorced from its natural context, considered abstractly as an absolute magnitude and declared to be a controlling principle as such, it loses the distinctiveness, originality and uniqueness which mark it off from the type of ethos common to the rest of the world and humanity and thus make it an appropriate designation of the distinctive manner of the Christian. . . . A self-glorifying Christian moralism, which tries to be

> such a principle itself, has always resulted in a relativising and leveling down of the difference between Christian and non-Christian existence and the practical sterilisation of the former, i.e., the loss of its offensive and defensive power. [57]

It is under this latter rubric that Barth raises serious questions about the classic understanding of vocation which sees the Christian as the recipient of grace and thus called to live a separate life in the world. Even though this also resembles his own understanding hitherto of vocation, Barth asks whether this is any longer sufficient. The first criticism Barth makes of this classical definition is that it would make the Christian ethos an end in itself instead of it being a component of the Christian life under the command of Jesus Christ. This definition tends toward a dualism of Gospel and Law, justification and sanctification. [58]

Secondly, the question must be raised about whether this presupposition is adequate to maintain the difference between the Christian and the non-Christian, particularly when the non-Christian quite often displays behavior which resembles that of the Christian but without the benefit of knowledge of Jesus Christ. Can one speak of the absolute uniqueness of the Christian ethos therefore?

Thirdly, the classical definition assumes that the ultimate goal of the Christian's vocation is to exist for Christ's sake and to be reassured of his salvation. But should this dominate his total Christian existence? Cannot this principle obscure and hinder the execution of this existence in the world? Barth disputes the classical idea of Christian vocation summoning us toward a state of grace. [59]

> We certainly have to read a great deal into the passage which speaks of the calling of Abraham, Moses and the prophets, or in the New Testament of the disciples and later in the special calling of Paul, to gather from them that their chief concern is with the saving of their souls, or their experience of grace and salvation, in short, with the establishment of their personal well-being in their relationship with God. [60]

Barth insists that an alternative understanding of vocation is living in order to be able to execute and do one's calling. Christians are possessed by the need and urgency to be witnesses to other people as God's Verbi divini ministri. This means that there is a prophetic element in vocation, a "being called out" and a "being sent" feature. This vocation at its very roots carries with it an obligation to be worldly, e.g., to be carried out in the world for the sake of the world. This suggests that at its very heart Christian vocation has to be exercised both societally and politically. It is this element which Barth sees as a call to so creatively exercise vocation that one might even describe such a doing of vocation as "cooperative":

> When service is rendered, two very different active subjects are obviously at work together in different ways, but with a clear differentiation of function. The One is the Lord, who quite apart from the superiority of His person is also superior in the fact that in the common work it is wholly and utterly a matter of His cause. The other is the servant, who quite apart from the littleness of his person is also subordinate to the fact that in his participation in the common work it can only be a matter of renunciating his own cause and treating that of the Lord as though it were his, or rather, of really making it his own. [61]

But it is a ministering servanthood, not a spectator-like or passive servanthood. The Christian brings creative work to the witnessing in the world on behalf of Christ. This is the cooperating aspect of vocation.

Because this vocation is so strange, even offensive in the world, Barth sees the Christian as disciple expecting and enduring particular afflictions and pressures, for which there are at least three sources. First, the world afflicts him because of its own alienation from God and its vulnerability to the constant threat of nothingness and chaos:

> His affliction arises quite simply from the fact that the world cannot accept this demand and challenge, and the less so the more clearly it realises what is at issue. Let there be no mistake! The world can tolerate, approve, and value a good deal in the way of religion. . . . And as long as it can understand Christianity too, as a religion, or so long as Christianity perhaps represents and evaluates itself as such, the world will be able to integrate Christianity into itself, i.e., into the picture which it makes of its reality, and it will thus have nothing really to fear from it. [62]

It is when the society tolerating Christianity as a religion suddenly feels threatened by its prophetic witness to Jesus Christ which may challenge its own mores and assumptions and alter its structures that the world inflicts affliction. Then the Christian vocation becomes dangerous for the world. And this affliction can occur in societies with liberal as well as conservative ideologies.

> For "think not that I am come to send peace on earth: I came not to send peace, but a sword" (Mt. 10:34). The context makes it quite clear that this is not a sword which the disciples have to draw, but the sword which is sharpened and drawn against them, the sword which Paul mentions in Rom. 8:35, where he then goes on to quote Ps. 44:22: "For thy sake are we killed all the day long; we are counted as sheep for the slaughter". [63]

The second source of affliction is the Christian himself, which Barth seems to understand as the Christian's insistence on being non-violent in the face of violent persecution. [64] At times the Christian may have to resort to violence in a very limited way, even though he knows this to be contradictory to the reconciling action by God with and in the world. But as one in solidarity with the rest of humanity, the Christian also exists under the conditions and presuppositions of the world. Therefore, he may have at times to resort to what Barth describes as "a very cautious, provisional, incidental and temporary use of the doubtful means of protection of a humanity not yet aware of its liberation." [65] In this way the Christian with the tension of inner affliction in the exercise of vocation is like a sheep amidst wolves (Lk. 10:3):

> Nor are they sent out as wolfhounds, who can bite no less powerfully than the wolves themselves, and are a good match for them, but as creatures who have no power to fight them and by human reckoning can only be chased and devoured by them. This is not a very heroic or comforting aspect of Christian existence. There is nothing here for Nietzsche. [66]

The third source of affliction is Jesus Christ Himself, who in His fellowship with the Christian summons him into situations which collide and conflict with the world's mores and values.

> The world would not be the world which has to oppose him, which has to be for him a world of wolves, were it not that it is already shaken and threatened to its foundations, and thus challenged to withstand and resist, by the self-witness of Jesus Christ. . . . Its opposition and resistance detected by the Christian in affliction is its reaction to the action of Jesus Christ in fulfillment of His prophetic office. . . . [67]

The world's resistance is shown by its affliction of the Christian. This means that the source both of the inner and the outer affliction is really the same: Jesus Christ. That is, Jesus Christ is both a source of worldly insecurity but also worldly security.

> In affliction, in face of it and through it, he is set in
> the ministry laid upon him, and summoned, engaged and
> challenged to discharge it, in order that in so doing he
> may be and become that man who is absolutely secure.
> [68]

Vocation and Political Consequences

Amidst such odds and experiences, what is the modus
operandi which impels Christians to execute their vocation in
such a world? Barth insists that it is the element of the new
which is shown in Jesus Christ--an element which may or may
not be recognized by the rest of the world but is known by the
Christian. That newness is that in Jesus Christ one is concerned
in a most fundamental sense with God and His work. But to say
this in the light of Jesus Christ also is to say that one is concerned with humanity, "the very impure, historical and sinful
humanity which has fallen away from God and fallen out with
itself, with the 'flesh of sin'." [69] The new is that He not only
became at one with it and identified with it in all its sinfulness,
but that He redeemed it.

> The Christian community hears this Word, sees this work
> and knows this person as it hears and sees and knows
> the One whose call is the basis and meaning of its own
> existence. Hence, what it perceives in this One is not
> merely an illumination of world history, but its correction
> and reformation. The gulf is not merely bridged; it is
> closed. [70]

World history and man's existence lose the character of alienation
and contradiction under the lordship of Jesus Christ the reconciler.

With this assurance and confidence, the Christian is
free to participate in political and social change and events,
for he knows that, whilst they are to be taken seriously and
worked at seriously, yet at the same time it is what Barth calls
a "penultimate seriousness". [71]

> Hence (the Church) can share neither the enthusiasm
> of those who regard the old form as capable of true
> and radical improvement nor the skepticism of those
> who in view of the impossibility of perfecting the old
> form think that they are compelled to doubt the possibility
> of a new form. . . . In face of the disorder of historical
> relationships and interconnexions it can yield neither
> to reactionary spasms on the one hand nor to revolutionary
> on the other; because in relation to the reality of history

> already present in Jesus Christ it knows how provisional
> and improper is all the construction and destruction of
> man. [72]

This is also the basis of hope which shapes the motivation of Christians acting in society--a hope grounded in the coming Lord who is already Lord.

Furthermore, it signifies that the Christian and the Christian community are to be active and visible in all aspects of human affairs. The Church cannot regard itself as a "disembodied spirit" in human society.

> There can be no excluding the attempts to understand
> it (the church) in the categories of general sociology
> as a union or society or specifically a religious fellowship,
> and therefore historically as a link in, or possibly as
> the supreme product of, the history of the development
> of such unions. . . . The Christian community is not merely
> ad extra and visible, ad extra and worldly. [73]

Yet there is also an invisible part of the Christian community's vocation, which, whilst not of immediate interest for purposes of this chapter, nevertheless ought to be noted. That is, the Christian community also distinguishes itself from other worldly institutions. It may even be in opposition to other institutions.

> It is the very fact that its historical existence in all
> its spatio-temporal and human concreteness is determined
> by the will and work and Word of God which constitutes
> the invisible essence of the people of God. We are thus
> dealing with its invisibly determined visible being even
> when mythological notions, images, and expressions are
> used. . . . [74]

This allows both for a dependence on and an independence from the conditions of political and social affairs because of the implicit eschatological and invisible character of the Church. This further allows the Christian community to adapt itself to a variety of political environments in order to witness to the prophecy of Jesus Christ, even though it may also oppose the principles of the society which dominate and surround it.

> There has never been anywhere a distinctive answer
> penetrating this circle, an intrinsically sacred sociology.
> Obviously, there is no such thing, just as there is no
> absolutely distinctive or intrinsically sacred language.
> In this respect, too, the people of God exist in worldly
> fashion within world-occurrence. [75]

It is the freedom to move across national and historical boundaries, says Barth, which gives the Christian community a great flexibility in acting socially and politically.

Such a vocation and witness place a special responsibility on the Christian community within the world-occurrence. First, the Christian community has the task of helping "men to know the world as it is." [76] The world cannot recognize itself in its divisions and its estrangement from God and within itself. It does not have a total perspective of the various forms and forces of estrangement. This is a part of learning about the world which is instructive for Christians also.

> To know man is to see and understand, how in fact all men, the strong and the weak, the clever and the foolish, the able and the needy, the leaders and their willing or unwilling followers, the indolent and the industrious, the religious and the irreligious, the apparently or genuinely law-abiding and the crude or refined transgressors, the Western and Eastern orators, newspaper men and liars, the men whose interest and orientation are academic, technical, aesthetic, political, or ecclesiastical, and the men who have no interests or orientation at all. . . . [77]

Secondly, the community can be the model where all people can see, know, and practice a common solidarity which exists amongst humanity. The Christian community cannot flee from the world, for in making such a flight, it would be unfaithful to its own Christ-given commission to be worldly.

> Solidarity with the world means full commitment to it, unreserved participation in its situation, in the promise given it by creation, in its responsibility for the arrogance, sloth, and falsehood which reigns within it, in its suffering under the resultant distress, but primarily and supremely in the free grace of God demonstrated and addressed to it in Jesus Christ, and therefore in its hope. [78]

Christians are to be like fools willing to be amongst other fools. Indeed, in an interesting reversal of the conventional idea about the Church endangering itself when it conforms to the world, Barth claims that when the Christian community is concerned with its own purity and reputation, it is in fact conforming to the world, for the world understands itself as having concern only for its own self and its own values, dividing people into factions and groups, parties and sects, each claiming a certain imperialism over against others:

> And it can quietly acquiesce in this lack and find justifica-
> tion for its sectarianism if it discovers that the community
> of Jesus Christ finally suffers from the same deficiency,
> that it takes the form only of another and perhaps more
> radical separation, that it does not accept the solidarity
> of its particular humanity with all other good or bad
> human manifestations. . . . Coming from the table of
> the Lord (the community) cannot fail to follow His example
> and sit down at table with the rest, with all sinners. [79]

Finally, the Church, like Christ, is under an obligation to help shape the world. As Christ suffered with the world and was active for it, so the Christian community must also act accordingly. The Church cannot be passive or neutral about problems and struggles in the world's political and social circumstances. [80]

Barth tries to identify the particular theological ways in which vocation is to be exercised in the immediate social and political conditions of the world at large. He describes them as the diaconate, [81] the prophetic, [82] and the establishment of fellowship (Gemeinschaftsbegründung). [83] The primary witness of the diaconate function of vocation is to serve those within and without the Christian community who are in material distress. This is manifested in helping people become masters of their situation. [84] Yet it also means identifying with the least able of society, the obscure and the marginal in society, "with those who are in obscurity and are not seen, with those who are pushed to the margin and perhaps the very outer margin of the life of human society, with fellow-creatures who temporarily at least, and perhaps permanently, are useless and insignificant and perhaps even burdensome and destructive." [85] The diaconate particularly seeks out such and identifies with them as brothers and sisters in Christ.

Such a diaconate takes several directions politically and socially. First, it is concerned with the whole environment and condition of all people. This means both intervening as advocate on behalf of the marginal or obscure person and at the same time recognizing the limitations of intervention in the light of certain fundamental disorders in the very fabric of human society. [86]

> This recognition will not cause the diaconate to refrain
> from fulfilling its task at the frontier set by these relation-
> ships. But it cannot refrain from expressing this recognition,
> from imparting it to the community in order that the
> latter may raise its voice and with its proclamation of
> the Gospel summon the world to reflect on social injustice
> and its consequences and to alter the conditions and

> relationships in question. In this situation there is need
> for the open word of Christian social criticism in order
> that a new place may be found for Christian action
> and a new meaning given to it. [87]

More often than not, says Barth, the Christian community has been silent or indifferent like a _stummer Hund_ serving the ruling powers in society. [88]

Secondly, the diaconate functions with the knowledge that it is limited and indeed always under threat by the state, particularly in the exercise of social welfare programs. The state has often taken over such social welfare functions formerly done by the church's diaconate. But this does not eliminate this function of the diaconate, for the state can only look after the material and physical needs of the neglected. The diaconate can serve the state by looking after the whole man and by helping to get people with a similar vision into public office. [89]

Thirdly, the entire Christian community must be engaged in the diaconate. It is not enough to let an order of deacons be responsible for the diaconate in society.

The carrying out of vocation in prophetic action means a witnessing to the tensions between the current events and structures of the present world and the commands of the kingdom of God. This provides perspective for Christian political and social action, which can also be service to the world. [90]

Finally, Christian vocation has to do with the establishment of fellowship between men. In a word this is a kind of secular ecumenicity and solidarity initiated and nourished by the Christian community as an obligation, but also as an important sustaining and renewing component of its own life. Such a fellowship transcends national and geographical boundaries. It neither removes nor sanctions these boundaries; it simply moves across them.

Politically, such a fellowship means that racism in any form cannot be tolerated by the Church on any account, even though it recognizes the values that cultural and racial differences carry with them.

> But this cannot in any sense or circumstance mean that
> appeal can be made to supposed orders of creation or
> sin, or even to Christian love, for the legitimate or even
> necessary dividing of the community into special white,
> black, and brown congregations. This cannot and must
> not happen because the community owes to the world
> a witness, not to the quality, but to the mutual fellowship
> of men. . . . [91]

Ecclesiastically, it means that no church can simply rely on its own national boundaries and historical similarity or tribalism as the basis for claiming a full consciousness of its vocation as a Christian community. Says Barth, very emphatically: "a national church in the strict and serious sense would necessarily be a sick church since it would resist the witness to the fellowship of all nations. . . . " [92]

Culturally, the establishment of fellowship signifies that there cannot be two Gospels--one for the cultured and intelligent and another for the uncultured and less intelligent or however expressed in similar cultural terms. Cultural patterns denote difference, but they cannot become barriers for the witnessing community. Under this heading, Barth also considers class differences, which he says cannot be taken seriously by the Church as a means of separating the community from the rest of the world. Rather the Christian community must relativize class differences:

> It has thus to address the middle classes neither positively nor negatively in terms of their capitalistic ideas and attitudes, nor the proletariat in terms of their socialistic, but both zealously on the basis of the fact that as men they are called and may be the children of God, that as such they may expect all good things only from His hand, that as such they are responsible only to Him, but that as such they are thus united and belong to one another. [93]

This attack on class divisions provides even more of an insight into Barth's claim that the constant dynamic of the Christian community internally is to realize the "revolution of God" and externally to make the "revolution of God" realizable. This may mean that the Church in various places in particular times can support a political program which is not always the same as that fellowship but which is intended to promote that fellowship:

> The Christian community both can and should espouse the cause of this or that branch of social progress or even socialism in the form most helpful at a specific time and place and in a specific situation. But its decisive word cannot consist in the proclamation of social progress or socialism. It can consist only in the proclamation of the revolution of God against "all ungodliness and unrighteousness of man" (Rom. 1:18), i.e, in the proclamation of His kingdom as it has already come and comes. [94]

The model for such action even with its relativity in terms of the final word of God is Jesus Christ as the royal man who ignored the high and mighty for solidarity with the lowly, the just for the sinners, Israel for the Gentiles. It was to those marginal groups in society in terms of possessions and success that Jesus particularly looked and with whom He established fellowship:

> In fellowship and conformity with this God who is poor in the world, the royal man Jesus is also poor, and fulfills the transvaluation of all values, acknowledging those who (without necessarily being better) are in different ways poor men as this world counts poverty. [95]

The revolutionary character of Jesus' action is that He sets all programs, principles, and societies into question. He is able to do this because He has a freedom which is only ascribed to royalty, independent of class or societal boundaries as a source of His authority. He simply reveals the limits and frontiers of groups and movements in the light of the kingdom of God and the freedom which accompanies that kingdom. [96] Jesus Christ is a revolutionary because He breaks all bonds and expectation and establishes new historical situations for those who can see and hear His word. All institutions are put into question because of this.

This is an important feature of God's revolution for, as Barth says, one does not know God if He is not known as the one who is the opposite of all the expectations and roles which man designs. God is absolutely opposed to our fallen world as the Judge of that world. Yet in spite of this, the last word of God, as well as Jesus, is that He is not against man but for him, even perverse man. Jesus Christ echoes the divine Yes as the royal man. That this is contrary to and opposite from man's expectations is shown in the decision of Jesus to be Himself a sufferer and a partisan of the poor. The fact of the new is shown in the revolutionary way that both the poor and the meek are called blessed in spite of their misery and the promise that they shall inherit the kingdom of heaven. [97]

Reconciliation and Political Directions

It remains to enquire about the concrete consequences of these processes in our society and world. How does Barth relate the theological understanding of the reconciliation between God and us, between us and our fellowman, and between the individual and himself with the concrete situation in reconciled and redeemed society? [98] What are the political and social actions characterizing the reconciled and redeemed society which do not characterize the unreconciled and unredeemed society? What political goals and directions undergo alterations, if any?

That is, in order to avoid simply an abstraction of society, to borrow an expression from Marx's critique of Hegel's idea of society and the state, what is the character of the particular "mundane existence" of mankind's actuality? [**99**]

First, in the redeemed society people are no longer driven toward unitary, private existences, but rather toward solidarity. In the light of God's grace which has been revealed to humankind and which has shaped the redeemed society, acting and speaking along the old lines are meaningless. The "Now" of God's grace marks off the present from the past and the future.

> "No" is what this Word says, and in so doing it forestalls the decision of those to whom it is spoken by confronting them with this accomplished inversion, this decision which is so pregnant for their own existence, as one which has taken place without any agreement or cooperation on their part, which their own decision in freedom must follow, but which it can only follow as a decision which is truly free. It is of this that the Word of the grace of God speaks as pronounced in Jesus Christ. [**100**]

When he was unreconciled, man felt free to be his own savior, to order his own relationship with God, with the world, and with himself. These efforts were analyzed by Barth under the headings of pride and the subsequent fall of man, sloth and the subsequent misery of man, falsehood and the subsequent condemnation. Related to this understanding of being free, the person who does not know his reconciliation thinks he is free to live in anxiety before God, his fellowman, and even himself. He thinks he is free constantly to complain, to worry, to accuse, to protest always, to be quarreling with someone or with something all the time. [**101**] Furthermore, he believes that he is free to be resigned in a kind of pathological way, to be a spectator to the affairs of society, to withdraw from the world and from the fellowship of others when he so chooses. But to each of these problems, the Word of God marks off a sharp demarcation.

In reply to the first point about our wanting to be our own reconciler, Barth says that the Word of God does not tell man that it is wrong or perverted in some moralistic sense. Rather

> it tells him that he cannot help himself because he is already helped. It thus tells him that all his activity in this respect belongs to the old aeon, that there is no place for it now that this has passed . . . it asks him what is the point of his life and thought and speech apart from and even against the grace of God. . . . [**102**]

With respect to the second problem about unreconciled man wanting to be able to live anxiously and to be negative all the time, Barth says that the Word of God does not lecture him, telling him that he must not bother other people or give way to anxiety. Rather

> it tells him something far more basic, namely, that he cannot do this, that he does not have the freedom, capacity or strength for this anxiety and its explosions, since the only convincing ground for it is removed, destroyed and overcome in and with that which has taken place as the reconciliation of the world. [103]

Nor is the assumed freedom of the unreconciled man to resign from being active in social and political affairs an alternative for the reconciled man.

> For in virtue of the establishment of the lordship of God on earth in Jesus Christ, it is decided that there is no further place for the existence of a non-participant who is neutral towards others and himself, who accepts no responsibilities or duties, who at any rate takes partial leave of absence, who is a mere spectator . . . . [104]

The justification, sanctification, and vocation of redeemed humanity established in Jesus Christ indicates and proclaims that we are now truly free to let ourselves go for and with others in solidarity and fellowship. Indeed this solidarity with others becomes a fundamental component of our humanity and our calling. It is no longer a question of whether reconciled Christians will or will not participate in and take responsibility for problems and issues in society; they simply do because God has bound the world to Himself and Himself to the world. [105] This is the goal and direction also of the redeemed society--solidarity and fellowship amongst each other.

> He cannot then be alone under a glass-case or behind asbestos sheeting. No, God has him now, and so, too, the world and men. For he has God, the world, and men, and therefore he cannot be alone but only in contact, solidarity and fellowship both vertically and horizontally. He can now be a lord only as in his own place and manner he is a servant. [106]

Barth insists that this is true liberation, that solidarity and fellowship by their very nature in light of God's reconciling event mean action socially and politically. To lose sight of this means that the Christian's humanity becomes inhumanity. [107]

Secondly, the character of the redeemed society and the redeemed man means a liberation from the enslavement by things and absolute principles. That is, there is the political direction aimed at a humanization of society in which people are the first priority instead of institutions, causes, and even ideologies:

> Hence, the smallest sigh or laugh of a man is surely more important to Him than the support of the most important institutions, the construction and working of the most marvelous apparatus, the development of the most lofty or profound ideas. Similarly, it is for the sake of men and not of things that the Christian, himself a man among men, is called to be a witness and exists as such. [108]

Under "sloth" Barth had pointed out the concealment of hypocrisy whose intention and achievement is the dehumanization of man through causes or principles. It occurs when systems, ideas, programs, institutions become more important than the human being whom they are to serve. Man is reduced to anonymity, to a thing.

> It can sometimes, as in Europe and America, disguise itself as ceaseless activity. It can cloak itself behind pure scholarship or pure art, or behind the promotion of the common interests of a national or economic or intellectual group, or behind officialdom with its concern for the regular functioning of an official apparatus. . . . Not least, the Church itself, the proclamation and hearing of the Word of God, the confession and doctrine and liturgy and order of the Church, and even its theology, offer a vast opportunity for philanthropic activity which is devoid of true humanity. All these things are "causes" which in their context do not lack the appearance of human justification, necessity and value. [109]

When one is treated like a thing, then the entire relationship between his body and soul collapses, for such treatment isolates him from his fellowman, without whom he is not human. Not even a preoccupation with good causes can restore this relationship or substitute for concern for man and humanity, since the danger is that the cause itself will become the dominant motivating factor. [110]

Within the redeemed society, one cannot ignore causes or even things which are important and necessary for the maintenance and improvement of one's daily life and existence in society. But the Christian, that is, the redeemed person who acknowledges this fact and whose vocation is determined by this fact, will take care that **things** do not tyrannize people:

> In the case of conflict he will always prefer man and
> the human to machinery and gadgets, and if need be
> he will joyfully renounce most, if not all, of the latter.
> As he stands on the basis of the decision for man taken
> in Jesus Christ . . . man takes precedence over things,
> and things--however great or even sacred--can never
> be preferred to man. [111]

Thirdly, liberation of humankind and society through
the reconciling act of God in Jesus Christ means that the possess-
ing role of capital as the operating motif in unredeemed society
is ended. Capital as the possessor of man in unredeemed society
means that the employer can be quite arbitrary with the distribu-
tion of labor. It is the individual employer who determines the
character of the productive process in such a society. Barth
maintains that it is to be society which must determine the goals
of labor and that it cannot delegate this to private ownership: [112]

> If the great mass of employees themselves think and
> judge in what is at bottom a "capitalistic" or unthinking
> way in relation to the question of ends, we need not
> be surprised if the proponents of these ends, the relatively
> few employers and politicians, do so to an even greater
> extent. [113]

In the capitalistic society the employer need not pay any attention
to the criterion of **humanity** when setting out the goals of jobs
offered. That is, one need think only or primarily of satisfying
oneself, forgetting that one must also be concerned for and work
with others. [114] It is a society resting on the foundation of
exploitation whose structural character is intimately linked with
private capital in spite of some progressive social programs:

> Finally, it can be urged that many of the arguments
> which could be brought against this system in its heyday
> are now out of date, that today there is in any case
> no such thing as pure and undiluted "capitalism", and
> that events have falsified . . . more than one of the
> prophecies of doom pronounced over it, e.g., the increasing
> enrichment of fewer and fewer wealthy persons, the
> developing proletarianisation of even the middle classes,
> and the cumulative misery of the masses, especially of
> the proletariat who have nothing to lose but their chains.
> Nevertheless, of what avail are all these arguments in
> face of the simple fact that this system does permit
> in practice and demand in principle that man should
> make another man and his work a means to his own
> ends, and therefore a mere instrument, and that this
> is inhuman and therefore constitutes an injustice? [115]

In the redeemed society, the Christian, in perceiving this disorder in the labor process, will keep to the "left", that is, on the side of the victims of this process and the oppressed. [116] Even if the Christian should have to support socialism, he needs to be mindful of its political relativity in terms of the "not yet" goal of God's reconciliation with the world.

> The relativity of even the most radical attempt at reform in the guise of "revolution" simply proves again that whatever can be done by men or said by Christians in the direction of such attempts can have only relative significance and force. It is again made clear that the root of the troubles lies deeper, namely, in a human aberration which necessarily gives rise to the exploitation of man by man in ever-changing forms--so necessarily that even the most well-meaning and rigorous attempts at counter-movement can arrest and modify but not entirely remove it. [117]

In the redeemed society the humanization of the socio-economical structure occurs decisively as that structure affects and shapes the labor process. This objective can be measured by the ways in which man's labor no longer enslaves him but frees him for service.

> (Man) is in no sense a reliable guarantor and custodian of his own freedom either as freedom for God or freedom for life. His work, therefore, must be protected against becoming this threat. It must not overwhelm him, neither must he be overwhelmed and enslaved by it. It must not become absolute, wholly engulfing and mastering him. . . . He may and should rest from all his work; otherwise he cannot do it aright. [118]

This service of the redeemed man in redeemed society is done both on behalf of his fellowmen and to the state, which again means that the Christian politically cannot be passive. Barth describes this service by Christians as the Church's guarantee given to the state:

> It then means that the essential service of the Church to the State simply consists in maintaining and occupying its own realm as Church. In so doing it will secure, in the best possible way, the position of the State, which is quite different. By proclaiming divine justification it will be rendering the best possible assistance to the establishment and maintenance of human justice and law. [119]

That Barth understands this direction of the redeemed society to be achieved through the political praxis of something akin to socialism or social democracy is evident from his criticism of the political and economic system of the West, which, he maintains, is founded upon and sustained by the exploitation of the weak by the strong. [120] The political praxis related to these directions and objectives in the redeemed society will be discussed later, but at this point it is important to notice that Barth, whilst not embracing Karl Marx, certainly understands the strength of his attack on capitalism:

> The injustice of the treatment of one man by another merely as a means to his own ends, as a mere instrument, once rested on a foundation of private capital, and still does so in the West. . . . (The Church) hardly has any right, therefore, to lay its finger today on the signs that state socialism, notwithstanding its pretended abolition of this injustice, might finally amount only to a new and perhaps even crasser form of the oppression and exploitation of man by man. This may or may not be so, but Christianity in the West has its main work cut out to comprehend the disorder in the decisive form still current in the West. . . . [121]

Barth advances the idea that the redeemed community in obedience to the command of God should measure man's labor by certain criteria in order to liberate it from the exploitative character which shapes that labor under capitalism. These criteria are:

1) **Objectivity,** by which is meant man strives for particular ends and goals in his life and that the righteous or "righteousness" of his work is to be measured by its doing justice to each specific goal and end. [122]

2) **The worth of human work** by which is meant whether human existence is served by the labor. [123]

3) **Humanity of human work** by which is meant work done in cooperation and co-existence with one's fellowman. [124]

4) **Reflection** by which is meant self-fulfillment in order that labor not become mechanical. [125]

5) **The limitation of labor and work** by which is meant that leisure is also essential for man's active life and work. [126]

All of this is a part of service to the state, even in its unredeemed areas, since the authority of the state and its foundations are included within the lordship of Jesus Christ. Even when acknowledging the unredeemed society within the state, the Church, maintains Barth, still "honors" the state, for it is by such acknowledgment that the Church defends the state against itself. That is, it seeks to remind the state of its true authority and role. [127] Barth suggests that such a role by the Church is particularly important when the state tries to claim "love" from its citizens and subjects:

> The just State requires, not love, but a simple, resolute, and responsible attitude on the part of its citizens. It is this attitude which the Church, based on justification, commends to its members. [128]

Hence, observes Barth, the Church cannot react to the state as though "it lived, in relation to the State, in a night in which all cats are grey." [129] The Church can make distinctions between states, both those of yesterday and those of today. The Church can be discerning in determining the correlation between the state's claim and demand of authority and loyalty and its true role in extending justice.

Therefore, in summarizing the effects of reconciliation on society and the world, Barth maintains that through justification, man's existence in society has been decisively altered, whether he acknowledges it or not. Those who do acknowledge their justification, namely, the Christian community, respond in the "work" of faith and exist in solidarity with, and therefore, in concern for all of mankind. Such an existence continues under a real freedom which liberates the Christian for new ventures and visions of society and the internal work of that society.

Through sanctification, the justified man is summoned to effecting the fact of justification in society. This is what Barth calls man's "work" of **discipleship**--people who work and exist for a new society in light of the knowledge that the new creation already is at work in the world through Jesus Christ. This is "God's revolution" which has definite social and political consequences in terms of property and possessions, value systems, the role of force and violence, and working for justice on behalf of all of mankind.

Through vocation, the reconciled man and the community make more explicit the service amongst their fellowmen which is implicit in justification and sanctification. Man's "work" to justification is **faith,** to sanctification **discipleship,** and to vocation **gratitude.** It is in the exercise of vocation that the worldliness of the Christian is particularly tested and affirmed. It results in various forms of affliction, as well as special obligations of service--service to the world in the sense of structures and institutions and service to society in terms of examining ideals and goals which shape that society. Here the Christian community has a summons to reflect something of the nature of the redeemed society for the benefit of the state, which is not and cannot be a second church or the kingdom of God. Barth understands this third aspect of man's task under reconciliation, namely, his vocation to be carried out particularly in **diaconia**, in the prophetic, and in the establishment of fellowship with others in the world. Each of these, in turn, also have particular social and political services attached to them as well as ecclesiastical roles for the internal life of the community.

It is when one tries to spell out these aspects of reconciliation in societal terms that one derives certain political directions and goals which will guide political praxis. Amongst these political directions and goals of the civil community under such a mandate are:

1) The goal of solidarity existence rather than unitary, private existence.

2) Humanity as the first priority in society rather than things, institutions, ideas, and causes.

3) The socialization of capital and the humanizing of labor rather than the institutionalizing of private capital and the exploitation of human labor, which will resemble social democracy.

These political directions and goals, however, must be linked with political praxis and institutions.

Chapter Six

POLITICAL CHRISTOLOGY AND PRAXIS

It has already been suggested in the previous chapter, Karl Barth uses what might cautiously be described as a method of correlation to determine the theological basis for political goals and directions in society. These goals and directions are related to what I am suggesting might be called "unredeemed" and "redeemed" society and therefore to two movements within the same society. That is, the nature of political goals and directions do indeed have a different character and telos in the unredeemed society than in the redeemed society, but they are two movements or dialectics which do occur together in one society.

One may summarize these differences as follows: the unredeemed society is characterized by an obsession for a unitary, private existence at all levels in that society, both privately and collectively, both economically and politically. One seeks to be his own savior and to order his own relationship with God, with his fellowman, and with himself apart from Jesus Christ. One is driven toward individualism (Individualismus) and egoism through pride, which leads to his fall; through sloth, which leads to his being miserable; and through lying, which leads to his anxiety of being condemned. In the redeemed society man is driven toward solidarity with fellowman, reconciliation with God, and true freedom within himself, which have been established in the event of justification, sanctification, and vocation in Jesus Christ. "(Man) can now be a lord only as in his own place and manner he is a servant." [1] These events also shape the political goals and directions of redeemed society.

A second difference in the political goals and directions is that in the unredeemed society the survival of things and institutions have a first priority. Such a priority results in the dehumanization of man through systems, programs, and even ideas, which reduce him to a commodity. Such a reduction leads toward isolation between people, which is really inhumanity, since authentic humanity is fellow-humanity (Mitmenschlichkeit). Within the redeemed society man moves toward solidarity with fellowman, and as such the enrichment and advancement of humanity rather than the enrichment and advancement of institutions, and even ideas or ideologies, have first priority. The fact that one gives things and institutions priority in the unredeemed society has the consequence of enslaving us to their preservation and at the same time allows these things and institutions to exercise a tyranny over us. Such a phenomenon is most noticeable in that one area of our creaturely existence which is fundamentally crucial to our own self-affirmation and identity as well as to our link with our fellowman, namely, our labor.

Barth's interpretation of labor and its function in society has been described in a previous chapter. His emphasis upon its crucial function as a link between man and his own self-identity and affirmation as well as between himself and nature, fellowman, and God reminds one of Karl Marx's understanding of labor's function. For Marx, labor is a fundamental vehicle for self-affirmation, self-worth, and self-creation:

> Labour is a process in which both man and nature participate, and in which man of his own accord starts, regulates, and controls the material reactions between himself and nature. . . . By thus acting on the external world and changing it, he at the same time changes his nature. He develops his slumbering powers and compels them to act in obedience to his sway. [2]

For this reason the division of labor on the basis of private ownership for Marx as for Barth leads always to internal alienation within the individual and the body corporate and to a privatization of labor as evident in the **Kampf ums Dasein**. As Marx remarks in **The German Ideology**:

> With the division of labour, in which all these conflicts are implicit and which is based on the natural division of labour in the family and in the partition of society into individual families opposing one another, there is at the same time distribution, indeed unequal distribution, both quantitative and qualitative, of labour and its products, hence property has its first form, its nucleus, in the family where wife and children are the slaves of the man. . . . Furthermore, the division of labour implies the conflict between the interest of the individual or the individual family and the communal interest of all individuals having contact with one another. The communal interest does not exist only in the imagination, as something "general", but first of all in reality, as a mutual interdependence of those individuals among whom the labour is divided. [3]

Barth speaks of alienation or dehumanization in the labor process resulting in the worker being plagued by anxiety and conflict within himself and by suspicion, isolation, and conflict between himself and his fellowmen. [4]

A third difference to be observed between the political goals and directions of the two societies is the role of capital and capitalism. Capitalism is privatization of property and human relations par excellence, according to Barth. Both the attitudes and actions of the holders and the beholden of capital are shaped by this possession:

> From this twofold evil root, namely, from this twofold thoughtlessness in respect of the social character of work and the true and vital necessity of the profit sought, everything else unfortunately follows. . . . [5]

This role of capital has particularly fostered and nurtured the class struggle within western industrial societies and results in exploitation in the labor process. But, as has already been pointed out in a previous chapter, the possibility of exploitation of the worker exists in socialist societies as well, although not by those privately owning capital.

The use of the term "correlation" as a possible character-istic of Barth's method of relating these political goals and direc-tions--goals and directions which implicitly are linked to and emerge from theological reflection--to political praxis [6] is an appropriate one, provided that it is not understood in Tillich's sense of correlation. Tillich sought to provide theological answers to what he called "existential questions" arising out of our experi-ence of the finiteness of human experience and the angst ensuing:

> Theology formulates the questions implied in human exist-ence, and theology formulates the answers implied in divine self-manifestation under the guidance of the ques-tions implied in human existence. This is a circle which drives man to a point where question and answer are not separated. [7]

Barth, using the category of the "humanity" of God as revealed and lived in Jesus Christ has God both posing the question of the "essentialness" of man's being in Jesus Christ and providing the answer in justification, sanctification, and vocation. That is, redeemed sinful man is to measure his being or humanity against the true humanity revealed by God in Jesus Christ. But the very category of **true humanity** is not to be under-stood apart from its correlation and acting out in political and social actions in society nor apart from the goals and directions of the redeemed society. Balthasar suggests that the modus operan-

_di_ for Barth in understanding Jesus Christ to be both the crisis and the resolution of the relationship between God and man, man and himself, and man and his neighbor is Barth's appropriation of Anselm's fides quaerens intellectum. [8]

It is in the concreteness of Jesus Christ that humankind's concreteness is first to be found with all the existential questions about his existence and essentialness or essence attached to that concreteness. [9] As Barth himself claims:

> As the Son of God and not otherwise, Jesus Christ is the Son of Man. This sequence is irreversible. God's independence, omnipotence, and eternity, God's holiness and justice, and thus God's deity . . . is the power leading to this superiority preceding subordination. **Thus we have here no universal deity capable of being reached conceptually, but this concrete deity--real and recognizable in the descent grounded in that sequence and peculiar to the existence of Jesus Christ.** [10]

Furthermore, as we affirm our humanity in the light of the true humanity in Jesus Christ, we are impelled to affirm not only the existence and situation of our fellowmen, but also to act on their behalf in political and social spheres. Indeed, Barth suggests that much of the appeal of Marxism to the working classes and much of the reason why the Church has not been able to refute it successfully in the past has been because Marxism understood and continues to understand the one important component of our humanity which the Church has neglected and even violated at times: the fundamental link between soul and body and the way that this unity between them is affected by economic and political stuctures and relations. [11] The problem with Marx, however, is that he neglected the soul and therefore, in the long run, violated true humanity. But he understood the interdependence between the two, particularly in seeking change in structures, relations, and environment:

> Man is (1) creaturely life--life which by the will and act of the living God is awakened, created and called into temporal existence as the individual life of a body. He is _living_ being. And he is (2) creaturely being--being which by the will and act of the same God has a certain spatial form or besouled body. He is living _being_. [12]

But Barth is not content only to have outlined the political goals and directions of the redeemed society. He seeks to give form and shape to these goals in political praxis. It is here that correlation becomes most apparent. As mentioned in the previous chapter, in redeemed society:

1) One is free through the grace of God to reorder his relationship to the world in that he no longer has to be a spectator in society because he is free from anxiety before God, himself, and his fellowman, knowing that he has already been helped in Jesus Christ.

2) One is free to establish solidarity and fellowship with his fellowman and thereby to realize the liberation established in Jesus Christ, both from the enslavement to things and absolute principles and for venturesome ideas and revolutionary action.

3) One is free to affirm the decision for man taken in Jesus Christ which means that humanity is given precedence and priority over things and causes.

4) One is freed from being possessed by a capitalistic value system which relies on exploitation of fellowman by fellowman in the unredeemed society and which Barth characterizes as a supreme example of thoughtlessness, and

5) One is free to act politically on the basis of the criteria established in the redeemed society as measuring rods for testing the worth of labor in society. [13]

Professor Helmut Gollwitzer, one of Barth's erstwhile students and interpreters, points out that Barth's understanding of the character of political praxis was really shaped by his experience and activities in Safenwil. They shaped his decision to move toward the left. Barth seldom uses socialism to characterize his own interpretation of political praxis in redeemed society because that expression for him has become too misleading, too idologically misunderstood, too cliche-ridden. But, claims Gollwitzer, it is the decisive character of his thinking about redeemed society. [14] Barth includes both reform and revolution as a part of the dynamic of political models for the redeemed society. [15] Jesus Christ gives substance to these kinds of models:

> But again, we do not really know Jesus (the Jesus of the New Testament) if we do not know Him as this poor man, as this (if we may risk the dangerous word) partisan of the poor, and finally as this revolutionary. We have to be warned, therefore, against every attempt to interpret and use Him as a further and perhaps supreme self-manifestation and self-actualisation of the old Adam. [16]

Gollwitzer describes this as Barth's steady determination that the theological modus operandi will always be the humanization (Vermenschlichung) of political practices and programs. [17] But it is a Vermenschlichung which first centers around advocacy and defense on behalf of the poor, oppressed, and the dispossessed groups in society. This is an important clue for Barth's criticism of western capitalism and eastern socialism.

> In the East there is arbitrary rule of the almighty party, propaganda, and police, but in the West we are surrounded by an equally tyrannous press, systems of private enterprize, snobbish presumption and public opinion. . . . Anyone who fails to resist the Western lion (reference to I Peter 5:9) with all his might will certainly not be able, either, to resist the Eastern lion. [18]

The first instrument or program for realizing these goals is, contrary to Prof. Marquardt's claim, not socialism, but rather social democracy, or what could be called "socialized democracy." This, too, has already been alluded to in the previous chapter, but ought to be spelt out in more detail. The link between social democracy as a political program for furthering the benefits of the person and work of Jesus Christ for the whole of mankind was already established and advanced by young pastor Barth in his sessions with the radical wing of the Swiss Social Democratic Party in Aargau:

> Jesus is the movement for social justice (soziale Bewegung), and the movement for social justice is Jesus in the present . . . The real contents of the person of Jesus can in fact be summed up by the words "movement for social justice". [19]

Barth devotes little attention to the ideological basis for social democracy as envisioned by such people as Ferdinand Lassalle (1825-1864) or August Bebel (1840-1913) or even the Gothaer Programm (1875). [20] Rather social democracy is seen by him as an institutionalized corrective program for political action aimed at ending the dehumanizing elements in unredeemed society. That is, for young Barth and for the older Barth in the **Church Dogmatics** the worker and the oppressed were both the central concern of and the testing measure for the worthiness of any political program:

> Socialism is the movement of the economically dependent, of those who earn wages working for somebody else, for a stranger; the movement of the proletariat. . . . The proletarian is not always poor, but is always dependent in his existence upon the means and the goodwill of his brother, the factory owner. Here socialism sets in. . . . It wants to make independent those who are dependent, with all the consequences for their external, moral, and cultural life which that would bring with it. Now one cannot say that Jesus also began precisely at this point . . .

> And yet it must strike everyone who reads his Old Testa-
> ment without prejudice that that which Jesus Christ was
> and wanted and attained, as seen from the human side,
> was entirely a <u>movement from below.</u> . . . [21]

One has to notice also that the dynamic of <u>untern nach
oben und oben nach untern</u> is significant for Barth both theologically in dialectical theology and politically in praxis. One also
has to notice that even in this model Barth does not exclude
the factory owners, the bosses, who are described as "brother"
and "co-worker", a phrase Barth used in an address to workers
in the radical left-wing of the Swiss Democratic Party in 1911:

> Capitalism is the system of production which makes the
> proletariat into the proletariat, <u>i.e.</u>, into a dependent
> wage earner whose existence is constantly insecure.
> The materials necessary for production (investment, capital,
> factories, machines, raw materials) are the <u>private property</u>
> of one of the co-workers, namely, the boss, the factory
> owner. The other co-worker (the "worker") possesses
> nothing but the power of his labour, which he furnishes
> to the factory owner. Socialism declares that it is unjust
> to pay the one co-worker for his production so disadvanta-
> geously, while the other pockets the full actual gain
> of the common production. . . . [22]

A second component of social democracy as envisioned
by Barth as the political program for advancing the goals and
directions of redeemed society is that of **solidarity.** This is directly
correlated with one of the benefits of man's sanctification in
Jesus Christ.

> (Social democracy) seizes and employs a means to lead
> this goal to realisation. The means is called organisation.
> The historic programmatic text of socialism, the **Communist
> Manifesto** of 1848, concludes with the famous words: "Pro-
> letarians of the world unite!" Socialism proceeds from
> the <u>solidarity</u> that is actually already imposed by the
> capitalistic system. In distinction to the crafts of the
> old guild type, modern factory work is collective work
> under conditions of solidarity. [23]

Solidarity is also a source of power and influence, particularly as it shapes and forms the thinking and action of the worker
and the working classes:

> To be a socialist means to be a "comrade" in consumers
> unions, in labour unions, and in political parties. He ceases
> to be an individualist, to be something for himself. . . . As
> a socialist he no longer thinks and feels and acts as

a private person, but rather as a member of the forward-
striding, fighting totality. Solidarity is the law and gospel
of socialism. [24]

Solidarity is a link between eschatology and society
for Barth as well. It is a part of realized eschatology which de-
clares that the Holy Spirit has already come into the world and
indeed participates in it through the organized community of
the working class as well as the religious community. Barth interprets the proletariat to be the suffering people waiting for the
new creation in Paul's letter to the Romans (1:18ff). But that
new creation is not simply a future event nor does it simply
negate the present creation. It has already taken place, and Christians as the adopted children of God have the mandate to make
the proletariat, which is a part of the suffering mentioned in
that passage, not only aware of this fact but also to act in solidarity with them to change the social situation so that it reflects
the new creation. [25]

Thus, in correlating the thoughtlessness engendered
by capitalism in the West and state authoritarianism in the East,
Barth would depend on social democracy to:

1) Humanize and socialize industrial relations and the
plight of the worker as well as that of the employer, and

2) Provide a solidarity between the workers themselves
and between the workers and non-workers. As Barth again said
in his early days as a pastor:

For in Jesus there was only a social God, a God of solidarity; therefore, there was also only a social religion, a
religion of solidarity. [26]

The second instrument or program for advancing the
goals and direction of the redeemed society in praxis is the Church
as advocate for and mirror of that society within the state.
Barth insists that the institutional role of the Church means
that it is the earthly-historical representation of all humanity
which has been justified, sanctified, and called in Jesus Christ
and that its internal life and order ought to mirror such in the
life and order of the larger society. [27] Barth cautions that
the Church is not the state nor the state the Church. The Church
in the state and society will display a loyalty to the laws of
the state which in fact is a service to the state. Its service is
that it reminds the state of its divinely-assigned role, but also
its divinely-assigned limitation and authority, which comes under
the authority of God. [28]

Yet, that service also embraces advocacy, particularly

for the justification of mankind in Jesus Christ and on behalf of the voiceless. Barth understands this to be a rightful interpretation of the "be subject unto" phrase of Romans 13.

> If the prayer of Christians for the State constitutes the norm of their "subjection" . . . and if this prayer is taken seriously as the responsible intercession of the Christians for the State, then the scheme of purely passive subjection which apparently--but only apparently--governs the thought of Romans 13 is broken. . . . Can serious prayer, in the long run, continue without the corresponding work? Can we ask God for something which we are not at the same moment determined and prepared to bring about, so far as it lies within the bounds of our possibility? [29]

Such subjection implicitly includes political concern and action by the Church, which is really an extension of the priestly function of the Church. It does not mean passivity, but rather vigilant activity, especially since the state is always in danger of exceeding its limitations. [30]

Hence, theology carries within itself at all times political seeds which will bear fruit in the active political life of the Christian and the Church as institution. This does not necessarily mean that there ought to be a formation of a "Christian" political party as some Roman Catholics in some western European states have done. But it does signify that if preaching is to include prophetic elements, it is by its very definition political and at times partisan, even when the preaching makes no direct references to community politics. The Kingdom of God, by its very nature, is intended to bring about political change.

One of the chief ways in which the role of advocate is fulfilled by the Church in society is the exemplary function, i.e., providing a model and patterns within itself as a service to the state and community surrounding it. Barth thinks that law and jurisprudence are particularly important to consider under this rubric since the New Testament is very concerned itself about the relationship between law and gospel. Barth admits that historically law and gospel have become so intertwined within the fabric of the Church as to lead both Church and state astray in the pursuit of justification and justice:

> To what end? Certainly not in order to claim that the law valid in the Church must also be the law of the state and other human societies. Certainly not to demand or invite these to appropriate the provisions of ecclesiastical law and therefore to replace their own law by canon law. Certainly not to ecclesiasticise the world and especially the state as the all-embracing form of human society. [31]

What Barth seems to mean by this is that church law ought to exemplify to the state the good news of Jesus Christ, namely, hope and an overcoming of human misery. [32] It is the alteration of the human situation in Jesus Christ that characterizes the message and example which the Church can provide to society, even if the society and the state refuse to acknowledge and recognize such an alteration.

> Again, it may be a model to the extent that in it every member of the community--irrespective of his estate, endowment, background or nature--is in the first instance treated absolutely as a brother. Worldly law sees a man in purely material relationships. It regulates his integration into society and the state, and the duties which this entails. . . . But it does not touch the man himself, although in all these relationships, it is first and last he who is concerned. In this respect, too, true Church law begins at the very point where all worldly law breaks off. Is it not salutary that the latter . . . should be concretely reminded that man is its true theme and subject-matter? [33]

By exemplification in its own internal life, the Church can hope to move and influence the application of law in the state in several directions. One of the first steps is that laws hitherto favoring a ruling class will be altered in the direction of the underprivileged and poor and have a goal of real equality. (Such an argument sounds similar to Marx's contention that bourgeoise democracy deliberately enacts laws and statutes to maintain the power and status of the bourgeoise to the detriment of the poor and the weak.)

> The poor, the socially and economically weak and threatened, will always be the object of (the Church's) primary and particular concern, and it will always insist on the State's special responsibility for these weaker members of society. . . . but it must not concentrate on this and neglect the other thing to which it is committed by its political responsibility: the effort to achieve such a fashioning of the law as will make it impossible for "equality before the law" to become a cloak under which strong and weak, independent and dependent, rich and poor, employers and employees, in fact receive different treatment at its hands: the weak being unduly restricted, the strong unduly protected. [34]

Another way in which advocacy can be exemplified is through the diaconate, which Barth understands to be both an order of the ministry as well as a feature of the whole community. It is a community ministry in which solidarity with the weak and marginal is affirmed and put into action. [35] The diaconate can function in several ways in this respect. First, it itself must be aware of the important link between the conditions and situation of the needy and poor in society and the political and economic structures. As such the diaconate must be engaged in constant action of "feeding the poor" as the New Testament admonishes by raising consciousness both with the religious and the civil communities and by being politically involved. Secondly, the diaconate, being knowledgeable and aware of the fact that the state has taken over many of the traditional welfare functions of the Church can find new and innovative ways to affirm and to be in solidarity with the "little ones", particularly in light of the state bureaucracy which often ministers such welfare programs and diminishes the humanity of the "little man." Thirdly, the diaconate can make the religious community constantly aware that such work is the service incumbent upon the entire community and not only a particularly ordained order, or individuals within the Church. [36]

A third form of political praxis is the obligation to be a social critic. This is related to the service of diakonia, but it is not the same as being prophetic, although it can embrace prophetic elements. It takes the form of what is called in parliamentary democracies "the loyal opposition" or the vigilant "shadow cabinet":

> (The Church) cannot deny that it is one human society with others, and that as such it comes within the jurisdiction of the state, of which its own members, individual Christians, are citizens, and which it regards and recognises as of divine appointment. It will thus adapt itself loyally to the ius circa sacra claimed and exercised by the state. [37]

Yet, in rendering such a service, the Church does not surrender its identity nor does it assume that it supercedes the state. Its role as a loyal critic is to preserve its own freedom to preach God's justification of humanity and to be able to worship in its own way in accordance with its own traditions. It is only as a free Church that it can remind the state of its limits and the dangers of it lapsing into either tyranny or anarchy. [38]

Barth calls this critical function a summons to maintain a "counter-movement" (Gegenbewegung). This may take the form of opposition to the state, but more often than not, it is to provide a perspective for the state's authority and an aid to the state so that it can more truly fulfill its mandate. Such counter-movements are not peculiar to the political involvement of the Christian community; indeed Barth seems to allow for some coalition between the religious community and other political groups and programs which have similar goals of social justice in society:

> Above all, perhaps as the main force behind the movement, and against the background of the great and radical analysis, questioning and criticism of the system particularly associated with the name of Karl Marx, there has been the awakening of the working class to consciousness of its power when properly organised. . . . [39]

> Again it has to be said that the command of God to the extent that it can and will be heard, is self-evidently and in all circumstances a call for counter-movements on behalf of humanity and against its denial in any form, and therefore a call for the championing of the weak against every kind of encroachment on the part of the strong. . . . [40]

It is because of the need for such counter-movements on behalf of the "little man" in the face of such obstacles and powers that more often than not such counter-movements are usually on the left politically.

Thus, the Church and the Christians are often protagonists in situations and antagonists in others; they are both revolutionary and reformist; they may be at one time liberal and at another time conservative. Much depends on the contextual ethic called for at the time. Barth is aware of the ambivalence at stake in the execution of political praxis by the religious community in society:

> It must now sometimes seem to be decisively for one side against another, sometimes refer equally decisively to a third quarter. . . . It will sometimes have to be surprisingly conservative and sometimes extremely revolutionary. It must be all these things at the proper time, namely, at the time shown to be the right time for a particular insight and judgment in the light of eternity. . . . [41]

There is no complacency in Barth's understanding of the link between theological thinking and political praxis. Even Reinhold Niebuhr, who criticized Barth for what he interpreted to be both irresponsibility and neutrality toward post-World War II communism has withdrawn that harsh criticism. [42] A more critical appraisal of Barth will come in the next section, but it ought to be noted that all through his career Barth had always understood christology to be fundamental to political activity and conceptualizing by the Church and the Christian. To **do** theology means political praxis. It is the Christ which not only puts all of society and its political orders under <u>krisis</u>, but also mobilizes men and women to move in solidarity. Even one of Barth's most critical Roman Catholic interpreters understood this dialectical dynamic between his theology and political praxis. [43] Early on in his career and in his theological writings, Barth established and maintained this link, a link which is perhaps best summarized in his **Church Dogmatics:**

> In this connexion it is important to notice that the people to whom God in His righteousness turns as helper and Saviour is everywhere in the Old Testament the harassed and oppressed people of Israel, which, powerless in itself, has no rights, and is delivered over to the superior forces of its enemies; and in Israel it is especially the poor, the widows, and orphans, the weak and defenceless. . . . What does all this mean? It is not really to be explained by talking <u>in abstracto</u> of the political tendency and especially the forensic character of the Old Testament and the biblical message generally. As a matter of fact, from the belief in God's righteousness there follows logically a very definite political problem and task. [44]

That is, one cannot avoid political praxis, for to do so, says Karl Barth, is to reject the divine justification established and effected by Jesus Christ.

The innovative and vigorous manner in which Karl Barth links his christological thinking with political praxis and the consequences of making such a link has been the theme of this investigation. Such a link has been a characteristic of Barth's ministry and thinking since he assumed his first position as pastor in the industrial village of Safenwil in 1909, which particularly grew after 1911. This interest takes on particular significance for Barth after his disappointment with his former theology mentors after 1914 and the events in Russia at that time.

It was not his intention to develop a "political theology". Rather he, on the one hand, sought to spell out the implications for man's world of a theology which insisted upon God's willingness and determination to be a partner with man in Jesus Christ. Since that world is a concrete world and not an abstract one, Barth was compelled to relate that divinely initiated partnership to concrete situations in man's world. And in so doing, on the other hand, Barth's theological understanding of political praxis was both a practical extension of that partnership and a logical one. That is, like Karl Marx, he too had little patience with the Hegelian abstract man and the Feuerbachian "real" man who seemed unaffected and unchanged by change in his world and who was not engaged in changing the world in preparation for the kingdom of God. Therefore, throughout his ministry and writings, Barth displayed a sensitivity to and affinity for thinking through and re-thinking the relationship between theological interpretation and praxis.

Such a relationship was not an artificial or a recent one for Barth. It was a consequential and implicit one which he considered most legitimate and authentic for the Christian community and for the Christian. It is this view which lies behind Barth's contention that ethics and dogmatics are not only to be always related to each other but also cannot be separated from each other. As Barth so sharply says early on in his **Dogmatics:**

> Therefore the theme of dogmatics is always the Word of God and nothing else. But the theme of the Word is human existence, human life and volition and action. This is challenged by the Word of God, questioned as to its rightness, and brought into the right way. It is for this reason and in this sense, not in virtue of its own previous competence, but by the Word of God, that human experience acquires theological relevance. . . . Dogmatics has no option: it has to be "existential," i.e., because it refers to the Word of God, it must also refer to human existence. [45]

To this extent, the claim made by J. Bettis that Barth is **not** a universalist is correct. [46] There is a universalist tendency in Barth in that God has established in Jesus Christ not only a concern, but a participation in human affairs in all areas of society. Barth is uneasy about restricting the apprehension of God's grace to Christians and most especially to Christian individuals. He fears that this removes the objective and cosmic nature of that grace both in nature and in the historical processes.

> It is the Church which with its perception and experience of the grace of God stands vicariously for the rest of the world which has not yet partaken of the witness of the Holy Spirit. It is the Church which in this particularity is ordained to the ministry of reconciliation and the witness of the grace of God in relation to the rest of the world. It is in its existence, therefore--and only in the sphere of its existence in that of individual Christians--that the salvation ascribed to the world is appropriated by man. [47]

When that reconciliation is restricted to individual apprehension, then the possibility exists that "psychologism", "sociologism", Platonism, personalism, and other "isms" become the determinative filter for truth and through which the Word is interpreted and exegeted. One can suggest that a determination not to restrict the good news of universal reconciliation to individual subjective apprehension spurred Barth always in his ministry and praxis to seek out solidarity with others, such as his talks to the study groups of the Swiss Social Democratic Party in his early ministry, his activities whilst in Germany, and his letters and travels in eastern Europe as well as his sermons to the inmates of prison in his native Switzerland demonstrate. And it has been no mistake that Barth sought to establish the enabling function and power of this reconciliation for the underclasses and the weak ones in man's society. As he pleaded in his **Dogmatics:**

> If this separation (of ethics and dogmatics) is insisted on, dogmatics incurs the grave suspicion of being no more than an idle intellectual frivolity. If it really has to accept this disjunction, we ought not to be surprised if in time it acquires the reputation of being aloof from life and of doubtful value, in view of its pure "intellectualism". In these circumstances it has every reason to retire in favour of ethics (even an untheological ethics) if this is regarded as worthwhile. [48]

It probably need not be repeated that it is corporate sin which shapes and binds mankind together as creatures in the world; it is the corporate nature of God's reconciliation in Jesus Christ which reveals true humanity and therefore provides a concrete situation of what mankind is called to be and how his society can be transformed. But as this is not always acknowledged or even known by all of mankind, the religious community has a particular witness to make in not only proclaiming this event but also practicing it. To this extent Barth might speak of "unredeemed" society and "redeemed" society as two directions which both show the distress of the one society. That is, they both can and do occur within man's total societal life.

If Thurneysen is correct that Barth abandoned his early Kierkegaardian affinity because of Christoph Blumhardt, then the question of dogmatics and ethics being linked together is carried a step further. Blumhardt insisted that God was particularly active in man's social and political circumstances, usually under the clothing of Religious Socialism and as such man's very existence was surrounded and infiltrated by God's activity and partisanship. Young Blumhardt ruled out indifference and neutrality regarding social problems and circumstances, believing that as all were living between the times, Christians ought to be socially and politically engaged in preparing the world for the time of the kingdom. This eschatological component of Blumhardt's thinking appealed to young Barth and gave him a perspective on the divine judgment under which all human institutions and ideologies stand. But it also offered him a clue to the renewal, reform, and establishment of institutions and causes. Marquardt perhaps quite rightly identifies this as the <u>totaliter aliter</u> component surrounding all political praxis for young Barth. [49]

Appraisal of Barth's Presumptions and Method

Yet at this point a more careful and critical appraisal of Barth's thought is called for, particularly in terms of the content of the political practices and goals which he sees growing out of the redeemed society and in terms of his theological method in linking christology with certain political models. The latter point is all the more important because Barth derives such models presumably after subjecting himself to his own criteria for testing the "truth" of such models. Those criteria are:

1) Agreement with the witness of scripture, which does not preclude non-biblical sources providing signposts for new ways of hearing scripture and determining a hermeneutic by the Church.

2) An interaction between the model and what Barth calls "world occurrences," by which he means the non-church or secular world.

3) Significance for activating the Christian community in social and communal activities.

In other words, there are other bearers of truth in a pluralistic state which the Church ought not to ignore, but at the same time ought not to confuse their truth with the truth revealed in Jesus Christ alone.

It is presumably in accordance with this idea that Barth identifies the political praxis of the redeemed society with social democracy or even socialism (Marquardt). Yet there is a certain shallowness and even an implied romance in Barth's use of social democracy which ought to be examined. To say socialism or social democracy means that one has to deal with Marx and Engels whether one makes claims along the Utopian Socialist line, the scientific socialist insights, the social democratic point of view or even the Christian Socialist world-picture. That is, in order to understand what Barth's view of socialized democracy is about means that one has to understand what social democracy is about, which is derived from Marx-Engels. It is this internal political praxis advocated by Barth which brings to mind three issues:

1) The adequacy of his theological and political foundations for the social democratic state.

2) The adequacy of his definition and understanding of labor in the redeemed society, especially as his model for labor is derived from his understanding of social democracy and the social democratic state.

3) An examination of his understanding of Aneignung, which is the main feature of the unredeemed society.

It has already been noted that Barth has at times an unclear and often ambivalent attitude toward the institution called the state. This may have something to do with his mistrust of ideology and its threatening entrapment for the doing of political theology. In part of **Romans**(1) Barth sees Paul as urging that Christians work for the coming of the kingdom of God by dissolving the state which is evil and corrupt. [50] At the same time in that first edition he shows a fear of possible anarchy resulting from such a dissolution. This tension is not resolved, even though he makes his strongest statements about the state having to disappear in **Romans**(1). In the **Church Dogmatics** he claims that the state is a created institution by God with a divinely derived authority and mandate to govern and guide man's collective life. Part of the need for such an institution is to hinder its citizens from practicing all forms of individualism, which should not be confused with individuality. [51]

This ambivalence and tension can be demonstrated by his interpretation of Romans 13:1: "Let every person be subject to the governing authorities (powers)." In his early writings, he suggests that this phrase does not mean the state can expect support from the Christian if the state uses its power to suppress the preaching of the gospel and to restrict the Church's freedom. [52] This Leitmotiv also is apparent in the Barmen Declaration which he wrote. Yet at the same time he insists that even when the state might be doing an unjust act, the Church is not called upon to demolish it or to coalesce with forces calling for its demolition because:

1) Justice can come forth even in the doing of injustice, such as was the case of Pilate passing sentence on Jesus.

2) The state is due respect even when it is critical respect.

Hence there is an ambiguous attitude toward the loyalty owed the state when the Church is certain that injustice is being done by the state. Barth admits this as much in his letter to the pastor in the German Democratic Republic. Replying to a query about the state curtailing the Church's freedom to speak out and to resist the Marxist state, Barth writes:

> Only God Himself can properly claim this freedom for His Word. The Church has no "right" to make such a claim for her own word. The state has a right to the faithful, accurate, and entirely unacclaimed service of the Church's word. The freedom to speak out and to receive a public hearing can only be granted to the Church as a gift of God's free grace. The "curtailment" of the Church's freedom ought therefore to be understood clearly as a divine work of love, carried out by the socialist state against its will, a work which it is not advisable to resist. [53]

The more significant question to raise in this respect is whether Barth has a model of the state which lies behind such an interpretation. This question can be answered by Barth himself, who insists in spite of his criticism of western democratic states and their economic systems, that the nearest model which will allow the Church the kind of freedom envisioned in the New Testament and mandated to it by Christ is the democratic state.

> It may be remarked (again, with pleasure or annoyance) that the Christian line that follows from the gospel betrays a striking tendency to the side of what is generally called the "democratic" state. Here again, we shall be careful not to deny an obvious fact, though "democracy" in any technical meaning of the word (Swiss, American, French, etc.), is certainly not necessarily the form of State closest to the Christian view. . . . It must be admitted that the word and the concept "democracy" ("the rule of the people") are powerless to describe even approximately the kind of State which, in the Christian view, most nearly corresponds to the divine ordinance. This is no reason, however, why it should be overlooked or denied that Christian choices and purposes in politics tend on the whole towards the form of State, which, if it is not actually realised in the so-called "democracies", is at any rate more or less honestly clearly intended and desired. Taking everything into account, it must be said that the Christian view shows a stronger trend in this direction than any other. There certainly is an affinity between the Christian community and the civil communities of the free peoples. [54]

Marquardt, perhaps rightly and incisively, has already suggested that one source of this ambivalence may have biographical roots in Barth. The first edition of **Romans** was written during the chaotic period of revolutions in Russia and throughout Germany near the beginning of this century, whereas the second edition of **Romans** was written during the period when many early supporters of the Russian Revolution and socialism had become disillusioned with the aftermath of that revolution and the many inhumanities and continuing chaos which they saw in the Soviet Union. The promises simply had not been fulfilled. [55] The ensuing insecurity and turmoil simply shattered a great groundswell of idealism which the Bolshevik Revolution had aroused for many in Barth's generation.

But this model of the state, even with a democratic or non-democratic form, seems really to be that of the nation-state growing out of the eighteenth and nineteenth centuries. On the one hand, one can speak of the political and philosophical ideals of freedom, liberty, and equality which are associated with the democratic state, including the so-called "rule of the people" being actualized in the populace being able to vote for their legislative and executive bodies along the lines suggested in Montesquieu. These are certainly the images of the democratic state which Barth thinks of. It is the redeemed society.

At the same time, on the other hand, the democratic state emerged not simply in quest of egalitarian ideals applicable to all its citizens, but rather as a structure embued with certain declared rights intended to advance and secure economic and political goals of the developing middle classes over against the propertied-classes and the gentry in the feudal and monarchial states of western Europe. [56] The advancement of the idea that democracy meant the rule of all people developed much later--in fact mostly during this century. During the nineteenth century it was mostly the socialists and the socialist trade union movement which agitated for universal suffrage, but even that excluded women and non-whites. [57] These factors together with the developing nationalist mood of European countries during the eighteenth and nineteenth centuries as well as the colonial expansionist policies of these states document the fact that the political philosophy and fabric of the democratic state cannot be considered without including the restrictive class interests that the state was intended to advance and maintain. Karl Marx rightly observed that in the democratic state some groups were deliberately excluded or not enfranchised, such as the French peasantry, who

> are incapable of enforcing their class interest in their own name, whether through a parliament or a convention. They cannot represent themselves, they must be represented. Their representative must at the same time appear as their master, as an authority over them, as an unlimited government power that protects them against other classes and sends them the rain and sunshine from above. The political influence of the small peasants, therefore, finds its final expression in the executive power subordinating society to itself. [58]

Even that most prized instrument and demonstration of western democracy, membership in the parliament or legislature, was restricted to certain estates, classes, and propertied groups or limited by hereditary or non-elected first or upper chambers. Even the United Kingdom, which was perhaps less restrictive than some of the other western European democracies, in the 1850's allowed only approximately one million out of some 27.5 million citizens to vote for Members of Parliament. [59] And even the Second Reform Act of 1866 introduced by the Liberals did not envisage universal suffrage for all male citizens. Less than eight percent of the population was enfranchised to vote in spite of the democracy ideology about "rule of the people". [60]

All of this has been mentioned in order that the content of Barth's model of the "state" and particularly the democratic state be clearly understood. Now if such a fabric and philosophy of the state is so intertwined with the very definition of the democratic state, and if this model, even with Barth's insistence that in the redeemed society the historical capitalist component of the democratic state will be diminished and humanized through social democracy, lies behind Barth's interpretation of the New Testament, particularly Romans 13 and Col. 2:15, then it is a legitimate question to ask whether Barth undeliberately may have a kind of Utopian Socialist idea of the state in view. [61] By failing to do some of the critical historical and political analysis of the concept of the state, might not the charge be brought that Barth is also a product of his time in this area or that he is struggling to provide a theological justification for an existing political model which meant a great deal to him in light of the turmoil of 1911-1922 as it did to most of western Europe and North America?

But there is a second aspect of this use of the democratic model by Barth which raises questions about his use of that model as the best possible vehicle for realizing the goals and directions of the redeemed society. Even the sacred language of the democratic state--freedom, equality, brotherhood or fraternity--cannot be understood in their historical sense apart from the economic interests of the middle classes at the time. Barth considers these words also important to characterize the redeemed society: freedom, [62] equality, [63] and fraternity or solidarity. [64] The question is whether these, even with a theological interpretation, can be invigorated with a new kind of political substance in a practical way. Might it not be that the political and historical baggage which these terms in the democratic state bring with them are so identified with their administration and practice that when considering the democratic state they cannot be liberated in any radical way, only reformed or expanded? That is, can these politically and historically conditioned terms be "revolutionized" theologically? Is it for nothing that very few of the western democratic states with the experience of a pluralistic, multi-cultural populace seldom have been able to come up with a multi-cultural system of values but rather have tried to impose a particular tribal set of values associated with a national economic history? [65]

It is known that when the middle-classes were establishing the modern democratic nation-state that the concept of freedom was understood as a personal freedom, political freedom, and freedom of assembly for those classes as they sought to compete with the gentry and properties classes. This concept also embraced economic freedom for the merchant classes in terms of ending duties on goods, laissez-faire competition and economics, and the freedom to organize business and finance organizations. It was not intended to cover personal freedoms for the poor and proletariat, even in the "Declaration of the Rights of Man and the Citizen", as novel as it was at the time.

Equality had to do with establishing the middle-classes as being equal before the law on the same footing as the gentry and aristocracy, entrance into the civil service, equal taxes, and equal consideration for the military offices. It did not include the poor and dispossessed being equal either before the law or with others in the population, particularly since they could neither vote nor be voted into office.

Fraternity, at least in the French Republic, had more to do with national and patriotic feelings than with political solidarity of all classes. This slogan was initially intended to undergird the central government of revolutionary France and to call on all Republicans to defend the state against the internal threats of the monarchists and the divisive radical groups like the Jacobins.

Therefore, the question is, when these terms are used within the context of the democratic state as a concrete situation and not as an abstraction--a method Barth would encourage--can they be redeemed? Might not Barth be accused of dealing with the democratic state in abstraction himself?

There is yet a third aspect of the question of Barth's model for interpreting the New Testament--the instant dismissal of anarchy as an alternative to the democratic capitalistic state. If Marquardt is correct, then the question of anarchy and chaos, as has already been mentioned, must have been an all-consuming concern for Barth's generation, particularly in Germany, as that state languished between numerous internal uprisings and revolutions and political dismemberment by the victorious allies. [66] That is, the disorder, destabilization, and the chaos evident in the democratic states and amongst themselves carried with them some analogies of what Barth later called "nothingness" and the "threat of nothingness and chaos" under which man and his society always stand.

Yet might not a theological question be raised as to whether disorder may not in fact be a vehicle for a new order or even grace and a new creation? Barth himself moves to such a brink in the first edition of **Romans,** but then retreats. Furthermore, in his **Dogmatics,** particularly when he discusses Jesus Christ as revolutionary/reformer who reversed the established order in many areas, he himself also suggests such a dialectical possibility which can become a reality. [67] Certainly in parts of the New Testament the ushering in of a new order through disorder within the old order is demonstrated in Jesus Christ, particularly in Luke's Gospel. [68]

Moreover, there are historical models of anarchistic order aimed at dismantling the old order bringing forth new insights and new models of a new order other than that of the western democratic nation-state with its internal fabric of industrialization. Certainly, this was the case with the Proudhonists, the followers of Bakunin, and even the Paris Commune. Proudhon railed against the concept of a central government which could claim to minister fairly, insisting instead on limited local authority and a decentralized, small group or factory kind of economy. Such models were practiced in Switzerland in the nineteenth century as well as in parts of France and Italy. Likewise the Russian Populist movement was closely related to the anarchist movement in seeking new forms and models of the state and central authority in the nation-state. [69] Even Marx, who steadily opposed anarchy, recognized the radical freshness of Proudhon's ideas about anarchy, particularly his idea that the class society can best be demolished and undermined by making all men into workers with equal pay and privileges for their doing equal amounts of work in society. [70]

Karl Barth moves to the edge of the Marxist analysis of the nation-state model as an instrument devised to maintain the right of private property and private ownership of the means of production, but he does not move with Marx in his wanting to abolish the state eventually and radically to transform its basis during the transition from socialism to communism. Nor does he claim the revolutionary step of the anarchists by wanting to demolish the nation-state altogether and replace it with other models. Early on Barth had already equated tyranny with anarchy as two extreme ends of the same pole. But surely the radical freedom effected in Jesus Christ, as he claims, and the freedom with which Christians in light of His justification, sanctification, and vocation can engage in new imaginative efforts to practice the goals and directions of redeemed society cannot preclude anarchy either as a vehicle for the new order or as a political instrument.

In addition to the question of whether Barth's model of the state is an abstraction or a cultural holdover of his own day and past, one may also raise a second set of questions about Barth's definition and understanding of labor in society. He defines work as a given in man's existence through which man affirms his creatureliness and gives service to God. This is what distinguishes him from animal creatureliness. [71] Labor is a form of man's obedience to God's command. It preserves, safeguards, develops, and shapes human life in order that human life may be a witness to the kingdom of God. It reaches toward the fulfillment of certain goals in the worker's life, but is often perverted and corrupted by the capitalist Kampf ums Dasein, which is based on egoistic individualism. Such individualism undermines the solidarity and cooperation which labor ought to generate. It is through the allurement of possessions and consumption used to entrap the worker as wage earner that a perpetual state of dependence on the part of the worker is furthered and maintained, thereby securing the dominant role of the capitalist as wage-giver and as exploiter. [72]

Barth suggests that social democracy would both liberate the worker from such a position as well as humanize industrial relations and the entire working process in the state. Certainly this sounds laudatory, but again it lacks some of the preciseness and sharpness which would have helped the reader in estimating how much depth there is to Barth's conception, particularly as one tries to think of the modern industrial and technological society. Certainly this sounds laudatory, but apart from occasional glances at Karl Marx, Barth displays no evidence of having wrestled with the single most important analyst of labor in the capitalist industrial world, Karl Marx, whose analyses have had to be considered in doing any hermeneutic of labor since the Industrial Revolution. Is the central role of work affirmed by Barth because of his own social democratic activities? Would his understanding and development of labor be also applicable in the Third World developing countries where marginal living and non-industrial kinds of labor are not resources of affirmation as much as necessities for daily survival? Might this interpretation of labor be a reflection of Barth's Reformed tradition with it work ethic, even though he criticizes and departs from this tradition from time to time? [73]

On the one hand, Barth would agree with Marx that one's labor is fundamentally intertwined with his identity and self-worth as well as his place and value in society. In the production of one's sustenance one affirms his relation to nature, self, and fellowman. Barth says this as well. It is through labor that a class consciousness develops, be it that of the capitalist or that of the worker. Class consciousness develops from common economic interests and experiences which shape one's being and thought, says Marx. Labor is intimately connected with one's creativity, although, as Barth cautions, being such a creator cannot be confused with the creative power of the divine. Subsequently, the alienation of the individual from his labor and his class through forms of exploitation is detrimental to self-identity and societal value, not to mention injurious to one's humanity as that humanity is fulfilled in fellow-humanity. For Barth, alienation and exploitation are characteristics of the unredeemed society; for Marx such things are characteristics of the unjust and inhuman society which more often than not can be seen in the modern industrial state under capitalism. [74]

On the other hand, Barth does not go far enough in resolving this matter or in analyzing some of the components of labor either in an industrial or in a non-industrial society. That is, his understanding of labor comes out of an industrial model, but the character of that labor and the forces which shape that labor seem to be dealt with in a too hurried manner similar to that of the Utopian Socialists or the Religious Socialists, although Barth would reject this idea. It is because of the division of labor that class divisions and antagonisms arise. Hence, not even a social democratic state would do away with the class divisions since social democracy would sustain the division of labor and thus greed, maximizing private profits, competition, and bourgeois interests. Likewise a social democratic state, according to the Marxists usually results in some form of mixed economy, meaning that both private enterprise and state-owned or regulated enterprises survive and compete side by side. It means that private ownership of the means of production still can shape and form social and political relations.

> Political economy proceeds from the fact of private property. It does not explain private property. It grasps the actual, material process of private property in abstract and general formulae which it then takes as laws. . . . Political economy does not disclose the reason for the division between capital and labour, between capital and land. . . . Similarly, competition is referred to at every point and explained from external circumstances. [75]

If Barth assumes that through a democratic vote class divisions will end and property and the means of production will be "socialized", then one can easily ask how significant and deep Barth's theological appraisal of labor is. Presumably with the freedom in Jesus Christ the Christian community, standing at the side of the poor, could engage in revolution in full knowledge that chaos will ensue if the systems within the state were overthrown. But Barth leaves us with a certain ambiguity at this point, since revolution by its very nature is disorderly and disruptive but also creative.

Sir Isaiah Berlin tellingly points out that when the sources which cause this alienation and division of labor are eliminated, then labor in a different socialized form can unite and liberate, be creative and expressive of man's solidarity and cooperation with his fellowman. [76]

Through Marx many sociologists agree that one's identity and consciousness are changed and altered by the kind of work one does and the working conditions in which that labor is produced. Such have an effect upon the social relations and the human relations of individuals and society. As Marx stated in his **Critique of Political Economy:**

> The sum total of these productive relations constitutes the economic structure of society--the real foundation on which rise legal and political superstructures, and to which correspond definite forms of social consciousness. The mode of production in material life determines the general character of the social, political, and spiritual processes of life. It is not the consciousness of men that determines their existence, but on the contrary their social existence determines their consciousness. [77]

It is clear that Barth cannot agree with the Marxist view that man's consciousness is shaped and determined by his social and productive existence and not vice versa because of his anthropology and doctrine of transcendence, although Barth does compliment "historical materialism" for reminding the Church that man's soul and "spiritual" life cannot be separated from his bodily and "material" life even in political and social circumstances, not to mention religious circumstances. [78] For Barth, man's identity and consciousness have already been established in Jesus Christ and his labor is the highest evidence of solidarity with fellow-man and service to God. But the imposition of a christology upon a Marxist idea of labor only adds unclarity and some ambiguity. This is all the more apparent in Barth's defense of "fair" wages and work contracts, something which Marx rejects altogether, claiming that the wage system under capitalism only reinforces the idea and power of private ownership. [79]

The central driving agent in this privatization and individualism in the unredeemed society is Barth's notion of Aneignung which motivate the Kampf ums Dasein in the capitalistic society or state. Once again, unless one defends a doctrine of natural aggressiveness and selfishness, then one has to ask whether there are social causes for this trait. Barth describes manifestation of this trait in the unredeemed society and traces its theological sources to man's pride, sloth, and falsehood. Through the overcoming of these aspects of man's sin in Jesus Christ and their replacement by true freedom and solidarity Barth provides a theological foundation for political praxis which will further these goals and directions in society, thereby overcoming Aneignung.

But Barth only gives a description of the Aneignung in the political or **real** world as it is manifested. What is lacking is why it took the particular forms it took in industrial democracies. Much of the criticism of Barth on this point is related to the previous observations about his model for the democratic state and his almost romanticized view of labor. But there are some additional points which ought to be noted.

One must again repeat that Barth appears to be concerned with the real, non-abstract situation in grasping the significance of his christology. It is not abstract man with which he wishes to be concerned, but the real man in concrete situations. The privatization of possessions and human relations must have historical and social causes.

Early in his career Barth criticized the way that the majority in the democratic state enforces often unjust decisions and actions upon the minorities, or even by powerful bourgeois minorities acting as though they were the majority. [80] Presumably, the "revolution of God" would usher in such a state, one of whose chief characteristics would be the dissolution of Aneignung. [81] But the resolution of this individual, ethnic, and national decision and act of privatization as proposed by Barth is less than clear when following his own insistence that Christian ethics and practice grow out of the concrete situation, not the abstract or the "narrowly intellectual" idea.

Lenin was expanding on Marx and Engels when he claimed that all forms of Aneignung could be traced to historical class economic needs and conflicts within capitalistic democratic states and between such states. Hence domestic political and economic policy is greatly shaped by such needs and conflicts as well as foreign policy. Barth himself hints at this both in his early **Romans** and in his **Dogmatics.** [82] But Barth does not go far enough with any careful analysis of the concrete situation. Again, one gains the impression that Barth puts the capitalistic concept of Aneignung under moralistic judgment and then imposes a theological **ideal** (or **Idea**) upon that moralistic judgment. By not devoting enough analysis to the kinds of power or sources and forces of power both economically and politically in the democratic state, Barth fails to understand that there are powers which themselves shape the actions and decisions of the capitalists who perpetuate Aneignung. One need only to mention the kind of national and international dependence inflicted upon states and economies by military, foreign alliances, and geo-political institutions and forces. Related to this is also the economic role of government and its supporting invisible bureaucrats, who, in effect, can and often do function as managers even in state corporations as well as state regulatory agencies. Is it not conceivable that Aneignung will only be ended when its causes and institutions are abolished?

Marx and Engels tried to demonstrate empirically that Aneignung is a derivative of the division of labor. The division of labor, which brought about the class system that Barth wishes to abolish in the redeemed society, came through the sale and purchase of land, the division of agriculture and industry, workers and managers, slaves and masters. As Engels comments:

> Civilisation opens with a new advance in the division of labour. At the lowest stage of barbarism men produced only directly for their own needs; any acts of exchange were isolated occurrences, the object of exchange merely some fortuitous surplus. . . . Civilisation consolidates and intensifies all these existing divisions of labour, particularly by sharpening the opposition between town and country . . . and it adds a third division of labour peculiar to itself and of decisive importance. It creates a class which no longer concerns itself with production, but only with the exchange of the products--the merchants. . . . Now for the first time a class appears which, without in any way participating in production, captures the direction of a production as a whole and economically subjugates the producers; which makes itself into an indispensable middleman between any two producers and exploits them both. [83]

The question is not whether one agrees with Engels; the question is whether such empirical analysis of the concrete situation and its roots must also be demanded of theologians like Barth who see the social democratic ethic as a proper development of his christology. The issue is whether one can understand the phenomenon of Aneignung without examining the reasons for its occurrence at the deepest level. The problem is whether one, having done this, can assume that its demise will be accomplished in any act less than concrete revolution and the establishment of new forms and instruments of political authority, albeit the risk that those newly established forms and instruments themselves could become perverted and corrupt.

Karl Marx often criticized social democrats and would-be socialists for wanting the comforts of socialism in society without engaging in or realizing the risks and dangers of the struggles necessary to achieve such a society. One must be cautious about attaching such a criticism to Barth, although there are a number of indications that his writings could lend themselves to such possibilities. That Barth's active ministry throughout his life shows otherwise is a witness which brakes such a label. But at times when reading Barth one cannot help recalling Marx's criticism of Feuerbach in his <u>Theses</u>:

> Feuerbach, who does not go into the criticism of this actual essence, is hence compelled 1) to abstract from the historical process, and to establish religious feeling as something self-contained, and to presuppose an abstract--isolated--human individual; 2) to view the essence of man merely as "species" as the inner dumb generality which united the many individuals <u>naturally.</u> [84]

Barth's engaging claim that christology has to do with political as well as theological solidarity prevents him from following the first point of Marx's criticism. The question is whether he might not be following the second point of Marx's criticism.

APPENDIX

Roman Catholic Theory of the Origin of the State

I am relying very much on Heinrich A. Rommen's rather exhaustive work, **The State in Catholic Thought: A Treatise in Political Philosophy.** (St. Louis: B. Herder Book Company, 1945), which is an expansion of his earlier work, **Der Staat in der katholischen Gedankenwelt** (Paderborn, Germany: Bonifacius Druckerei, 1935). Also for historical influences on Aquinas' ideas about the origin of the state and political authority of the state, Thomas Gilby's **Principality and Polity: Aquinas and the Rise of State Theory in the West** (London: Longmans, Green and Company, 1958) was helpful.

Catholic thought about the state begins with the presupposition that man as a social and political being is in a state of becoming. That is, he depends on other beings of his own likeness for identity and affirmation as he strives toward perfection. This striving toward perfection is intentional and teleologically directed even with the Fall of man, which did not destroy the original divine nature of man; it only wounded it.

But this social life and the realization of "self-sufficiency" for the individual in community is only possible if the community of individuals adhere to a set of acknowledged common rules and norms. That is, there has to be a "must" component in following these rules and norms if the community is to survive. Such a "must" means that an authority must exist which can be appealed to for the enforcement of the rules or for the resolution of conflict in different interpretations of the rules:

> We base our security in society on the certainty that the rules or, if you like, the habits of the members will be observed voluntarily and that if not so observed they will be enforced. [1]

It is the state which comes into being as the overseer of the norms and rules necessary for the realization of human perfection and the full-enjoyment of man's social nature. Thus, some kind of state would have been formed even had man continued to live in his original perfect state. That is, the state is a natural development which is a necessary entity. It is a natural community which is given an authority to decide the common good and to enforce it as well as to punish or place sanctions against those who injure the common good and order.

The state is not the consequence of sin, as some sects have tried to maintain, say the Catholics. To suggest this is to move to their next point that the redeemed Christian does not have to obey the state. This would suggest statelessness, which, for the Thomist, is estrangement and homelessness for man:

> The end of the state is coincident with the individual end; therefore again, obedience to authority and authority itself are measured by an objective end, the perfection of man's nature. . . . To live in a state, then, is a command of natural law and of God as the Creator and supreme Lawgiver. Thus, to be obedient to the new order, which does not derive its authority from the free will and is not a transfer of individual natural rights but a protection of them, is of natural law. [2]

Because the state originates as part of the development of human nature, which has been created by God, one can speak of the state as part and subject of the created order.

Such a theory has important consequences for a Catholic appraisal of revolutionary movements which aim either at overthrowing the existing state or radically changing the existing political authority of the state. This is particularly the case when the Roman Church has to deal with Marxist theory and ideology aimed at the perfect communist society occurring with the withering away of the existing state.

Classical Catholic doctrine of the origin of the state mitigates against Marxist or social democratic ideas about a classless society. Rommen claims that such a goal is akin to anarchy and man's longing for a society without any enforcing or compulsive authority, without what he calls an imposing "must". [3] But this "must" is necessary and must be imposed for the survival of the fabric of the community of individuals. The state is teleologically necessary and directed, therefore it cannot wither away. Though it exists by the free consent of individuals, it takes on an objective moral order of its own, independent of the will of the individuals. Yet it must continue to promote justice and the good for the sake of its constituents.

The question after establishing the natural origin of the state is how does the state get its authority and what is the basis for obeying that authority. The authority of the state comes about and is necessary as people freely join together in a unitas ordinis. Francis Suarez (1548-1617), one of the major Catholic proponents of democratic theory, maintains that all political authority, including that of monarchs, rests with the body politic and is derived from the body politic itself. The body politic in a freely given consent establishes authority and is the final legitimization of that authority. [4] But the new moral and political authority assumed by the state, the ordo justitiae legalis, cannot abolish what are called inalienable rights of the citizen or individual.

Catholic political thought has fathered two theories of the origin of political authority in the state: the designation theory and the translation theory. The first has had considerable latitude in Europe, the latter considerable influence in America and 20th century Europe.

The designation theory maintains that political authority is transferred to the executor of that authority by God. This does not mean the divine right of kings, however. Rather individuals guided by providential direction through voting or the electorate or some other means, freely consent to designate someone or a group of people to be the political authority. But these means are only the conditions providing for the transfer of authority. God transfers authority and power through these secondary sources. Though political authority originates in God as the source of all authority and power, it is transferred by Him to the body politic at the moment of its formation. The citizens freely subject themselves to the designated authority as a moral duty. The person designated can be said to have a divine vocation to govern.

The translation theory maintains that no single member because of his wealth or prominence or influence has an innate right to rule, as does the designation theory. All men are born free and equal. To become the sovereign authority the individual or group of individuals must be transformed or translated by a free act of the people such as an election into another constitutional form, like the presidency or parliament. This is immediate democracy which leads to self-government by the people without a divine or royal intermediary, but its roots rest in the translation of power and authority from the people. It is this latter theory, which, according to Rommen, is more widely held by modern day Catholic thinkers. Other than a supernatural act of God, in whatever form that may take, the translation or transfer of power is the only natural source of authority in the state.

NOTES

Chapter One - Beginnings and Boundaries of Barth's Career

1. Quoted from his "Remembrances of America," in The Christian Century. (January 2, 1963), 9, which is cited in How I Changed My Mind. (Edinburgh: Saint Andrew Press, 1969), 80.

2. Ralph Crimmann, "Der junge Karl Barth in Kreuzfeuer der Kritik, 1909-27." (Ph.D. Thesis, University of Erlangen, 1975). See especially James D. Smart, **The Divided Mind of Modern Theology,** (Philadelphia: Westminster Press, 1967); the introduction in Helmut Gollwitzer's Karl Barth's Church Dogmatics. trans. and ed. G. W. Bromiley. (Edinburgh: T. & T. Clark, 1961), 1-28; Karl Kupisch, **Karl Barth in Selbstzeugnissen und Bilddokumenten.** (Hamburg: Rowohlt, 1971); T. F. Torrance, **Karl Barth: An Introduction to His Early Theology.** (London, SCM Press, 1962); and Eberhard Busch, **Karl Barths Lebenslauf.** (München: Chr. Kaiser Verlag, 1975), Eng. trans. (London: SCM Press, 1976).

3. Evangelical Theology in the Nineteenth Century," **The Humanity of God.** (London: Collins, 1961), 19.

4. Ibid., p. 24

5. Karl Kupisch, **Karl Barth in Selbstzeugnissen und Bilddokumenten,** 26.

6. Eberhard, Busch, **Karl Barths Lebenslauf,** 56. English translation, 44. I have made my own translation from the German edition of Busch throughout this book.

7. Ibid.

Notes to pp. 2-5

8. Ibid., 57; (E.T., 45).

9. Quoted from an interview, ibid.

10. Smart, op. cit., 46. See also Wilhelm Pauck, **Karl Barth: Prophet of a New Christianity?** (New York: Harper & Brothers, 1931), 42-44.

11. Smart, op. cit., 46.

12. Pauck, op. cit., 43.

13. Ibid.

14. See a description of Safenwil and the position of the Hüssy family in Eberhard Busch, op. cit., 81; E.T. 69.

15. A discussion of how the Swiss Arbeiterverein was established on the model of the German trade unionists in Switzerland, who were political refugees and who sought through an organization (Junges Deutschland, 1841) to realize some of the teachings of the Utopian Socialists, is found in **Schweizerische Arbeiter-bewegung: Dokumente zu Lage, Organisation und Kämpfen der Arbeiter von der Frühindustrialisierung bis zur Gegenwart.** (Zürich: Limmat Verlag, 1975), 32-33.

16. Busch, op. cit., 82. "Ich halte die sozialistischen Forderungen für ein wichtiges Stück Anwendung des Evangeliums . . . realisieren lassen." ("I regard the demands of the Socialists as an important example of how the gospel is applied, though I also believe that those demands cannot be realized without the gospel.") 82; E.T. 70.

17. Ibid.

18. See Thurneysen's review of the development of young Barth along with their correspondence from 1914 to 1922 in "Die Anfänge," **Antwort** (Zürich, Evangelisher Verlag, 1956), 831-64.

19. Ibid., 831.

20. Kupisch, op. cit., 34

21. Cited in Pauck, op. cit., 47.

22. Ibid., 49-50. See also a helpful and illuminating article by John Glasse, "Barth on Feuerbach," Harvard Theological Review, Vol. 57, No. 3 (April, 1964), 69-96.

23. **The Epistle to the Romans,** 6th Edition. Edwyn C. Hoskyns, trans. (London: Oxford University Press, 1933) 57.

24. Cited from Barth's 1937-38 Gifford Lectures in an unpublished thesis by Ian Grimmett, "The Doctrine of Man in Karl Barth's Commentary on the Epistle to the Romans," (S.T.M. Thesis. New York: Union Theological Seminary, 1953) 94.

25. Introductory essay on Feuerbach in **The Essence of Christianity**, trans. George Eliot (New York: Harper and Brothers, 1957), xxiv.

26. See the SPS's historical and political development in **Schweizerische Arbeiterbewegung**, op. cit., 97-99. (Hereafter SAB).

27. The SPS's political progamme can be found in the SAB, 97-99.

28. Friedrich-Wilhelm Marquardt, Theologie und Sozialismus (München: Kaiser-Grünewald Verlag, 1972) 39; see also Busch, op. cit., 95-96, and Kupisch, op. cit., 36-37. Marquardt, who defends the controversial thesis that Barth in fact was and remained a socialist (39), suggests that his entrance into the SPS was a theological statement, which was not so much an issue of theological debate as a matter of theological existence ("christliche Antwort auf eine politische Situation, mithin auch eine Gestalt politischer Existenz", 40). He was forced to take this step as a practical and theological consequence of his sermons ("Predigen führt in die Politik", 40), as a sign of solidarity with the workers in his congregation ("Verstehens hilfe für einen Teil der Gemeinde", 40), as a token of his support for the aims of the party, which however did not mean that he would withhold criticism of Socialism ("Polemik ist Liebe", 40), and as authentication of the theological motives for acting politically, 40-41.

29. Kupisch, op. cit., 36.

30. Ibid., 36-37.

31. Ibid., 37; Busch, op. cit., 95; E.T. 83.

32. Kupisch, op. cit., 37.

33. Ibid., 37; Busch, 96; E.T. 84.

34. Antwort, 841-2; see also Smart's book for biographical sketches and outlines of the ideas of the two Blumhardts, Christoph and Johann Christoph (1805-80), Ragaz and Kutter, 59-64; Kupisch, 37-38.

35. The text of this speech is found in **Anfänge der dialektischen Theologie**, I. (München: Chr. Kaiser Verlag, 1977), 3-37. Religious Socialism, see Renata Breipohl, **Religiöser Sozialismus und bürgerliches Geschichtsbewusstsein zur Zeit der Weimarer Republik** (Zürich: Theologischer Verlag, 1971), 237f, for a reaction to Barth's introduction to Germany as a whole through this meeting with the Religious Socialists at Tambach, "Karl Barth war der Oeffentlichkeit der deutschen Kirche und Theologie bis zum Herbst 1919 ein Unbekannter." ("Karl Barth was

Notes to pp. 6-8

unknown to the German church and German theology until autumn, 1919.") see George Merz's article, "Die Begegnung Karl Barths mit der deutschen Theologie," **Kerygma und Dogma** (Göttingen, 1956), 157-175. The reaction of the Religious Socialists to the Tambacher speech can perhaps best be glimpsed in Carl Mennicke's polemical critique entitled "Disagreement with Karl Barth," which he published after the Tambach in his <u>Blätter für religiösen Sozialismus</u>, 1. Jg., Nr. 2, (Pfingsten, 1920), 5-8.

36. Quoted from Thurneysen's article, "Zum religiös-sozialen Problem" in <u>Zwischen den Zeiten</u> (1927), 514-515 in Pauck, <u>op. cit.</u>, 59.

37. Marquardt, <u>op. cit.</u>, 83.

38. See Barth's correspondence with Thurneysen during the start of this period (1st September, 1916 -23rd October, 1916 in **Antwort**, 847-8). Kupisch points out that Barth was inwardly compelled to produce his **Romans** as a means of self-contentment ("Selbstbefreiung"), 40-41.

39. Busch, 93; E.T. 81.

40. "Evangelical Theology in the Nineteenth Century," **The Humanity of God**, 14.

41. Pauck, 55-6.

42. Smart, 81.

43. <u>Ibid.</u>, 82.

44. "The Humanity of God," **The Humanity of God**, 40.

45. Busch, 116; E.T., 103.

46. "Unsere Dialektik ist auf einem toten Punkt angelangt und, wenn wir gesund und stark sein wollen, müssen wir von vorn anfangen." ("Our dialectic has reached a dead end, and if we want to be healthy and strong, we must start from the beginning.") Busch, 104; E.T., 92.

47. "Es war immer schon alles fertig ohne Gott. Gott sollte immer gut genug sein zur Durchführung und Krönung dessen, was die Menschen von sich aus beginnen. Die Furcht des Herrn stand nicht objektiv am Anfang unserer Weisheit, sondern seine Zustimmung wurde immer nur so im Vorbeigehen zu erhaschen ge- sucht." ("Everything was always settled without God. God was supposed to be sufficiently good to put the crowning touch on whatever men started on their own. The fear of the Lord did not stand objectively at the beginning of our wisdom; rather we always tried to get His agreement in passing." Busch, 112; E.T. 99.

48. Kupisch, 41-43. This obituary can also be found in **Anfänge der dialektischen Theologie**, I, 37-49; E.T. in Robinson, James, ed., **The Beginnings of Dialectic Theology**, I (Richmond, VA: John Knox Press, 1968), 35-45. This is only a partial translation of Vol. I, 39-49; 77-197; 322-347, and Vol. II, 1-218.

49. See Barth's impact on the conference and the reactions to him in Germany on pp. 39-45 of Chapter Two. Also see Kupisch, 43-45 and Busch, 122-127, E.T., 109-115; Smart, 87-89.

50. Kupisch, 44; Busch, 122, E.T. 110-111.

51. "Ja, Christus zum soundsovielten Male zu säkularisieren, heute z.B. der Sozialdemokratie, dem Pazifismus, dem Wandervogel zu Liebe, wie ehemals den Vaterländern, dem Schweizertum, dem Liberalismus der Gebildeten zu Liebe, das möchte uns allenfalls gelingen." **Anfänge der dialektischen Theologie**, I, 6; ("Indeed, to secularize Christ today for the nth time, e.g., for the sake of social democracy, pacifism, the Wandervogel, such as the fatherland, Swiss identity, liberalism of the intelligentsia—all that we could probably succeed in doing.")

52. Kupisch, 45.

53. See the description of this rupture and quarrel in Busch, 119-120; a description of the general strike itself and the issues can be found in SAB, 158-192.

54. Busch, 119; E.T. 107.

55. Busch, 135, E.T. 123; Kupisch, 45.

56. Busch, 163, E.T. 149-150.

57. Letter to the author from Dr. Walter Mogk, Akademischer Rat, Historisches Seminar, University of Munich dated 9th March, 1977.

58. Marquardt, 179.

59. See a summary of his initial apprehensions as lecturer in Busch, 140, E.T., 127.

60. Letter of 18th March, 1921, **Antwort**, 862.

61. Busch, 141, E.T., 128.

62. Letter of 31st January, 1922, **Antwort**, 864.

63. See his discussion of Overbeck's ideas and their subsequent influence on Barth's early eschatology, op. cit., 100-4; see also Kupisch, 47; Busch, 128, E.T., 115-116.

64. Busch, 128, E.T., 115.

65. Ibid.

66. Smart, 101.

67. Ibid.

68. Ibid., 101-102.

69. Ibid., 102; see also Professor Marquardt's incisive discussion about B. Wielenga's work on the parallels between Lenin's idea of revolution and those of Barth in the first and second editions of the **Romans,** op. cit., 126-168. "Der zweite **Römerbrief** interpretiert den 'existentialen', der erste aber einen im engeren Sinn 'sozialen' und im weitesten Sinn 'kulturellen' Sinn der späteren Dogmatik . . . " ("The second edition of **Romans** interprets the 'existential' element, the first edition, however, the social in a narrower sense and the cultural in the broadest sense of the later **Dogmatics.** . . . ") See also Barth's review of Overbeck's papers published by a student, Carl Albrecht Bernoulli, posthumously, in a collection called **Christentum und Kultur.** Barth wrote that were the theologians to follow through on all the implications of Overbeck's theology, they would be led not only to a new theology, but to a new Christianity. "Unsettled Questions for Theology Today" (1920), **Theology and Church,** Louise Pettibone Smith, trans. (London: SCM Press, 1962), 73. Cf. **Church Dogmatics,** II/1, 634-6.

70. Smart, 104.

71. "A Thank You and a Bow: Kierkegaard's Reveille," Canadian Journal of Theology, IX (1965), No. 1, p. 5.

72. Ibid., 6.

73. Ibid., 7.

74. Letter of 26th March, 1925, in **Revolutionary Theology in the Making,** trans. James Smart (Richmond, VA: John Knox Press, 1964), 217-218. (Hereafter, **Revolutionary Theology.**)

75. For a summary of his faith and activities, see Smart, 59-62.

76. Ibid., 61.

77. Ibid.

78. II/i, 633.

79. Smart, 62.

80. **Epistle to the Romans,** 6th Edition. (London: Oxford University Press, 1933), 56.

81. Ibid., 69.

82. **The Humanity of God,** 41.

83. See a summary of this review in Smart, 117-122. See also Busch, 148-149; **Anfänge der dialektischen Theologie.** I, 119-142, E.T. 100-120.

84. Letter of 26th March, 1922, **Revolutionary Theology** 94.

85. Smart, 132-134.

86. Busch, 153; E.T., 140.

87. Ibid.

88. Ibid., 157; E.T., 144.

89. "Ob diese Einfahrt in den Tunnel der Dogmatik . . . nicht das Ende unserer Sendung bedeutet", Marquardt, 179. ("If this entrance into the tunnel of dogmatics . . . does not mean the end of our mission.")

90. **How I Changed My Mind,** 39-40.

91. Ibid., 45.

92. Letter of 13th September, 1923, **Revolutionary Theology,** 149.

93. Ibid., 101.

94. See his correspondence of 28th June, 9th May, 18th December, 1922 and 23rd January, 1923. **Revolutionary Theology,** 98, 104.

95. Busch, 169; E.T. 156.

96. See his letters in **Revolutionary Theology,** 163 and 166.

97. Ibid., 167 and 182.

98. Busch, 187-188; E.T., 174.

99. Cited from the **Christian Dogmatics** in Torrance, op. cit., 107.

100. Ibid., 109.

101. Ibid.

Notes to pp. 15-18

102. See Barth's introductory essay on Feuerbach in **The Essence of Christianity.** Trans. George Eliot, xxvii.

103. Cited in Smart, 166.

104. Torrance, 110.

105. Smart, 167.

106. Torrance, 121.

107. Ibid., 123-124.

108. **Church Dogmatics,** I/i, vii. (Hereafter the **Church Dogmatics** will be cited by its respective part volumes.)

109. III/iv, xiii.

110. Busch, 298-200; E.T., 185-187.

111. Ibid., 177; E.T., 164.

112. Busch, 198-199; E.T., 185.

113. Busch, 202; E.T., 189.

114. Ibid., 211-214; E.T., 198-201. For the growing conflict between Barth and the Landeskirchen, see Kupisch, 68-72, especially for his debate with Bishop Otto Dibelius (1880-1967). See also Smart, 208-211.

115. Busch, 215; E.T., 202.

116. Ibid., 217; E.T., 204.

117. Quoted in Busch, 217; E.T., 204.

118. Torrance, provides an adequate summary discussion of this event and the subsequent publication, 182-193.

119. **How I Changed My Mind,** 43.

120. Barth, **Anselm: Fides Quaerens Intellectum,** trans. I. A. Robertson (Pittsburgh, PA: The Pickwick Press, 1975), 11.

121. Ibid., 18.

122. Ibid., 24. See also 74f where Barth analyzes how Anselm uses this principle in his famous argument about that which cannot be conceived of as greater than God.

123. Ibid., 28.

124. Ibid., 31.

125. Barth's explication of ratio is found on p. 19 of this work.

126. Ibid., 48.

127. Ibid., 78. See Barth's rather lucid discussion of the nature of the language used by Anselm and the presupposition behind this language, 73-78.

128. Ibid., 60, 64.

129. Ibid., 71.

130. Smart, 197.

131. **How I Changed My Mind**, 43.

132. I/i, vii-xiii.

133. Busch, 225-226; E.T., 212-213.

134. See an account of this speech and the reactions to it in Smart, 208-211 and in Kupisch, 68-72.

135. Kupisch, 72.

136. I/i, xiii.

137. Cited in Smart, 209.

138. Kupisch, 72-75; Marquardt, 47; Busch, 231, E.T., 218.

139. A. C. Cochrane, **The Church's Confession Under Hitler**, (Pittsburgh, PA: The Pickwick Press, 1976), p. 52. Also see the note on p. 283; Kupisch, 73; Marquardt, 47-48.

140. The text of these principles can be found in Cochrane, 222-3. See also the German texts in **Der Nationalsozialismus: Dokumente 1933-1945**, Hsgr. Walther Hofer (Frankfurt: Fischer Taschenbuch Verlag, 1957), 131-32.

141. Cochrane, 79-80.

142. See Barth's reaction to this in Busch, 236-240; E.T., 223-227.

143. Cochrane, 97, and the text of these Theses on 229.

144. Ibid., 99.

145. Busch, 238; E.T., 225.

146. Ibid.

147. Ibid.

148. Cochrane, 101.

149. **How I Changed My Mind**, 46.

150. Cochrane, 103.

151. Busch, 240; E.T., 227.

152. See the text of the new constitution in Cochrane, 224-228.

153. Quoted in Cochrane, 104.

154. Ibid.

155. Busch, 241; E.T., 228.

156. Busch, 241, E.T., 229; Cochrane, 107.

157. Busch, p. 242; E.T., 229.

158. Cochrane, 109.

159. Ibid., 112.

160. Ibid., 113.

161. Ibid., 119.

162. See the complete translated text of these Theses and Barth's reply in Cochrane, 120-122.

163. Ibid., 121-122.

164. Ibid.

165. Ibid., 123.

166. Ibid., 130.

167. Ibid., 131.

168. Ibid., 132.

169. Ibid., see the full text on 230-234.

170. Ibid., 232. See also Busch, 248-254; E.T., 235-241.

171. Ibid., 234.

172. Ibid., 237. See full text of the resolutions and motions at this synod on 237-247.

173. II/i, 177.

174. How I Changed My Mind, 47; Busch, 254; E.T., 242.

175. Busch described the details of Barth's last days in Bonn very well, 268-275; E.T., 255-262.

176. Ibid., 270; E.T., 257.

177. Ibid., 272; E.T., 259.

178. Ibid., 272-273; E.T., 259-260.

179. Ibid., 274; E.T., 261.

180. Ibid., 279; E.T., 266.

181. II/i, xi.

182. Busch, 302; E.T., 289.

183. Ibid., 319, 321; E.T., 305-306, 307-308.

184. How I Changed My Mind, 55.

185. Busch, 345; E.T., 332-333. See also Barth's description of his relationship to Brunner even after his famous Nein in Busch, 494; E.T., 476-477.

186. Busch, 356; E.T., 342.

187. Busch, 367-368; E.T., 354-355.

188. How I Changed My Mind, 64.

189. See Barth's own admission of suspicions and his reactions at the Assembly in Busch, 370-373; E.T., 357-360.

190. Ibid., 372; E.T., 359.

191. Ibid., 373; E.T., 359.

Notes to pp. 31-35

192. Ibid., 472-477; E.T., 457-460.

193. Cited in H. Gollwitzer's **The Demands of Freedom**, 149.

194. Busch, 485; E.T., 468; **How I Changed My Mind**, 76.

195. Busch, 484-485; E.T., 467-468.

196. See all the details of Barth's last days in Busch, 512-517; E.T. 496-500.

197. Ibid., 517; E.T., 499.

Chapter Two - **The Emerging Model for Political Dogmatics**

1. See F. Marquardt, **Theologie und Sozialismus: Das Beispiel Karl Barth**, 39-40; E. Busch, **Karl Barths Lebenslauf**, 72-138; H. Gollwitzer, **Reich Gottes und Sozialismus bei Karl Barth.** (München: Chr. Kaiser Verlag, 1972), 7-30.

2. See Busch, 81-84.

3. "Die Anfänge", **Antwort**, 832-3.

4. "Jesus Christus und die soziale Bewegung," Der Freie Aargauer, December 12, 1911. English translation in **Karl Barth and Radical Politics,** ed. and trans. George Hunsinger (Philadelphia, PA: Westminster Press, 1976), 19-46.

5. II/2, 512.

6. I/1, xiv.

7. I/2, 362-457.

8. II/2, 509-782.

9. III/4, 3-685.

10. **Kirchliche Dogmatik** IV/4, (Das christliche Leben), 1-73.

11. I/2, 783.

12. See Chapter One, 9-10.

13. I/2, 790.

14. Ibid.

15. Ibid., 791.

16. Ibid., 795.

17. Ibid., 793.

18. "Vergangenheit und zukunft: Friedrich Naumann und Christoph Blumhardt" in Moltmann, Jürgen, ed. **Anfänge der dialektischen Theologie**, 1, 40; E.T. 37.

19. Ibid., 41; E.T. 38.

20. Ibid., 41-2; E.T. 38-39.

21. Ibid., 43; E.T. 40.

22. Ibid., 44; E.T. 41.

23. "Es gibt im einzelnen auch ohne Religion viel Gutes und Hoffnungsvolles, viele Gleichnisse des Göttlichen in der Welt, sie bedarf und harrt aber im Ganzen einer durchgreifenden Erlösung und Neuordnung nicht durch Religion, sondern durch die realen Kräften Gottes. Man kann das Neue und Neutestamentliche . . . zusammenfassen in das eine Wort: Hoffnung: Hoffnung auf eine sichbare und greifbare Erscheinung der Herrschaft Gottes über die Welt (im Gegensatz zu dem blossen, oft so gotteslästerlichen Reden von der Allmacht Gottes). Hoffnung auf eine radikale Hilfe und Errettung aus dem gestrigen Weltzustand. . . . An 'Gott' glauben, das heisst für beiden Blumhardt: diese umfassende Hoffnung ernst nehmen, ernster als alle andern Erwägungen; alle Dinge von dieser Hoffnung aus betrachten und behandeln, sich und sein Leben bis ins einzelne in das grosse Licht dieser Hoffnung stellen." ("There are in individual cases even without religion much that is good and hopeful, including many metaphors of the divine in the world. Taken as a whole it needs and awaits a thoroughgoing redemption and reordering, not through religion, but through the real forces of God. The new world and the New Testament can be comprehended in a single word: hope--hope is a visible and tangible appearance of the lordship of God over the world (in contrast to mere talk of God's omnipotence, which is blasphemous); hope in radical help and deliverance from yesterday's world. . . . To believe in "God" means for the two Blumhardts to take this all-embracing hope seriously, more seriously than all other considerations; to consider and deal with everything on the basis of this hope; to place one's self and one's life in all particulars in the great light of this hope." Ibid., 45; E.T. 41-42.

24. Ibid., 48; E.T. 44.

25. See footnotes Chapter I, 6.

26. Moltmann, 4; Marquardt, 87-94, for an analysis of his early sermons.

Notes to pp. 39-42

See also Marquardt, **Der Christ in der Gesellschaft, 1919–1979** (München: Chr. Kaiser Verlag, 1980), 7–38.

27. Ibid., 5–6.

28. Marquardt, 186.

29. Ibid., 187.

30. See Barth's speech, "Der Christ in der Gesellschaft" in Moltmann, 8. "Die Gesellschaft ist nun beherrscht von ihrem eigenen Logos oder vielmehr von einer ganzen Reihe von gottähnlichen Hypostasen und Potenzen. . . . Dass die Götzen Nichtse sind, das beginnen wir zu ahnen, aber ihre dämonische Macht über unser Leben ist damit noch nicht gebrochen." 7 ("Society is ruled at present by it own logos or even more by a whole range of divinized hypostases and powers. . . . We begin to suspect that the idols are ciphers, but their demonic power over our life is not yet broken." 7) Marquardt has made an appraisal of the continuing importance of this address in a monograph, **Der Christ in der Gesellschaft, 1919– 1979**, 81–120.

31. Ibid., 7.

32. Ibid., 8.

33. Ibid., 11; Marquardt, 204.

34. Ibid., 14; see also Marquardt's discussion of the development of the Ursprung both philosophically and theologically in Barth, 207–219.

35. Ibid., 9; cf. Marquardt, **Der Christ in der Gesellschaft, 1919–1979**, 41–42.

36. Ibid., 10; cf. Thurneysen's appraisal of Barth's use of eschatology in Tambach in **Antwort**, 833.

37. Ibid., 11.

38. Ibid., 14.

39. Ibid., 17.

40. Ibid., 18.

41. Ibid.

42. Ibid., 20.

43. Ibid.

44. Ibid., 28.

45. See Marquardt, **Theologie und Sozialismus,** 204. See especially his view that Barth in this speech is exploring a "Logos Gottes" to confront the "Logos des Gesellschaft", 206-7.

46. Ibid., 204-5.

47. Moltmann, 34.

48. Ibid., 35.

49. Ibid.

50. Ibid., 36.

51. Ibid., 36-37.

52. Kupisch, 45.

53. See the text of this address in Moltmann, 49-78.

54. Kupisch, 47.

55. **Kerygma und Dogma,** 159.

56. Blätter für religiösen Sozialismus, 1. Jg. Nr. 2, (Pfingsten, 1920), 6.

57. Ibid. See also the discussion of his social ethic and understanding of Socialism from which he criticized Barth in R. Breipohl, **Religiöser Sozialismus und bürgerliches Geschichtsbewusstsein zur Zeit der Weimarer Republik** (Zürich: Theologischer Verlag, 1971), 232-233.

58. Ibid., 7.

59. Marquardt, 109.

60. Ibid, 109-110.

61. Ibid., 110.

62. Ibid., 111.

63. Op. cit., 240.

64. Busch, 118, E.T. 105.

65. Ibid.; Kupisch, 41.

66. Ibid.

67. Ibid.; Kupisch, 41.

68. **Der Römerbrief,** 1st ed., (Bern: G. A. Bäschlin, 1919; reprint ed., Zürich: EVZ-Verlag, 1963), 7-8.

69. Ibid., 12.

70. Ibid., 13.

71. Ibid., 376.

72. Ibid.

73. Ibid., 377.

74. Ibid.

75. Ibid., 378.

76. Ibid., 379.

77. Ibid.

78. Ibid.

79. Ibid., 380.

80. Ibid.

81. Ibid.

82. Ibid., 388.

83. Ibid., 385.

84. Ibid., 381.

85. Ibid., 382.

86. Ibid., 385. "Die Parole 'Gott mit uns!' ist eine begehrte und brauchbare Waffe auf dem politischen Kampfplatz. . . . Aber aller Glanz und alle Wucht einer 'christlichen Politik' können nicht darüber täuschen, dass sie gerade als solche den Wurm in sich trägt. Gott ist nicht dabei, gerade wenn und weil wir ihn dabei haben wollen." (The slogan, "God with us!" is a worthy and useful weapon on the political battlefield. . . . But all the glory and all the pressure of a "Christian

politics" cannot conceal the past which carries the seeds of its own destruction. God is absent, precisely when and because we want Him to be present.)

87. Ibid.

88. Ibid., 386.

89. Ibid., 387.

90. Ibid., 388.

91. Ibid.

92. Ibid., 390.

93. Ibid., 391.

94. Ibid., 392.

95. Marquardt, **Theologie und Sozialismus,** 127-142.

96. Ibid., 129.

97. Ibid.

98. Ibid., 131. "Er spricht von Ersetzung und Ablösung. So teilt er die Intention der Leninschen Schrift. Denn Lenin polemisiert gegen das Missverständnis des Engelsschen Gedankens vom 'Absterben des Staates', als wäre damit der gewaltsame Umsturz, die Revolution unnötig geworden. Er hebt Engels Unterscheidung des 'absterbenden" von dem gewaltsam 'aufhebenden' Staat hervor. 'Absterben' wird der Staat in der bereits erreichenten kommunistischen Gesellschaft. Gewaltsam 'aufzuheben' ist der bürgerliche Gewaltstaat. Zu 'ersetzen' und 'abzulösen' ist auch nach Barth der 'jetzige Staat'," 132. ([Barth] speaks of replacement and dissolution. As such he shares the ideas of Lenin's works. Lenin was polemical against the misunderstanding of Engel's thinking about "the withering away of the state," as if violent overthrow and revolution were unnecessary. He stressed Engel's distinction between the withering away of the state and the violent dissolving of the state. The state will "wither away" when the communist society is achieved. The bourgeois state rooted in violence must be uprooted by violence. The present state must also be replaced and dissolved according to Barth, 132).

99. Ibid., 136.

100. Ibid., 134.

101. Ibid., 134-145.

102. Ibid., 135.

216

103. Ibid., 136.

104. Ibid., 139.

105. **Die Grundlegung der Ethik in der Theologie Karl Barths** (München: Manz Verlag, 1966), 13.

106. Ibid., 22-26.

107. Ibid., 22.

108. Cited from **Römerbrief**(1), 423: ibid., 24.

109. H. Gollwitzer, **Reich Gottes und Sozialismus bei Karl Barth**, 7-8, 21-22.

111. Quoted from Der freie Aarguaer, 23rd December, 1911, cited in E. Lessing, **Das Problem der Gesellschaft in der Theologie Karl Barths und Friedrich Gogartens** (Gütersloh: Gütersloher Verlagshaus, 1972), 64.

112. Der freie Aarguaer, op. cit., 1; E.T. in Hunsinger, op. cit., 19-37.

113. Busch, op. cit., 133; E.T. 120.

114. **Epistle to the Romans,** vi.

115. Ibid., 314; cf. **Römerbrief**(2), 304; E.T. 314. See also J. Smart's appraisal of this transition which he says was induced by 1) Barth's more intensive study of St. Paul, particularly I and II Corinthians, 2) Overbeck's challenge to his understanding of history, leading him to include all of history under God's judgment of sin and death, 3) his better understanding of Plato and Kant, and 4) his better understanding of Kierkegaard and Dostoevsky, **The Divided Mind of Modern Theology,** 109-112.

116. Ibid., 42.

117. Ibid., 43.

118. Ibid., 44.

119. Ibid., 52.

120. Ibid., 65.

121. Ibid., 91.

122. Ibid., 92.

123. Röm. 130.

124. **Epistle to the Romans** 169.

125. Ibid., 428.

126. Ibid., 430.

127. See **Kirchliche Dogmatik**, IV/2, 565-694; **Church Dogmatics**, IV/2, 499-613.

128. **Epistle to the Romans**, 431.

129. Ibid., 435.

130. Ibid., 468.

131. Ibid., 469.

132. Marquardt points out that the first **Römerbrief** was written during the Bolshevik Revolution and the related revolutions in Germany and Switzerland in 1918. It was a sign of Barth's wistful participation in the revolution after his own theological manner. **Romans**(2) was written after many were disappointed over the outcome of these revolutions including Barth's own disappointment with the way they had gone. Barth was also motivated by a knowledge that many people misunderstood his theological position on revolution. Op. cit., 160-166.

133. **Epistle to the Romans**, 477.

134. Ibid., 478.

135. Ibid., 479.

136. Ibid., 478.

137. Ibid., 480.

138. Ibid.

139. Ibid., 481. See also Marquardt on "the honour of God" in which he suggests that this concept is a political as well as a theological vehicle in Barth which relativizes both revolution and reaction: "Gott als Gott wirkt immer demonstrativ, in bestimmten Bejahungen und Verneinungen, Relativierungen und Relationierungen," (156). **Theologie und Sozialismus**, 149-159. (God as God always works demonstratively in concrete Yeses and Noes, in relativities and relationships.)

140. **Epistle to the Romans**, 482.

141. Ibid., 484. Marquardt maintains that Barth is not so much against revolution as against the revolutionary, since he does not want to overturn the existing order with violence, fearing that the new will quickly relapse into the

old institutions only under a new heading. For Barth, revolution is a theological problem, for it is the negative mask of the evil man, a phenomenon which can only be eventually overcome by good. ([Barths] Vorwurf des Gottlosigkeit meint einen Mangel der Revolution als Revolution: ihre Erstarrung zum Prinzip . . . ihr schnelles Streben nach Etablierung neuer Gegebenheit und die Unfähigkeit, radikal, permanent die Revolution alles, auch des 'neuen' Bestehenden zu sein, 148. [Barth's] charge of godlessness points to a defect in revolution qua revolution—its deification into an absolute principle . . . its rapid tendency to establish a new system and its incapacity to be radically and permanently the revolution of everything, even of the new order.) He is anxious to preserve the "honour of God" so that God will not be identified with any revolutionary movement. (151)

142. Ibid., 496.

143. Ibid., 496-497.

144. See Marquardt's discussion of this point and its relationship to the Marxist principles of how social and economic relationships determine and shape man's historical and political situations. **Theologie und Sozialismus,** 152.

145. Ibid., 168.

146. I/2, 785.

Chapter Three - **Theological Foundations of the State and Society**

1. See Chapter 1, 27-32 for a summary of the **Christian Dogmatics.**

2. Loc. cit., (London: Paternoster Press, 1956), 18. See Barth's reply to this charge in IV/3, 173-180.

3. (Boston: The Pilgrim Press, 1928).

4. (London: SCM Press, 1930 and Hodder and Stoughton, 1935).

5. Op. cit.

6. Op. cit. For the initial reactions to Barth in the English-speaking world, see John McConnachie, "Der Einfluss Karl Barths in Schottland und England,," **Theologische Aufsätze: Karl Barth zum 50. Geburtstag,** (München: Chr. Kaiser Verlag, 1936), 529-570.

7. **Theologie und Sozialismus: Das Beispiel Karl Barths.** See also the essay by Marquardt which summarizes much of this book in **Karl Barth and**

Radical Politics 47-76. See the documentation of the debate about this controversial work in Ingrid Jacobsen, ed., **War Barth Sozialist?** (Berlin: Verlag die Spur, 1975).

       8. (München: Chr. Kaiser Verlag, 1975), 72-138. E.T. 1976.

       9. Ibid.

     10. **The Humanity of God** (London: Collins, 1961), 40.

     11. **Anselm: Fides Quaerens Intellectum,** trans. Ian W. Robertson, Pittsburg, PA: The Pickwick Press, 1975), 11. See also a rather brief but very useful summary of this period in Prof. Torrance's book, **Karl Barth: An Introduction to His Early Theology, 1910-1931,** 182-198.

     12. "Church and State," **Community, State, and Church,** trans. A. M. Hall, G. Ronald Howe, and Ronald Gregor Smith, (Gloucester, Mass.: Peter Smith, 1968), 101-148.

     13. See significantly recent research about Barth's attitude and conduct during this period in Hans Prolingheuer. **Der Fall Karl Barth, 1934-1935.** (Neukirchen: Neukirchener Verlag, 1977). See also Prof. Scholder's evidence for Barth's a-political conduct and writings during his early years in Germany. Klaus Scholder, **Die Kirchen und das Dritte Reich** (Frankfurt: Propyläen Verlag, 1977), 153-159.

     14. **Community, State, and Church** (Hereafter CSC), 107. Paul Lehmann points out that this confrontation really has to do with a confrontation which centers around the exercise of power that becomes detached from the purpose of power, a crisis develops and the possibility of revolution ensues. Since the state, according to Lehmann, is always attempting to validate and justify its use of power, then Pilate here is reacting to politics as the state would be expected to act, given its own understanding of how power is exercised: politics is always understood as power politics. But Jesus in this confrontation really has another view of power, which is eschatological, meaning that for Him politics includes both ultimate purposes and penultimate purposes. This is the clue to Jesus' rejoinder to Pilate that even the state's source of power and therefore authority comes from a source beyond the state. **Transfiguration of Politics.** (New York: Harper & Row, 1975), 52, 53-59.

     15. Ibid., 110.

     16. Ibid., 113.

     17. Ibid., 111.

     18. Ibid., 113-114.

     19. Ibid., 107.

     20. III/3, 458f. See also E. Lessing's discussion of a natural foundation for the state and political indifference and inactivism in his **Das Problem der Gesell-**

Notes to pp. 67-70

schaft in der Theologie Karl Barths und Friedrich Gogartens. (Gütersloh: Gütersloher Verlagshaus, 1972), 261-266.

21. **CSC,** 116-117.

22. Ibid., 118.

23. III/4, 301-313.

24. "The form of the command particularly in question is its political form which we shall have to consider in the context of the doctrine of reconciliation, namely the call of God to the state, which is not an order of creation but a genuine and specific order of the covenant." III/4, 303. Cf. Cullmann's similar discussion of the state being a part of the Bundesordnung as a penultimate institution which will disappear when the final kingdom of God appears. Oscar Cullmann, **Christ and Time.** Rev. ed. trans. Floyd V. Filson. (Philadelphia, PA: Westminster Press, 1964), 191-210.

25. Op. cit., 259-267.

26. See Barth's reply to the formulation of his colleague in Bonn, Hans Weber, who insisted that pastors as civil servants (Beamten) could support the Hitler oath. In his reply Barth points to totalitarian claims by the fascist state being measured over against scripture for the evangelical Christian. Prolingheuer. Op. cit., 67-68.

27. III/1, 59-61; Lessing, op. cit., 268.

28. III/1, 59.

29. Ibid., 60-61.

30. Ibid., 73.

31. Ibid.

32. Ibid., 75.

33. Ibid., 80.

34. Ibid., 83.

35. Ibid., 78.

36. **CSC,** 122.

37. **CSC,** 156. For a summary of Roman Catholic views of the origin of the state, see Appendix.

38. Ibid., 129.

39. Ibid., 157. (The more exacting consequences of this idea in political praxis will be explored in the latter part of this book.)

40. Prof. Hans Maier deals especially with the question of the ideology of the European Christian Democratic parties and the relation of these parties to the state which provide a useful historical and social background to Barth's resistance to "Christian Democratic" parties and ideologies. **Revolution und Kirche: Zur Frühgeschichte der christlichen Demokratie.** (München: DTV, 1973), 9-67, 248-268.

41. **CSC**, 161.

42. Ibid., 132.

43. Lessing, op. cit., 79.

44. **CSC**, 138. The issue of what "subjection" means in Rom. 13:1-7 has obviously had a lively and long exegetical, theological, and hermeneutical history. For a summary of the theological interpretation of this text, both in Catholic and Protestant, as well as Anglican thought, see the editorial in Journal of Church and State. Vol. 18. Nr. 3 (Autumn, 1976), 433-442. For a very comprehensive article on the actual historical situation being addressed by Paul in this text, see Johannes Friedrich, et. al. "Zur historischen Situation und Intention von Röm. 13.1-7." Zeitschrift für Theologie und Kirche. 73. Jg. (1976), 131-166. Friedrich, et. al. maintains that since 49 A.D. the Jewish Christians were no longer under the protection of statutes allowing certain privileges to synagogues. Driven from the synagogue, gathering primarily in house churches, and looked upon suspiciously by the Roman officials as a superstitious cult, Paul tries to advise the Christians in 58 A.D. how to live in this new, more precarious situation. Thus Rom. 13:1-7 primarily is intended to advise Christians about the right way of obedience and loyalty in their new situation. This is all the more crucial, according to Friedrich, et. al., because Nero had brought in a number of administrative tax reforms to which there was resistance. Therefore, according to the authors, Paul chooses his language very deliberately because of similarities between it and that of the bureaucrats, in order to dampen any resistance on the part of the Christians in this new situation. (161-166)

Paul Lehmann sees a link between Paul's admonition to "submit" to the political authorities in vv. 1 and 5 and Paul's advice in v. 8: "Owe no one anything, except to love one another, for he who loves his neighbor has fulfilled the law." Opheilein may mean either "owe" as in the case of indebtedness or "to be obligated". This obligation to neighbor provides a more radical form of obedience in the state. It is the instrument through which there can occur a transfiguration of values and society as contrasted with simply a change or transformation of society.

> Submission to the state, then takes the form of negative
> obedience amounting to indifference. Making sure that

Notes to pp. 71-74

> the state has no claim against you, paying "tax and toll
> . . . " is simply a realistic attempt at being as wise
> in one's own generation. . . . The obligation to the neigh-
> bor, however, is a positive obedience, which admits of
> no exceptions, including the exception of the state. The
> state and neighbor are thus joined in a single obedience
> to the "higher law" of love. Submission and responsibility
> both express the revolutionary perspective upon life in
> the world. . . . Op. cit., 37-38.

He insists that this has been an overlooked connexion in Barth's Römerbrief, particularly where he discusses the "negative possibility of revolution" and the "positive
possibility of love." (43-48)

45. Ibid., 110.

46. Ibid., 111.

47. Ibid., 114. For an analysis of why Barth persisted even during
the Third Reich to hold this view, see Scholder, op. cit., 681-682.

48. III/3, 73.

49. **Systematic Theology** II. (Chicago: University of Chicago Press,
1957), 61.

50. III/3, 76.

51. Ibid., 77.

52. IV/1, 220.

53. Ibid.

54. "War itself is neither Christian nor unchristian, neither moral nor
immoral. In certain historical circumstances it is the imperative expression of human
nature as this has developed with civilisation to political life. (Hence) we can
participate with a good conscience only in a state which pledges its might for
the right, not merely within its own borders against the criminal, but also against
another state which uses force against it." Quoted from Herrmann in III/4, 457.

55. Ibid., 458. See Barth's appraisal of war in the state in III/4, 450-470,
which he includes in the sub-chapter on "The Protection of Life". See also his
critique of Herrmann's position in Busch, op. cit., 93, and in W. Huber, "Evangelische
Theologie und Kirche beim Ausbruch des Ersten Weltkrieges," **Studien zur Friedensforschung**, Bd. 4. (Gilching: Käsel Verlag, 1970), 207.

56. Ibid.

57. Ibid., 459.

58. Ibid.

59. Ibid.

60. III/4, 452.

61. Ibid., 453.

62. Ibid., 454.

63. Ibid.

64. Ibid., 467.

65. Ibid., 462. Barth does suggest that war might possibly be legitimated when what he calls "the time of a state in its present form of existence has expired, that its independent life has no more meaning nor basis, and that it is thus better advised to yield and surrender, continuing its life within a greater nexus of states". Such legitimization could take place, for example, were the Swiss confederation to have to defend itself or when a stronger state is bound to the defense of a weaker state by treaty. 461-464.

66. Ibid., 466ff.

67. Op. cit., 185-192.

68. Ethik I, Dietrich Braun, ed. (Zürich, Theologischer Verlag, 1973), 273.

69. Ibid., 274.

70. III/4, 117.

71. Ethik I, 276.

72. Ibid., 277.

73. Ibid., 274.

74. Ibid., 283.

75. Ibid., 284.

76. Ibid.

77. III/4, 459.

224

78. Ibid., 452.

79. Ibid., 517.

80. Ibid., 518.

81. Ibid., 520.

82. Ibid., 527-529.

83. Ibid., 529-534.

84. Ibid., 534-536.

85. Ibid., 537.

86. Ibid., 537-538.

87. Ibid., 538. Lessing suggests that Barth's polemic against the privatization of economic and social relations has to do with his break with liberalism and its view of society. He suggests three reasons for this polemic: 1) With his attack on liberal theology, Barth could not justify the private spheres of human life and societal values and thus saw the crises of the private sphere connected with the crisis of liberal theology, 2) This moved Barth to pay more attention to the public sphere and use of power in light of his understanding of injustices and sinfulness of society to be particularly reflected in private property and private control of the means of production in western society, a tendency already detected in the two commentaries on **Romans**. 3) The real goal became his warning to Christian congregations incorporating and legitimizing in their own structures the privatizing and individualizing tendencies of the economic and social spheres. Op. cit., 279. Cf. Helmut Gollwitzer, **Reich Gottes und Sozialismus bei Karl Barth.** (München: Chr. Kaiser Verlag, 1972), 55-56 and IV/3.2, 734-742, where Barth discusses the dependence and independence of the Christian congregation in relation to the surrounding society.

88. Ibid., 542.

89. Ibid., 543.

90. Ibid., 544.

91. Ibid.

92. Ibid., 545. See also Gollwitzer's commentary on this aspect of Barth in **Reich Gottes**, 14.

93. **Theology and the Church**, 334-354.

94. Ibid., 341.

95. Ibid., 343.

96. Ibid., 349.

97. Ibid., IV/1, 188.

98. Ibid., 198.

99. Ibid.

100. Ibid., 194-200.

101. IV/3.1, 388-393.

102. Ibid., 405-411.

103. IV/1, 295.

104. III/4, 301.

105. II/2, 721.

106. Ibid., 722.

107. Ibid., 723.

108. **CSC**, 163.

109. Ibid., 167.

110. Ibid., 168.

111. IV/1, 396.

112. A more detailed analysis of the reconciling act of Christ for man and his society will be given in another part of this book.

113. Ibid., 413-432.

114. Ibid, 420-421.

115. Ibid., 421.

116. Ibid.

117. Ibid., 432-445.

Notes to pp. 84-88

118. Ibid., 436.

119. Ibid., 437.

120. Ibid., 445.

121. Ibid., 445-458.

122. Ibid., 449.

123. Ibid., 451.

124. Ibid., 458-478.

125. Ibid., 463.

126. Ibid., 465.

127. III/4, 470-564.

128. Ibid., 474.

129. Ibid., 477-478.

130. "Rechtfertigung und Recht" (translated as "Church and State"), CSC, 145.

131. Ibid., 146.

132. Ibid., 147.

133. Ibid., 146.

134. Ibid., 147-148.

135. **Reich Gottes**, 9.

136. **Eine Schweizer Stimme, 1938-1945**. 2. Auflage, (Zürich: Evangelischer Verlag, 1948), 272-302.

137. Ibid., 293.

138. **CSC**, 181. See also Marquardt, "Theologische und politische Motivationen Karl Barths im Kirchenkampf," **Junge Kirche**, 34. JG., 294-295.

139. Ibid.; Cf. discussion of these points in Busch, 367-370; also **Die Kirche zwischen Ost und West**. (Zürich: Evangelischer Verlag, 1949); **How I Changed My Mind**. (Edinburgh: Saint Andrew Press, 1969) 61-67.

140. Busch, loc. cit., 397; E.T., 383.

141. Barth discusses these points in a letter which is partially quoted in Busch, 354; E.T., 341.

142. III/4, 544.

143. Ibid., 545.

144. Ibid., 551-552.

145. "Die Kirche zwischen Ost und West," **Der Götze Wackelt.** (Berlin: Käthe Vogt Verlag, 1964), 141.

146. Ibid., 137.

147. **Eine Schweizer Stimme,** 292.

Chapter Four - Jesus Christ as Servant, Lord, and Witness

1. **Humanity of God,** 44-45.

2. Ibid., 46.

3. Ibid., 53.

4. IV/ 3.1, 174-175.

5. III/1, 94-329.

6. IV/1, 7.

7. Ibid., 26-28.

8. Ibid., 27. See a very helpful analysis of the role of the covenant in the ancient Near East by George Mendenhall, **Law and Covenant in Israel and the Ancient Near East.** (Pittsburgh: The Biblical Colloquium, 1955).

9. Ibid., 28.

10. Ibid., 32.

Notes to pp. 94-96

11. Ibid., 32-34. " . . . for they shall know me, from the least of them to the greatest," says the Lord, "and I will forgive their iniquity, and I shall remember their sin no more."

12. Ibid., 34.

13. Ibid.

14. Ibid., 35.

15. Ibid., 39-43. Barth suggests that this covenant has four implications for Christians. 1) God in His freedom chooses to initiate the reconciling act through the atonement of Jesus Christ. 2) The grace of the covenant is beneficial for man. 3) Its grace evokes an act of gratitude on the part of man. 4) As a creature of God chosen to be His partner, man cannot be neutral toward God.

16. Ibid., 43.

17. Ibid., 49-50.

18. Ibid., 52.

19. See Tillich's discussion of this term in **Systematic Theology.** I. (Chicago: University of Chicago Press, 1951), 163-292.

20. Ibid., 54.

21. Barth's analysis of Johann Cocceius (1603-1669) and Federal theology would seem to suggest that he himself could agree with their approach to the preexistence of the covenant of grace with the single exception of Cocceius' idea that the covenant of grace is based on an intratrinitarian decision within the Godhead. Ibid., 59-68.

22. Barth pays particular attention to this problem in III/3, under his doctrine of evil (289-368) and his doctrine of angels (369-531).

23. IV/1, 67.

24. Ibid., 72-73.

25. Ibid., 72-73.

26. Ibid., 76.

27. See his discussion of the traditional rendering in IV/1, 123-124, 127-128.

28. Ibid., 128.

29. See his discussion in IV/1, 132-135.

30. Ibid., 135.

31. See a discussion of christology from below toward above and from above downward in Wolfhart Pannenberg, **Jesus: God and Man.** trans. Lewis L. Wilkins and Duane A. Priebe (Philadelphia: Westminster Press, 1968), 23ff.

32. IV/1, 159f.

33. Ibid.

34. Ibid., 166.

35. Ibid., 168.

36. Ibid., 170.

37. "Deity of Christ" appears to mean something similar to what one might also call the "dignity of Christ", that is, a non-loss of face even in his humiliation as man. Barth discusses this concept quite fully in IV/1, 177-183.

38. Ibid., 181. See particularly Barth's appraisal of the kenosis controversy, 181-183.

39. Ibid., 184.

40. Ibid., 185.

41. Ibid., 192-193.

42. Ibid.

43. Ibid., 202.

44. Ibid.

45. Ibid., 202-203.

46. Ibid., 204.

47. Ibid., 208-209.

48. Ibid., 217.

49. Ibid.

50. Ibid., 222.

51. Ibid., 231-232.

52. Ibid., 233. "We are threatened by it because there is a complete turning of the tables. He who has acted therefore as Judge will also judge me, and He and not I will judge others."

53. Ibid., 234. "I am not the Judge. Jesus Christ is Judge. The matter is taken out of my hands. And that means liberation. A great anxiety is lifted, the greatest of all. I can turn to other more important . . . activities."

Notes to pp. 101-103

54. Ibid., 235-244.

55. Ibid., 236

56. Ibid., 237.

57. Ibid., 240. "He does it by coming amongst us in the character and form and role of a man like that, and therefore showing us by example what the being of every man is in His eyes and therefore, in truth. . . . In that He takes our place it is decided what our place is."

58. Ibid., 241.

59. Ibid., 243. "The only possibility which is still open to us as we look at Him and at ourselves is that of repentance, of turning away from the being and activity . . . of turning to what can be made our evil case now that it is the case of Jesus Christ. . . . "

60. Ibid., 244-256.

61. Ibid., 248.

62. Ibid., 256-283.

63. Ibid., 257.

64. Ibid., 259.

65. Ibid., 296.

66. IV/2, 20-154.

67. Ibid., 21. The phrase "homecoming of the Son" is apparently taken from Gollwitzer's work, **Die Freude Gottes**, deliberately in order to refute some of his exegesis and to improve on others, particularly as Gollwitzer's exegesis of the Prodigal Son story maintains that Jesus Christ is to be seen implicitly in the actions of the father in the story (22-23).

68. Ibid., 24.

69. Ibid., 28. See also a discussion of Christ's humanity as developed by Barth in relation to the classical terms of anhypostasia and enhypostasia in John Thompson, **Christ in Perspective: Christological Perspectives in the Theology of Karl Barth.** (Grand Rapids, Mich.: Wm. B. Eerdmans, 1978), 28-29. Barth's own appraisal of his relationship to these categories can be found in IV/2, 49-50, 91-95. Prof. Friedrich Marquardt insists that these classical terms have undergone a reinterpretation in Barth through his political praxis. **Theologie und Sozialismus: Das Beispiel Karl Barths,** 265-275.

70. Ibid., 31-36.

71. Ibid., 36-116.

72. Ibid., 116-154.

73. Ibid., 49. See also Barth's views of what are the distinctions of man's creaturehood as contrasted with the creatureliness of other creatures in III/2, 71-132, 222-285.

74. Ibid., 50.

75. Ibid., 52.

76. Ibid., 53.

77. Ibid.

78. Ibid., 53-54.

79. Ibid., 60.

80. Ibid., 65.

81. Ibid., 62-63.

82. Ibid., 63-64.

83. Ibid., 92.

84. Ibid., 100.

85. Ibid., 101.

86. Ibid., 106.

87. Ibid., 115.

88. Ibid., 151.

89. Ibid., 154.

90. Ibid., 168.

91. Ibid., 169.

92. Ibid., 172.

93. Ibid., 180-181.

94. Ibid., 173-175.

95. Ibid., 175.

96. Ibid.

97. Ibid., 177.

98. Ibid., 189-190.

99. Ibid., 191.

100. Ibid.

101. IV/3.1, 5-6. See a useful historical summary of the development of Calvin's doctrine of the three-fold ministry of Jesus in John F. Jansen, **Calvin's Doctrine of the Work of Christ.** (London: James Clarke & Co., 1956).

102. Ibid., 12.

103. Ibid., 46.

104. Ibid., 46-47.
105. See his description of the Old Testament prophets, Ibid., 48-49.
106. Ibid., 50.
107. Ibid., 50-51.
108. Ibid., 51-52.
109. Ibid., 52.
110. Ibid., 53-65.
111. Ibid., 66.
112. Ibid., 69.
113. Ibid., 89.
114. Ibid., 81.
115. Ibid., 93.
116. Ibid., 86.
117. Ibid., 100.
118. Ibid., 101.
119. Ibid., 111.
120. Ibid.
121. Ibid., 119.
122. Ibid., 120.
123. Ibid., 124.
124. Ibid., 126.
125. Ibid.
126. Ibid., 126-127.
127. Ibid., 127.
128. Ibid., 127-128.
129. Ibid., 128-129.
130. Ibid., 130.
131. Ibid., 132.
132. Ibid., 139.
133. Ibid., 139.
134. Ibid., 142.
135. Ibid., 148.

136. Ibid., 154-157.

137. Ibid., 160.

138. Ibid., 192-193.

139. Ibid., 246.

140. Ibid., 247.

141. Ibid., 248.

142. Ibid.

143. Ibid., 248-249.

144. Ibid., 150-152.

145. Ibid., 154.

146. Ibid., 255.

147. Ibid., 155-157.

148. Ibid., 267.

149. Ibid., 270.

150. Ibid., 270-271.

151. Ibid., 271.

152. IV/1, 359-360.

153. Ibid., 361. See also Hans Küng's chapter on the basis for the methodology in Barth's christology. **Justification: The Doctrine of Karl Barth and a Catholic Reflection**, trans. Thomas Collins, et. al., (London: Burns & Oates, 1964), 42-52.

154. Ibid., 365.

155. Ibid., 369.

156. Ibid., 373.

157. Ibid.

158. Ibid., 375. See also Barth's appraisal of Hegel's anthropology and theism in **Die protestantische Theologie im 19. Jahrhundert**, Band 1. (Hamburg: Siebenstern Verlag, 1960), 330-339. See also a rather interesting thesis by James Yerkes who maintains that the Christ event really provides the historical fulfillment of absolute spirit. Through the cross, Hegel understood Christ to be negating his naturalness as man and returning to his initial unity with God as absolute spirit. **The Christology of Hegel**, American Academy of Religion Dissertation Series, no. 23. (Missoula, Montana: Scholars Press, 1978).

159. Ibid., 375.

160. Ibid., 376.

161. Ibid.

Notes to pp. 118-123

162. _Ibid._

163. _Ibid._, 377.

164. _Ibid._, 377-381.

165. _Ibid._, 391.

166. _Ibid._, 397-399.

167. _Ibid._, 399-403.

168. _Ibid._, 403-407.

169. _Ibid._, 407-413.

170. _Ibid._, 410.

171. _Ibid._, 413.

172. _Ibid._, 414.

173. _Ibid._, 418-419.

174. _Ibid._, 420.

175. _Ibid._, 421.

176. _Ibid._

177. _Ibid._, 421-422.

178. _Ibid._, 422.

179. _Ibid._, 432-433.

180. _Ibid._, 435.

181. _Ibid._

182. _Ibid._, 436.

183. _Ibid._, 437.

184. _Ibid._, 445-446.

185. _Ibid._, 447.

186. _Ibid._, 449.

187. _Ibid._, 451.

188. _Ibid._

189. _Ibid._, 452.

190. _Ibid._, 458-459.

191. _Ibid._, 459.

192. _Ibid._, 464-465.

193. _Ibid._, 464.

194. Ibid., 465.

195. Ibid., 478.

196. Ibid., 480.

197. Ibid., 481.

198. Ibid., 484.

199. Ibid., 486.

200. Ibid., 487.

201. Ibid., 488.

202. Ibid., 489.

203. Ibid.

204. Ibid., 492.

205. Ibid., 494.

206. Ibid.

207. Ibid., 495.

208. Ibid., 496.

209. Ibid., 500.

210. See Barth's defence in IV/1, 499-501.

211. Ibid., 501.

212. Ibid., 502.

213. IV/2, 382.

214. Ibid., 386.

215. Ibid., 387-388.

216. Ibid., 389.

217. Ibid., 392.

218. Ibid., 393.

219. Ibid., 396.

220. Ibid., 401.

221. Ibid., 403.

222. Ibid., 405.

223. Ibid.

224. Ibid., 407.

225. Ibid., 408.

Notes to pp. 128-132

226. Ibid., 409.

227. IV/1, 418-432.

228. Ibid., 411.

229. Ibid.

230. Ibid., 420.

231. Ibid., 421.

232. Ibid., 422-423.

233. Ibid., 433.

234. Ibid.

235. Ibid., 433.

236. Ibid., 436. See also his discussion of man and woman in III/4, 116-239.

237. Ibid., 438.

238. Ibid.

239. Ibid., 439.

240. Ibid.

241. Ibid., 442.

242. Ibid., 443.

243. Ibid., 444.

244. Ibid., 452.

245. Ibid., 453.

246. Ibid., 460.

247. Ibid., 462.

248. Ibid., 463.

249. Ibid., 468-470.

250. Ibid., 471.

251. Ibid., 474. See also Barth's work ethic in III/4, 472ff. Cf. Marquardt, op. cit., 331-333.

252. Ibid., 475-476.

253. Ibid., 477.

254. Ibid., 477-478.

255. Ibid., 483.

256. Ibid., 484.

257. Ibid., 489-490.

258. Ibid., 490.

259. Ibid., 494.

260. Ibid., 495.

261. IV/3.1, 368-480.

262. Ibid., 369.

263. Ibid., 371.

264. Ibid., 373.

265. Ibid., 376.

266. Ibid.

267. Ibid., 377.

268. Ibid., 434.

269. Ibid., 436.

270. Ibid., 440.

271. Ibid., 446.

272. Ibid., 452-453.

273. Ibid., 462.

274. Ibid., 470.

275. Ibid., 470-471.

276. Ibid., 472-473.

Chapter Five - **Effects of Reconciliation: Our Justification, Sanctification and Vocation**

1. IV/3.1, 315

2. Ibid., 316.

3. Ibid., 328.

4. Ibid., 339.

5. Ibid., 340.

6. IV/1, 310.

Notes to pp. 139-144

7. Ibid., 316.

8. Ibid., 323.

9. IV/3.1, 340.

10. IV/1, 573.

11. Ibid., 575-576.

12. Ibid., 615.

13. Ibid., 614.

14. Ibid., 619.

15. Ibid.

16. Ibid., 621.

17. Ibid., 627.

18. Ibid., 632.

19. Ibid., 634.

20. IV/2, 500.

21. Ibid., 503.

22. Ibid., 504.

23. Ibid., 505.

24. Ibid., 511.

25. Ibid.

26. Ibid., 511-513.

27. Ibid., 516.

28. Ibid., 519.

29. Ibid., 524.

30. Ibid., 527.

31. Ibid., 529.

32. Ibid., 530; IV/3.2, 489-490.

33. Ibid., 533. See also Dietrich Bonhoeffer, **The Cost of Discipleship,** trans. R. H. Fuller. (New York: Macmillan Company, 1955), 37-85.

34. Ibid., 536-538.

35. Ibid., 538-553.

36. Ibid., 544.

37. Ibid., 545.

38. Ibid., 548.

39. Ibid., 549. It is interesting to compare Barth's "transvaluation" with Paul Lehmann's "transfiguration" of power. **Transfiguration of Politics,** 73-226.

40. Ibid., 550. Barth lists other concrete manifestations of discipleship in society with social and political aspects on 550-552. Amongst them are personal relationships and loyalties, particularly those of family and nation.

41. Ibid., 553.

42. IV/3.2, 484.

43. Ibid.

44. Ibid., 485.

45. Ibid., 493.

46. Ibid., 494.

47. Ibid., 522.

48. Ibid.

49. Ibid., 524.

50. Ibid., 530-531.

51. Ibid., 532.

52. Ibid., 533.

53. Ibid., 535.

54. Ibid., 536.

55. Ibid.

56. Ibid. 548.

57. Ibid., 559.

58. Ibid., 565.

59. Ibid., 566.

60. Ibid., 572.

61. Ibid., 601.

62. Ibid., 621.

63. Ibid., 625.

64. Ibid., 628.

65. Ibid.

66. Ibid., 630.

67. Ibid., 634.

Notes to pp. 152-158

68. Ibid., 646.

69. Ibid., 711.

70. Ibid., 712.

71. Ibid., 717.

72. Ibid.

73. Ibid., 723.

74. Ibid., 730.

75. Ibid., 739.

76. Ibid., 769.

77. Ibid., 770.

78. Ibid., 773.

79. Ibid., 775.

80. Ibid., 776.

81. Ibid., 889-895

82. Ibid., 895-898.

83. Ibid., 898-901.

84. Ibid., 891.

85. Ibid.

86. Ibid., 892.

87. Ibid.

88. Ibid., 893. See also William O. Shanahan, **Der deutsche Protestantismus vor der sozialen Frage, 1815-1871.** (München: Chr. Kaiser Verlag, 1962). He analyzes the prevalent attitudes in the Prussian Church regarding the poor and the workers and the dominant conservatism of the German Church in general toward a social and political diaconate at the time of industrialization. Likewise Klaus Scholder extends this analysis into the 20th century in **Die Kirchen und das Dritte Reich.** I. (Berlin: Propyläen, 1977), 124-150.

89. Ibid., 893.

90. Ibid., 896.

91. Ibid., 899.

92. Ibid.

93. Ibid., 901.

94. III/4, 545.

95. IV/2, 169.

96. Ibid., 172. Marquardt maintains that the "royal" man really means the new man who is able to break through the class character of society. **Theologie und Sozialismus,** 295.

97. Ibid., 192. Marquardt suggests that Barth refers here not to the "natural" man, but to the man under grace, the forgiven man in Christ, who is really free to be revolutionary in the christological sense. This is not a sociological or simply a psychological revolution. It is a theology of revolution. As such it is a theology which has to do with being partisan on the side of the poor. A definite political obligation follows from the belief in the justice and fairness of God. This takes the character of God standing at the side and for the defense of the oppressed poor, the widows, the orphans, and the strangers, always against those who already have their rights and for those from whom it has been taken. "Die Parteilichkeit Gottes stellt den Christen nach links." Op.cit., 296-297. Cf. Henrikus Boers' interpretation of Matt. 25:31-46, where he maintains that the revolutionary and radical character of that passage has to do with claiming that acts of social and political action, be they from Christians or non-Christians, can in fact disclose what it means to be a Christian. "With that, in a very radical way, it allowed itself to be let in on a dialogue with the world by allowing itself to be confronted and interpreted by worldly acts. **Theology out of the Ghetto.** (Leiden: E. J. Brill, 1971), 73. Barth seems to confirm this claim also as a possible acting out of Christian vocation. See also Jose Miranda, **Marx and the Bible,** John Eagleson, trans. (Maryknoll, N.Y.: Orbis Books, 1974). Miranda understands the knowledge of justice on behalf of both the victim and perpetrators of injustice and oppression. See especially 44-76.

98. See my earlier chapter in which the definition and the character of unredeemed and redeemed society as aspects of God's reconciliation are analyzed.

99. "Up to now the political constitution has been the religious sphere, the religion of the people's life, the heaven of their universality in contrast to the particular mundane existence of their actuality." From "Critique of Hegel's Philosophy of the State" cited in **Writings of the Young Marx on Philosophy and Society.** Lloyd D. Easton and Kurt H. Guddat, ed. (Garden City, New York: Anchor Books, 1967), 176.

100. IV/3.1, 242.

101. Ibid., 243.

102. Ibid.

103. Ibid., 244.

104. Ibid.

105. Ibid., 248.

106. Ibid., 248-249.

107. IV/3.2, 664-671.

108. Ibid., 666.

Notes to pp. 161-165

109. IV/2, 438.

110. Ibid., 441.

111. IV/3.2, 667.

112. III/4, 532.

113. Ibid., 533.

114. Ibid., 537.

115. Ibid., 543. Cf. Helmut Gollwitzer, **Reich Gottes und Sozialismus bei Karl Barth,** 14.

116. Ibid., 544.

117. Ibid., 544-545.

118. Ibid., 551.

119. **Community, State and Church,** 146; cf. 153-159.

120. III/4, 543.

121. Ibid., 544.

122. Ibid., 528. "Right work is righteous work, i.e., work which to the best of its ability does justice to each specific task and end; whereas dilettante or botched work, however profitable or well-meaning in other respects, and whatever the effort incurred, cannot possibly be right work . . . and therefore obedience to the divine command. . . . " 528-529.

123. Ibid., 530. "If we are not to leave the world of work and workers to themselves as though they were only links in a great nexus of fate in which there is no responsibility, there is need to put quite sharply the question of worthy or valuable work which serves the cause of humanity." 531.

124. Ibid., 535. This has already been dealt with in the early part of the chapter, 30-32.

125. Ibid., 546. "Only in this reflection can and will he assert himself as a man in his external work. . . . Yet neither his self-assertion in face of the ever-threatening autarchy of his external work, nor his indispensable devotion to it, is in any sense self-evident. Hence the reflection . . . must be an inward work." 546.

126. Ibid., 551. "(The Sabbath) is the concrete reminder of the day of the Lord which preceded all man's working days as the day of completed creation and of the Lord's resurrection, and which will follow them all as the day of judgment and of death. This day is the day of God's freedom and rest and therefore of man's freedom and rest . . . God demands . . . that he should rest. . . . "

127. **CSC,** 140.

128. Ibid., 143-144.

129. Ibid., 119.

Chapter Six - **Political Christology and Praxis**

1. IV/3, 249.

2. Cited from <u>Capital</u> in David McLellan. **Karl Marx.** (New York: The Viking Press, 1975), 36.

3. **Writings of the Young Marx on Philosophy and Society.** trans. and ed., Lloyd D. Easton and Kurt H. Guddat. (Garden City, New York: Doubleday & Company, 1967), 424. Cf. the full context from which this was selected in: **Karl Marx, Die Frühschriften.** Hsgr. Siegfried Landshut. (Stuttgart: Alfred Kröner Verlag, 1974), 378-408.

4. III/4, 539f.

5. <u>Ibid.</u>

6. For some verification of this, see Barth's views on the relation of contemplation to what he calls the "active life" in III/4, 560-564. There can be no worthwhile active life for the Christian without some theological reflection and perspective permitted through the discipline of contemplation. But contemplation can become a <u>cul-de-sac</u> without relating it to the active life.

7. **Systematic Theology.** I, 61.

8. Hans Urs von Balthasar. **Karl Barth: Darstellung und Deutung seiner Theologie.** (Köln: Jacob Hegner, 1962), 244-245.

9. <u>Ibid.</u>, 243.

10. **The Humanity of God**, 48. Emphasis added.

11. See Barth's comments and critique of Marx in III/2, 387-390.

12. <u>Ibid.</u>, 367.

13. III/4, 528-551.

14. Gollwitzer, **Reich Gottes und Sozialismus bei Karl Barth**, 13.

15. <u>Ibid.</u>, 14; cf. III/4, 545.

16. IV/2, 180; cf. Barth's interpretation of the political role of Christ in His own society. III/4, 472.

17. Gollwitzer, <u>op. cit.</u>, 15.

18. **How to Serve God in a Marxist Land**, trans. Henry Clark and James D. Smart. (New York: Association Press, 1959), 52.

19. Cited in **Karl Barth and Radical Politics**, ed. and trans., George Hunsinger, 19. See also Wolfgang Huber's criticism of this point of view of the young Barth in **Studien zur Friedensforschung.** Bd. 4 (Gilching: Käsel Verlag, 1970), 202-209; Gollwitzer's observations in **Reich Gottes**, 20.

20. This has been commented upon and more thoroughly noted in the first chapter of this book. For excerpts and documentation of the social

democratic movement in Germany, see Helga Grebing. **Geschichte der deutschen Arbeiterbewegung.** (München: Deutscher Taschenbuch Verlag, 1970), 50-68, 87-93; in Switzerland see **Schweizerische Arbeiterbewegung,** 96-236.

21. Hunsinger, op. cit., 23.

22. Ibid., 29. See also Barth's criticism of both East and West in "Die Kirche zwischen Ost und West," **Der Götze wakelt,** 124-143.

23. Ibid., 33.

24. Ibid.

25. Friedrich Marquardt. "Socialism in the Theology of Karl Barth." Cited in Hunsinger. op. cit., 63-65. See also Barth's letter to Paul Tillich cited in Ernst Wolf, "Politischer Gottesdienst," Blätter für deutsche und internationale Politik, XI (1966), 289-301. In this letter Barth calls the politics of the SPD a "healthy politics" in that the political program fulfilled the mandate for political action in the New Testament. Their politics included 1) concern and advocacy for the working classes, 2) advocacy of democracy, 3) advocacy for demilitarization in Europe.

26. Cited in Hunsinger, 34.

27. IV/2, 620f, 719. See also Joseph Bettis' refutation that Barth is in fact a universalist: "Is Karl Barth a Universalist?" Scottish Journal of Theology. XX (1967), 423-436.

28. IV/2, 689; see also "Justification and Justice" in **Community, State, and Church,** 118-122.

29. Ibid., 144-145.

30. Ibid., 139.

31. IV/2, 720.

32. Ibid., 721.

33. Ibid., 724.

34. **CSC,** 173.

35. IV/3.2, 889-895.

36. Ibid., 900-901.

37. IV/2, 688. See also Helmut Thielicke's characterization of Barth's understanding of the relationship between church and state as two concentric circles. **Theological Ethics.** II, ed. and trans., William H. Lazareth, (Philadelphia: Fortress Press, 1969), 278, 502.

38. IV/2, 689.

39. III/4, 543.

40. Ibid., 544.

41. Ibid., 511.

42. "Toward New Intra-Christian Endeavors," Christian Century. 86 (December 31, 1969), 1662-1663.

43. Balthasar, op. cit., 54.

44. II/1, 386.

45. I/2, 793.

46. See page 174 of this chapter.

47. IV/1, 149-150.

48. I/2, 787. Cf. Bastiaan Wielenga's comments on how Barth's political engagement and interest in the Russian revolution was examined by Barth himself in theological categories and what effect this had on his interpretation of the avant garde role of the Christian community in **Romans**. In **Lenins Weg zur Revolution**. (München: Chr. Kaiser Verlag, 1971), 434-436.

49. Marquardt. op. cit., 110-111. See also Barth's insistence on the tie between Christian ethics and socialism in his 1922 essay, "Grundfragen der christlichen Sozialethik," **Anfänge der dialektischen Theologie**. I, 152-165.

50. **Römerbrief**. 1. Auflage, 380ff. See also Chapter Two, 45ff of this book.

51. III/2, 721.

52. "Justification and Justice," **CSC**, 138.

53. **How to Serve God in a Marxist Land**, 69.

54. "The Christian Community and the Civil Community," **CSC**, 181-182.

55. Marquardt, op. cit., 160-166.

56. For a very illuminating account tracing the development of the merchant and middle classes economically see **The Emergence of Industrial Societies-1**, ed. Carlo M. Cipolla, (Glasgow: William Collins Sons, 1973), 7-227. For some observations about their political development see J. M. Roberts, **The French Revolution**. (Oxford: University Press, 1978); Karl Marx. **Class Struggles in France, 1848-1850**. (New York: International Publishers, 1964).

57. E. J. Hobsbawm. **The Age of Capital, 1848-1875**. (New York: New American Library, 1979), 107-109.

58. The Eighteenth Brumaire of Louis Bonaparte in **Werke**. VIII, 198-199. Cited in Hobsbawn, op. cit., 110.

59. Ibid., 111. See a fuller description of England's cautiousness about universal suffrage in Richard Shannon. **The Crisis of Imperialism, 1865-1915**. (London: Hart-Davis Macgibbon, 1974), 62-64.

60. Hobsbawn, 111.

246

61. For a fuller explanation of this pre-Marxist or pre-scientific socialist movement as well as the idea of the state amongst the Religious Socialists see **Die frühen Sozialisten.** 2 vols. (München: Deutscher Taschenbuch Verlag, 1972). For the Marxist appraisal of this movement and its ideas, see Engels' **Herr Eugen Dühring's Revolution in Science (Anti-Dühring),** trans. Emile Burns. (New York: International Publishers, 1966), and **Socialism: Utopian and Scientific,** trans. Edward Aveling. (New York: International Publishers, 1948).

62. IV/3.1, 242-249; IV/3.2. Barth includes an entire chapter on freedom and liberation, but particular attention ought to be paid to the social consequences of freedom and liberation on 664-670.

63. "Christian Community and Civil Community," **CSC,** 182-184; III/2, 271-278. See also Barth's discussion of equality within the Church under church law. IV/2, 719-726.

64. IV/2, 511-533. See Chapter Five where the theological and political significance of solidarity is discussed.

65. For a rather comprehensive interpretation of what the framers of the American Declaration understood about these words and the concept, see Garry Wills. **Inventing America.** (New York: Random House, 1978). See also Roberts, op. cit., 1-22, 137-159.

66. One can perhaps best understand how such apprehension was articulated in Germany during this period by reading the writings, letters, etc. of a number of German literati writing at the time. Many of these are compiled in **Deutsches Mosiak: Ein Lesebuch für Zeitgenossen.** (Frankfurt: Suhrkamp Verlag, 1972), 65-141.

67. "But it was not these incidental disclosures of the freedom of God which made Him a revolutionary far more radical than any that came either before or after Him. It was the freedom itself, which could be classified. . . . " IV/2, 172. See Jesus' reversal of the family, economic orders, etc. 173-179.

68. See particularly the radical political hermeneutic of Luke in Richard J. Cassidy. **Jesus, Politics, and Society: A Study of Luke's Gospel.** (Maryknoll, New York: Orbis Books, 1978). See also the tension between the New Testament idea of property and the Roman idea in the life of the early church in Martin Hengel. **Property and Riches in the Early Church,** trans., John Bowden, (Philadelphia: Fortress Press, 1974), 23-46; Robert M. Grant. **Early Christianity and Society.** (New York: Harper & Row, 1977), 13-43, 96-123.

69. Hobsbawm. op. cit., 177-179.

70. David McLellan. **Karl Marx: His Life and Thought.** (London: Macmillan, 1973), 163ff.

71. III/4, 518.

72. See the development of Barth's conception of labor in Chapter Three, 78-80.

73. In a rather illuminating chapter, Prof. Robert Grant points out that most of what we learn about work in the New Testament is in Paul, who directed most of his thoughts in this area to the Corinthians. Corinth was the home of the proto-Gnostics who saw themselves as wise men because of their wisdom and did not encourage manual labor. Prof. Grant also describes the various kinds of occupation in the early church. Op. cit., 67-96.

74. "The object of labour is thus the **objectification** of man's **species-life;** he produces himself not only intellectually, as in consciousness, but also actively in a real sense and sees himself in a world he made. In taking from man the object of his production, alienated labour takes from his **species-life,** his actual and objective existence as a species." Karl Marx, "Economic and Philosophic Manuscripts." **Writings of the Young Marx on Philosophy and Society,** 295.

75. Ibid., 287-288.

76. **Karl Marx: His Life and Environment.** Third Edition. (Oxford: University Press, 1963), 131. Cf. **The German Ideology,** 31f. Cited in McLellan. **Karl Marx: His Life and Thought,** 145-146.

77. Cited in Berlin. op. cit., 133. See Carl Landauer's rather strong refutation of the traditional idea that "historical materialism" is a proper description of Marxism. Rather, he asserts, the technological element is the active agent in history and society making for change, even in the ideas of the philosophers and intellectuals. **European Socialism.** I, (Berkeley: University of California Press, 1959), 153-155. Barth also gives his interpretation of "historical materialism" in III/2, 387-390.

78. III/2, 389.

79. McLellan, op. cit., 112.

80. Barth describes this as the teufliche Kunst der Majorisierung (the devilish art of those in the majority) in **Röm.**(1), 377. Cited in Marquardt, 129. See also Chapter Three of this book. Marquardt interprets Barth's early criticism of the state as a political expedient intended to abolish the present bourgeois democratic state in order to establish a truly just state. This is supposed to parallel Lenin's similar tactic. 131.

81. Marquardt, 139. See also Chapter Three of this book, 75-80.

82. See III/4, 450-459.

83. Friedrich Engels. **The Origin of the Family, Private Property, and the State,** trans. Alec West, (New York: International Publishers, 1972), 224-225. Cf. **The Communist Manifesto:** Sections on "Bourgeois and Proletarians," "Conservative, or Bourgeois, Socialism," and "Critical-Utopian Socialism and Communism."

84. **Writings of the Young Marx on Philosophy and Society,** 402.

Appendix

1. Rommen, 225.
2. <u>Ibid.</u>, 239-240.
3. <u>Ibid.</u>, 224.
4. <u>Ibid.</u>, 447.

SELECTED BIBLIOGRAPHY

Barth's Works

Anselm: Fides Quaerens Intellectum. Translated by Ian W. Robertson. 1958. Reprint. Allison Park, Pennsylvania: Pickwick Publications, 1985.

The Christian Life. Translated by J. Strathearn McNab. London: SCM Press, 1930 & Hodder & Stoughton, 1935.

Church Dogmatics. Edited by G. W. Bromiley and T. F. Torrance. Edinburgh: T. & T. Clark, 1956-1962.

I/1   **The Doctrine of the Word of God.** Prolegomena. Translated by G. T. Thomson, 1936.

I/2   **The Doctrine of the Word of God.** Prolegomena. Translated by G. T. Thomson and Harold Knight, 1956.

II/1   **The Doctrine of God.** Translated by T. H. L. Parker, W. B. Johnston, Harold Knight, J. L. Haire, 1957.

II/2   **The Doctrine of God.** Translated by G. W. Bromiley, J. C. Campbell, Iain Wilson, J. Strathearn McNab, Harold Knight, R. A. Stewart, 1957.

III/1   **The Doctrine of Creation.** Translated by J. W. Edwards, O. Bussey, Harold Knight, 1958.

III/2   **The Doctrine of Creation.** Translated by Harold Knight, G. W. Bromiley, J. K. S. Reid, R. H. Fuller, 1960.

III/3   **The Doctrine of Creation.** Translated by G. W. Bromiley and R. Ehrlich, 1960.

III/4   **The Doctrine of Creation.** Translated by A. T. Mackay, T. H. L. Parker, Harold Knight, Henry A. Kennedy, John Marks, 1961.

IV/1   **The Doctrine of Reconciliation.** Translated by G. W. Bromiley, 1956.

Church Dogmatics - continued

    IV/2   **The Doctrine of Reconciliation.** Translated by G. W. Bromiley, 1958.

    IV/3.1 **The Doctrine of Reconciliation.** Translated by G. W. Bromiley, 1961.

    IV/3.2 **The Doctrine of Reconciliation.** Translated by G. W. Bromiley, 1962.

    IV/4   **The Christian Life.** Translated by G. W. Bromiley, 1969.

Community, State, and Church. Translated by A. M. Hall, G. Ronald Howe, Ronald Gregor Smith. Introduction by Will Herberg. Gloucester, Mass.: Peter Smith, 1968.

Der Götze wackelt. Berlin: Käthe Vogt Verlag, 1964.

Der Römerbrief. 1st ed., Bern: G. A. Bäschlin, 1949; Reprint ed., Aürich: Evangelischer Verlag, 1963.

Die Kirchliche Dogmatik. IV/4. Zürich: Theologischer Verlag, 1976.

Die Kirche zwischen Ost und West. Zürich: Evangelischer Verlag, 1949.

Die protestantische Theologie im 19. Jahrhundert. 2 vols. Hamburg: Siebenstern Verlag, 1960.

Dogmatics in Outline. Translated by G. T. Thomson. London: SCM Press, 1949.

Eine Schweizer Stimme, 1938–1945. 2nd ed. Zürich: Evangelischer Verlag, 1948.

The Epistle to the Romans. 6th ed. Translated by Edwyn C. Hoskyns. London: Oxford University Press, 1933.

Ethik I. Edited by Dietrich Braun. Zürich: Theologischer Verlag, 1973. (Karl Barth Gesamtausgabe)

Ethik II. Edited by Dietrich Braun. Zürich: Theologischer Verlag, 1978. (Karl Barth Gesamtausgabe)

Evangelical Theology: An Introduction. Translated by Grover Foley. London: Weidenfeld and Nicolson, 1963.

Final Testimonies. Edited by Eberhard Busch. Translated by G. W. Bromiley. Grand Rapids, Mich.: William B. Eerdmans Company, 1977.

The German Church Conflict. Translated by P. T. A. Parker. Richmond, Virginia: John Knox Press, 1965.

Barth's Works – continued

How I Changed My Mind. Introduction and Epilogue by John D. Godsey. Edinburgh: The Saint Andrew Press, 1969.

How to Serve God in a Marxist Land. Translated by Henry Clark and James D. Smart. New York: Association Press, 1959.

The Humanity of God. Translated by John N. Thomas and Thomas Wieser. London: Collins, 1961.

"A Thank You and a Bow: Kierkegaard's Reveille." Canadian Journal of Theology. IX (1965) No. 1, 3-7.

Theology and Church. Translated by Louise Pettibone Smith. London: SCM Press, 1962.

The Word of God and the Word of Man. Translated by Douglas Horton. Boston: The Pilgrim Press, 1928.

Revolutionary Theology in the Making: Barth-Thurneysen Correspondence, 1914– 1925. Translated by James D. Smart. Richmond, Virginia: John Knox Press, 1964.

Works of Other Authors

Arbeitsgruppe für Geschichte der Arbeiterbewegung Zürich. **Schweizerliche Arbeiterbewegung: Dokumente zu Lage Organisation und Kämpfen der Arbeiter von der Frühindustrialisierung bis zur Gegenwart.** Zürich: Limmat Verlag, 1975.

Balthasar, Hans Urs von. **Karl Barth: Darstellung und Deutung seiner Theologie.** Köln: Jacob Hegner, 1962.

Berkouwer, Gerrit C. **The Triumph of Grace in Karl Barth.** Translated by Harry R. Boer. London: Paternoster Press, 1956.

Berlin, Isaiah. **Karl Marx: His Life and Environment.** 3rd ed. Oxford: Oxford University Press, 1963.

Bettis, Joseph. "Is Karl Barth a Universalist?" Scottish Journal of Theology. XX (1967): 423-436.

_____, "Political Theology and Social Ethics: The Socialist Humanism of Karl Barth." Scottish Journal of Theology. XXVII (1974): 287-305.

Boers, Herikus, **Theology Out of the Ghetto.** Leiden: E. J. Brill, 1971.

Bouillard, Henri. **Karl Barth: Genèse et évolution de la théologie dialectique.** 3 vols. Paris: Aubier, 1957.

Breipohl, Renata. **Religiöser Sozialismus und bürgerliches Geschichtsbewusstsein zur Zeit der Weimarer Republik.** Zürich: Theologischer Verlag, 1971.

Busch, Eberhard. **Karl Barths Lebenslauf.** Munich: Chr. Kaiser Verlag, 1975. English trans. London: SCM Press, 1976.

Cassidy, Richard J. **Jesus, Politics and Society: A Study of Luke's Gospel.** Maryknoll, New York: Orbis Books, 1978.

Cipolla, Carlo M. ed. **The Emergence of Industrial Societies–I.** The Fontana Economic History of Europe. Glasgow: William Collins Sons, 1973.

Cochrane, Arthur C. **The Church's Confession Under Hitler.** Philadelphia: Westminster Press, 1962; Reprint. Pittsburgh, Pennsylvania: Pickwick Press, 1962.

Crimmann, Ralph. "Der junge Karl Barth im Kreuzfeuer der Kritik, 1902-27." Ph. D. Dissertation, University of Erlangen, 1975.

Cullmann, Oscar. **Christ and Time.** Rev. ed. Translated by Floyd V. Filson. Philadelphia: Westminster Press, 1964.

Dehn, Günther. "Engel und Obrigkeit: Ein Beitrag zum Verständnis von Römer 13, 1-7." **Theologishe Aufsätze: Karl Barth zum 50. Geburtstag.** Munich: Chr. Kaiser Verlag, 1936: 90-109.

Deutsches Mosiak: Ein Lesebuch für Zeitgenossen. Introduction by Gustav Heinemann. Frankfurt: Suhrkamp Verlag, 1972.

Easton, Lloyd D. and Guddat, Kurt H., eds. **Writings of the Young Marx on Philosophy and Society.** Garden City, New York: Anchor Books, 1967.

Engels, Friedrich. **Herr Eugen Dühring's Revolution in Science (Anti-Dühring).** Translated by Emile Brims. New York: International Publishers, 1966.

_____, **Socialism: Utopian and Scientific.** Translated by Edward Aveling. New York: International Publishers, 1978.

_____, **The Origin of the Family, Private Property and the State.** Translated by Alec West. New York: International Publishers, 1972.

Feuerbach, Ludwig. **The Essence of Christianity.** Translated by George Eliot. Introduction by Karl Barth. New York: Harper & Brothers, 1957.

Friedrich, Johannes; Pöhlmann, Wolfgang; and Stuhlmacher, Peter. "Zur historischen Situation und Intention von Röm 13, 1-7." Zeitschrift für Theologie und Kirche. 73. Jg. (1976): 131-166.

Gilby, Thomas. **Principality and Polity: Aquinas and the Rise of State Theory in the West.** London: Longmans, Green and Company, 1958.

Glasse, John. "Barth on Feuerbach." Harvard Theological Review. 57 (April, 1964): 69-96.

Gollwitzer, Helmut. **The Demands of Freedom: Papers by a Christian in West Germany.** Translated by Robert W. Fenn. Introduction by Paul Oestreicher. London: SCM Press, 1965.

_____, **Karl Barth's Church Dogmatics: A Selection.** Translated and edited by G. W. Bromiley. Edinburgh: T. & T. Clark, 1961.

_____, **Reich Gottes und Sozialismus bei Karl Barth.** Munich: Chr. Kaiser Verlag, 1972. English trans. in **Karl Barth and Radical Politics.** Translated and edited by George Hunsinger.

Grant, Robert M. **Early Christianity and Society.** New York: Harper & Row, 1977.

Grebing, Helga. **Geschichte der deutschen Arbeiterbewegung.** Munich: Deutscher Taschenbuch Verlag, 1970.

Grimmett, Ian. "The Doctrine of Man in Karl Barth's Commentary on the Epistle to the Romans." S.T.M. thesis, Union Theological Seminary, 1953.

Gunton, Colin E. **Becoming and Being: The Doctrine of God in Charles Hartshorne and Karl Barth.** Oxford: Oxford University Press, 1978.

Hengel, Martin. **Property and Riches in the Early Church.** Translated by John Bowen. Philadelphia: Fortress Press, 1974.

Hobsbawn, Eric J. **The Age of Capital,** 1846-1875. New York: New American Library, 1979.

Hofer, Walther, ed. **Der Nationalsozialismus: Dokumente 1933-1945.** Frankfurt: Fischer Taschenbuch Verlag, 1957.

Huber, Wolfgang. "Evangelische Theologie und Kirche beim Ausbruch des Ersten Weltkrieges." **Studien zur Friedsforschung.** Vol. 4. Gilching: Käsel Verlag, 1970.

Hunsinger, George, ed. and trans. **Karl Barth and Radical Politics.** Philadelphia: Westminster Press, 1976.

Jacobsen, Ingrid, ed. **War Barth Sozialist? Ein Streitgesprach um Theologie und Sozialismus bei Karl Barth.** Berlin: Verlag die Spur, 1975.

Jansen, John F. **Calvin's Doctrine of the Work of Christ.** London: James Clarke & Company, 1956.

Journal of Church and State. 18 (Autumn 1976): 433-442.

Klotz, Leopold, ed. **Die Kirche und das Dritte Reich: Fragen und Forderungen deutscher Theologen.** Gotha: L. Klotz, 1932.

Kool, Fritz and Krause, Werner, eds. **Die frühen Sozialisten.** 2 vols. Munich: Deutscher Taschenbuch Verlag, 1972.

Küng, Hans. **Justification: The Doctrine of Karl Barth and a Catholic Reflection.** Translated by Thomas Collins, Edmund E. Tolk, and David Grandskou. London: Burns and Oates, 1964.

Kupisch, Karl. **Karl Barth in Selbstzeugnissen und Bilddokumenten.** Hamburg: Rowohlt, 1971.

Landauer, Carl. **European Socialism.** 2 vols. Berkeley: University of California Press, 1959.

Landshut, Siegfried, ed. **Karl Marx: Die Frühschriften.** Stuttgart: Alfred Kröner Verlag, 1974.

Lehmann, Paul. **The Transfiguration of Politics.** New York: Harper & Row, 1975.

Lessing, E. **Das Problem der Gesellschaft in der Theologie Karl Barths und Friedrich Gogartens.** Gütersloh: Gütersloher Verlagshaus, 1972.

Macquarrie, John, **God-Talk: An Examination of the Language and Logic of Theology.** New York: Seabury Press, 1967.

McConnachie, John. "Der Einfluss Karl Barth in Schottland und England." **Theologische Aufsätze: Karl Barth zum 50. Geburtstag.** Edited by Ernst Wolf. Munich: Chr. Kaiser Verlag, 1936: 559-570.

McCord, James I. and Parker, T. H. L., eds. **Service in Christ: Essays presented to Karl Barth on his 80th Birthday.** London: Epworth Press, 1966.

McLellan, David. **Karl Marx.** New York: The Viking Press, 1975.

_____, **Karl Marx: His Life and Thought.** London: Macmillan, 1973.

Maier, Hans. **Revolution und Kirche: Zur Frühgeschichte der christlichen Demokratie.** Munich: Deutscher Taschenbuch Verlag, 1973.

Marquardt, Friedrich-Wilhelm. **Der Christ in der Gesellschaft, 1919-1979.** Munich: Chr. Kaiser Verlag, 1980.

_____, "Theologische und politische Motivationen Karl Barths im Kirchenkampf." Junge Kirche. 34. Jg., 283-303.

_____, Theologie und Sozialismus: Das Beispiel Karl Barths. Munich: Kaiser-Grünewald, 1972.

Marx, Karl. Class Struggles in France, 1848-1850. New York: International Publishers, 1964.

Marx, Karl and Engels, Friedrich. The Communist Manifesto. Translated by Samuel Moore. Introduction by A. J. P. Taylor. New York: Penguin Books, 1977.

Mendenhall, George. Law and Covenant in Israel and the Ancient Near East. Pittsburgh: The Biblical Colloquium, 1955.

Merz, Georg. "Auseinandersetzung mit Karl Barth." Blätter für religiösen Sozialismus. 1. Jg. (Pfingsten, 1920): 5-8.

_____, "Die Begegnung Karl Barths mit der deutschen Theologie." Kerygma und Dogma. 2 Jg. Göttingen: Vandenhoeck & Ruprecht, 1956.

Miranda, José. Marx and the Bible. Translated by John Eagleson. Maryknoll, New York: Orbis Books, 1974.

Moltmann, Jürgen, ed. Anfänge der dialektischen Theologie. I. Munich: Chr. Kaiser Verlag, 1977.

Niebuhr, Reinhold. "Toward New Intra-Christian Endeavors." Christian Century. (December 31, 1969): 1662-63.

_____, "Barth's East German Letter." Christian Century. 76 (February 11, 1959): 167-168.

Pannenberg, Wolfhart. Jesus: God and Man. Translated by Lewis L. Wilkins and Duane A. Priebe. Philadelphia: Westminster Press, 1968.

Pauck, Wilhelm. Karl Barth: Prophet of a New Christianity? New York: Harper & Brothers, 1931.

Pöhlmann, Horst G. Analogia entis oder Analogia fidei? Der Frage der Analogie bei Karl Barth. Göttingen: Vandenhoeck & Ruprecht, 1965.

Prolingheuer, Hans. Der Fall Karl Barth, 1934-1935. Neukirchen: Neukirchener Verlag, 1977.

Roberts, J. M. The French Revolution. Oxford: University Press, 1978.

Rommen, Heinrich. Der Staat in der katholischen Gedankenwelt. Paderborn, Germany: Bonifaciius Druckerei, 1935.

256

_____, **The State in Catholic Thought.** St. Louis: B. Herder Book Company, 1945.

Scholder, Klaus. **Die Kirchen und das Dritte Reich.** Frankfurt: Propylaen Verlag, 1977.

Shanahan, William O. **Der deutsche Protestantismus vor der sozialen Frage, 1815–1871.** Munich: Chr. Kaiser Verlag, 1962. Original in English, **German Protestants Face the Social Question.** Notre Dame, Indiana: University of Notre Dame Press, 1954.

Shannon, Richard. **The Crisis of Imperialism, 1865–1915.** London: Hart-Davis Macgibbon, 1974.

Smart, James D. **The Divided Mind of Modern Theology: Karl Barth and Rudolf Bultmann, 1908–1923.** Philadelphia: Westminster Press, 1967.

Thielicke, Helmut. **Theological Ethics.** 2 vols. Edited and translated by William H. Lazareth. Philadelphia: Fortress Press, 1969.

Thompson, John. **Christ in Perspective: Christological Perspectives in the Theology of Karl Barth.** Grand Rapids, Michigan: Wm. B. Eerdmans Company, 1978.

Tillich, Paul. **Systematic Theology.** 3 vols. Chicago: University of Chicago Press, 1951–1963

Torrance, T. F. **Karl Barth: An Introduction to His Early Theology.** London: SCM Press, 1962.

Van Dijk, Joseph. **Die Grundlegung der Ethik in der Theologie Karl Barths.** Munich: Manz Verlag, 1966.

Wielenga, Bastiaan. **Lenins Weg zur Revolution.** Munich: Chr. Kaiser Verlag, 1971.

Williamson, René de Visme. **Politics and Protestant Theology.** Baton Rouge, Louisiana: Louisiana State University Press, 1976.

Wills, Garry. **Inventing America.** New York: Random House, 1978.

Wolf, Ernst. "Politischer Gottesdienst." Blätter für deutsche und internationale Politik XI (1966): 289–301.

Wolf, Ernst Kirschbaum, Ch. von and Frey, Rudolf, eds. **Antwort: Karl Barth zum siebzigsten Geburtstag.** Zürich: Evangelischer Verlag, 1956.

Yerkes, James. **The Christology of Hegel.** American Academy of Religion Dissertation Series, no. 23. Missoula, Montana: Scholars Press, 1978.

NAME INDEX

257

SUBJECT INDEX